A Companion to Translation Studies

D1563258

TOPICS IN TRANSLATION
Series Editors: Susan Bassnett, *University of Warwick, UK*
Edwin Gentzler, *University of Massachusetts, Amherst, USA*
Editor for Translation in the Commercial Environment:
Geoffrey Samuelsson-Brown, University of Surrey, UK

For more details of these or any other of our publications, please contact:
Multilingual Matters, Frankfurt Lodge, Clevedon Hall,
Victoria Road, Clevedon, BS21 7HH, England
http://www.multilingual-matters.com

TOPICS IN TRANSLATION 34
Series Editors: Susan Bassnett, *University of Warwick* and
Edwin Gentzler, *University of Massachusetts, Amherst*

A Companion to Translation Studies

Edited by
Piotr Kuhiwczak and Karin Littau

MULTILINGUAL MATTERS LTD
Clevedon • Buffalo • Toronto

Library of Congress Cataloging in Publication Data
The Companion to Translation Studies/Edited by Piotr Kuhiwczak and Karin Littau.
Topics in Translation: 34
Includes bibliographical references and index.
1. Translating and interpreting. I. Kuhiwczak, Piotr. II. Littau, Karin
P306.C655 2007
418' .02–dc22   2006031783

British Library Cataloguing in Publication Data
A catalogue entry for this book is available from the British Library.

ISBN-13: 978-1-85359-957-6 (hbk)
ISBN-13: 978-1-85359-956-9 (pbk)

Multilingual Matters Ltd
UK: Frankfurt Lodge, Clevedon Hall, Victoria Road, Clevedon BS21 7HH.
USA: UTP, 2250 Military Road, Tonawanda, NY 14150, USA.
Canada: UTP, 5201 Dufferin Street, North York, Ontario M3H 5T8, Canada.

The policy of Multilingual Matters/Channel View Publications is to use papers that are natural, renewable and recyclable products, made from wood grown in sustainable forests. In the manufacturing process of our books, and to further support our policy, preference is given to printers that have FSC and PEFC Chain of Custody certification. The FSC and/or PEFC logos will appear on those books where full certification has been granted to the printer concerned.

Typeset by Wordworks Ltd.
Printed and bound in Great Britain by the Cromwell Press Ltd.

Contents

Notes on Contributors

Gunilla Anderman is Professor of Translation Studies at the University of Surrey, UK. Her research interests include translation theory, drama translation and the translation of children's literature. She is the author of *Europe on Stage: Translation and Theatre* (2005), and co-editor with Margaret Rogers of *Words, Words, Words: The Translator and the Language Learner* (1996), *Word, Text, Translation: Liber Amicorum for Peter Newmark* (1999), *Translation Today: Trends and Perspectives* (2003), and *In and Out of English: For Better, For Worse* (2005).

Susan Bassnett is Professor in the Centre for Translation and Comparative Cultural Studies at Warwick University, UK. She is the author of over 20 books, including *Translation Studies* (3rd edn, 2002) which first appeared in 1980, and *Comparative Literature: A Critical Introduction* (1993) which has been translated into several languages. Her more recent books include *Sylvia Plath: An Introduction to the Poetry* (2004), *Constructing Cultures* (1998) written with André Lefevere, and *Post-Colonial Translation* (1999) co-edited with Harish Trivedi.

Luise von Flotow is Professor of Translation Studies at the University of Ottawa, Canada. Her research interests include gender and other cultural issues in translation, audiovisual translation, translation and cultural diplomacy, and literary translation. She is the author of *Translation and Gender: Translating in the Era of Feminism* (1997), co-editor of *The Politics of Translation in the Middle Ages and the Renaissance* (2001), and co-editor and translator of the anthology *The Third Shore: Women's Fiction from East Central Europe* (2006).

Theo Hermans is Professor of Dutch and Comparative Literature at University College, London (UCL), and Director of the Centre for Intercultural Studies. He has published extensively on translation theory and history, and on Dutch and comparative literature, and his work has been translated into Chinese, Dutch, German, Spanish and Turkish. He is the author of *Translation in Systems* (1999) and, amongst other books, editor of the seminal volume *The Manipulation of Literature: Studies in Literary*

Translation (1985), *Crosscultural Transgressions: Research Models in Translation Studies II* (2002) and *Translating Others* (2006).

Piotr Kuhiwczak is Associate Professor of Translation Studies at the University of Warwick, UK. He has published extensively in the fields of comparative literature, cultural studies and translation studies, and is currently researching the impact of translation on Holocaust memoirs and testimonies. His book *Successful Polish–English Translation: Tricks of the Trade* published in 1994, is now in its third edition. He is on the Advisory Board of the British Centre for Literary Translation, and the Editorial Board of *The Linguist*, a journal published by the Institute of Linguists.

Karin Littau is Senior Lecturer in English and Comparative Literature, and Director of the Centre for Film Studies at the University of Essex, UK. She has published widely on translation, rewriting and adaptation; and is especially interested in the intermedial relations between literature and film, and the historical receptions of print and new media. She is the author of *Theories of Reading: Books, Bodies, and Bibliomania* (2006), and co-editor of a special issue on 'Inventions: Literature and Science' for *Comparative Critical Studies* (2005). Since 1998 she has been on the executive committee of the British Comparative Literature Association (BCLA).

Lynne Long is Senior Lecturer in Translation Studies, and Director of the Centre for Translation and Comparative Cultural Studies at the University of Warwick, UK. She has published on Bible translation and on translation history, and is the author of *Translating The Bible: From the 7th to the 17th Century* (2001), and editor of *Translation and Religion: Holy Untranslatable?* (2005). She is involved with American Bible Society projects, with the Arts and Humanities Research programme 'Translation and Translation Theories East and West' at the Centre for Asian and African Literatures. She is also a member of the ACUME European Research Project in Cultural Memory based in Bologna.

Eithne O'Connell is Senior Lecturer at the Centre for Translation and Textual Studies at Dublin City University (DCU), Ireland. Her professional qualifications include the Final Translators' Examination (Institute of Linguistics) and a Certificate in Teletext Subtitling from the S4C/University of Wales. In 2000, she completed her doctoral research on screen translation at DCU. She is the author of *Minority Language Dubbing for Children* (2003), and a founder member of both the Irish Translators' and Interpreters' Association, and the European Association for Studies in Screen Translation.

Anthony Pym is Director of Postgraduate Programs in Translation at Universitat Rovira i Virgili, Tarragona, Spain. He works on sociological approaches to translation and intercultural relations. His recent publications include *Pour une éthique du traducteur* (1997), *Method in Translation History* (1998), *Negotiating the Frontier: Translators and Intercultures in Hispanic History* (2000), and *The Moving Text: Localisation, Distribution, and Translation* (2004). He is also the editor of *L'Internationalité littéraire* (1988) and *Mites australians* (1990) and the co-editor of *Les formations en traduction et interprétation: Essai de recensement mondial* (1995) and *Sociocultural Aspects of Translating and Interpreting* (2006).

Christina Schäffner is Reader in German and Translation Studies, and Director of Postgraduate Studies at Aston University, Birmingham, UK. She has published numerous articles on text linguistics and critical discourse analysis, especially of political texts. She is the author of *Translation Research and Interpreting Research* (2004) and co-author with Uwe Wiesemann of *Annotated Texts for Translation: English–German: Functionalist Approaches Illustrated* (2001). She has edited numerous books: most recently, *Translation and the Global Village* (2000), *The Role of Discourse Analysis for Translation and Translator Training* (2002) and *Translation Research and Interpreting Research* (2004).

Mary Snell-Hornby taught at the Universities of Munich, Heidelberg and Zürich, before taking up a professorship at the University of Vienna. She is also Honorary Professor at the Centre for Translation and Comparative Cultural Studies at Warwick University, UK. She is the author of more than 100 essays, and has published numerous books on translation studies (as well as on lexicography, linguistics and literary studies), including the influential *Translation Studies: An Integrated Approach* (1988, 1995). Her most recent book is *The Turns of Translation Studies: New Paradigms or Shifting Viewpoints* (2006). She was a founding member of the European Society for Translation Studies (EST) and the European Association for Lexicography (EURALEX).

Acknowledgements

The editors would like to thank the contributors of this volume for their patience in seeing this project through, and express their gratitude to Tommi Grover at Multilingual Matter for his unfailing support. Finally, we would like to thank the series' editors Susan Bassnett and Edwin Gentzler for asking us to put together this volume.

Introduction

PIOTR KUHIWCZAK AND KARIN LITTAU

In his introduction to the revised edition of *Contemporary Translation Theory* (2001) Edwin Gentzler wrote:

> Ironically, when it was first published, this book was initially criticised for including too many theories; many scholars in the field felt that the proliferation in theory was a passing phenomenon. Today, the book may appear to be theoretically limited, covering, as it does, a mere five approaches. As the field continues to grow with new scholars from different countries and different linguistic and cultural traditions conducting research, additional theories will begin to emerge, further complicating the map. (Gentzler, 1993/2001: x)

Gentzler's book, which first appeared in 1993, was written at a time when theorising about translation was changing fast. A fruitful exchange of views on what translation was and how it could, or should, be theorised and studied had taken place during the 1980s and early 1990s. Much of this debate had come in the aftermath of the 'explosion of theory' in the human sciences (see Bergonzi, 1990; Kreiswirth & Cheetham, 1990; Krieger, 1994). Susan Bassnett's *Translation Studies* (1980) was written in the midst of these critical upheavals, which questioned the traditional boundaries by which disciplines had been divided in the academy since the 19th century. It was published as part of the New Accents series for Methuen (later Routledge). The series' general editor, Terence Hawkes, claimed in the preface that each of its volumes was to 'suggest the distinctive discourse of the future' (in Bassnett, 1980: x). Thus, while Bassnett's book had laid important groundwork for the discipline of translation studies as a discipline, Gentzler's book by contrast was already looking back to systematise the knowledges belonging to this new discipline.

While both books were written in English, the upsurge in the academic interest in translation, of which the revised editions of both titles are an indicator, is by no means restricted to an Anglo-American context. The innovative thinking, which has characterised translation studies from its

very inception, has come from several geographical directions simultaneously, as well as from diverse critical traditions. When the *European
Society for Translation Studies* was formed in Vienna in 1992, multi-national
links were being forged between scholars. Soon, a new wave of new translation studies periodicals was to emerge: *Perspectives: Studies in Translatology*
in Copenhagen, *The Translator* in Manchester, *Translation and Literature* in
Edinburgh, *Across Languages and Cultures* in Budapest, *Forum* in Paris and
Seoul, and *Przekladaniec* in Krakow. This is only an indicative list, and does
not include the countless on-line journals that also sprang up in the 1990s.
In addition, well-established literary and linguistic journals, which had not
shown much interest in translation before, began putting together special
editions devoted to translation. For instance, the British journal *Forum for
Modern Language Studies* (1997) devoted a whole issue to translation, as did
the Italian journal of English Studies *Textus* (1999). There was also what can
only be described as 'frantic' activity on the conference front. While in the
1980s each translation conference, held mainly in Europe or Canada, had
constituted a major event that attracted often hundreds of participants, the
1990s saw an increase in conferences and seminars on such a scale that it
was difficult to keep up with participation. But it is not only that the
number of events increased dramatically; the events that traditionally had
been located in Western Europe and North America were now common in
Asia, the former Eastern Europe and South America. This internationalism
signalled that translation studies had finally 'arrived'.

  While its status as a discipline was less and less in question, the sheer
proliferation of discourses on translation made it necessary to take stock of
that discipline. Thus, dictionaries, encyclopedias and anthologies began to
appear with an astonishing frequency in an attempt to guide, but also
channel, the reading in the field. Just as anthologists in the 18th and 19th
centuries – faced with the multiplication of print in an ever-increasing
literary marketplace – selected what they thought was worthy of reading,
so editors in translation studies chose key texts for their readerships.
Throughout the 1980s and 1990s John Biguenet's and Rainer Schulte's
(1985, 1989) anthology, together with Andrew Chesterman's (1989), served
as the two basic standard teaching texts in English. Since then, Lawrence
Venuti's *The Translation Studies Reader* (2000) has appeared, as well as two
anthologies of primary historical material on translation, one by André
Lefevere (1992c), the other by Douglas Robinson (1997b/2001). Anthologies, or their modern-day equivalent, the 'Reader', are not just useful
sources that save readers time, and even prevent readers 'from reading all
the editor did' (Price, 2000: 2), but are also instruments of canon-formation
insofar as they shape curriculum design. In this sense their 'business' is, as

Matthew Arnold might well have said, to allow the reader 'simply to know the best that is known and thought' (1865/1907: 18–19) in a given field of study. Conversely, the encyclopedia does not select parts from an unmanageable whole, but tries to make the whole manageable by being as comprehensive and all-encompassing of all the parts as it can possibly be. Both forms of publication are designed, then, to help readers navigate amongst a proliferation of discourses on translation. The fact that the end of the 20th century and the beginning of the new millennium saw a mini explosion of such titles as Mona Baker's *Routledge Encyclopedia of Translation Studies* (1998), Olive Classe's *Encyclopedia of Literary Translation* (2000) and, in the same year, Peter France's *Oxford Guide to Literature in English Translation*, will undoubtedly be of note for future book historians. At present all we can say is that all these publications have contributed towards legitimising the disciplinary status of translation.

A similar pattern can be discerned with textbooks. While in the 1980s and 1990s Peter Newmark's (1981, 1987) and Mona Baker's (1992) texts constituted the canon, the situation changed radically with a host of new publications in the field – notably, Jeremy Munday's *Introducing Translation Studies* (2001), Basil Hatim's and Jeremy Munday's *Translation: An Advanced Resource Book* (2004), as well as the series of language specific textbooks regularly published by Multilingual Matters. The electronic bibliographical resources (such as those offered by the publishers John Benjamins and St Jerome) which complement print publications, have also helped research and placed translation studies firmly within 21st century humanities scholarship. Such a concentration of publishing projects was possible only because several well-established publishers (such as Routledge, Multilingual Matters and John Benjamins) expanded their translation studies lists considerably. The founding of St Jerome in Manchester as the first specialist translation studies publisher was also crucial in this respect, since its success sent out a signal that translation studies is not only an intellectually reputable subject but also a subject that can attract a substantial readership among students and academics.

In giving this necessarily short and schematic account of the institutional trajectory of translation studies, we are aware that we have not been able to do justice to the vast research, manifold publications and related developments in languages other than English. Nevertheless, we are convinced that certain paradigm shifts, largely due to theoretical debate instituted since the 1960s, have not left many departments untouched. Indeed, much of the influx of theory, which has so fundamentally influenced the ways in which we now think of language, approach literature or study culture, has come from outside an Anglo-American context. This is, of course, where the practice of translation has played a major role insofar as translation has been at the very heart of disseminating theory. For, without the translations of de Saussure from the French for instance, the ideas of structuralism would not have had the impact they have had. Similarly, without the translation of Anglo-American feminist theory into various European languages and, conversely, without the translation of French feminist theory into English, gender studies would not have developed as fast as it did. The rapidity of the spread of critical theory is therefore largely due to translation. This does not explain, however, why the development of translation studies was so rapid, and why it happened in the last two decades.

Gentzler (2001: x) attributes the rapid development of the discipline mainly to political and social change: the end of the Cold War, the re-awakening of China, the emergence of the developing world, and growing self-awareness among ethnic communities. With hindsight, one can also add to Gentzler's list globalisation and its mixed effects, as well as the growing and fluctuating self-awareness of not only ethnic but also religious communities. If these are some of the major socio-political reasons for change, what is the explanation for the rapidity by which the discipline established itself? For one thing, new disciplines such as translation studies, or cultural studies or film studies, have had to define themselves against older disciplines, and therefore absorbed new ideas more readily. While English was openly hostile to theory, film studies is almost entirely dominated by theory, initially a mix of structuralism and ideology-critique, and more recently a mix of psychoanalysis and feminist theory. Similarly, cultural studies adopted Marxist, feminist, post-colonial theory – theories, in other words, that helped to explain the position of minorities in society, a concern at the very heart of the cultural studies project. Translation studies, unlike other new disciplines, was far more eclectic in its use of theory, not least because those academics who had an interest in translation were housed in a variety of different departments (modern languages, English, comparative literature, classics, philosophy, linguistics, schools of interpreting, etc.), and thus brought with them a host of different theoretical tools with which to analyse translation. Translation studies is therefore informed by a Babel of theories.

While this has not produced a new 'theory' of translation, the transfer ('*translatio*') of theories from different disciplines into the arena of translation has hastened the development of the field of translation studies. It has also made it far richer than many of the other new disciplines that in defining their boundaries as disciplines have adopted a much more circumscribed body of theories. Theory has now largely been absorbed into the curriculum of even the most theory-hostile literature department, and the heydays of high theory are over. Instead, the last few years have seen a gradual diversification of theory into particularised theoretical praxes that have given rise to strategies of reading (including strategies of translation) within what might be called cultural politics. Questions to do with textual difference, so pressing in the 1980s and early 1990s, have now become supplanted by questions to do with cultural difference, including racial, ethnic, gender or sexual difference. This is because the questions that are now asked by theory no longer have to do with a priori conditions of translatability, but with a posteriori ideological and cultural factors that affect, not just translation, but also the translator. Thus, rather than expect new theories of translation, we should perhaps expect a prolonged period of eclecticism (cf. Bassnett, 2005). Alternatively, and in alignment with current trends in literary studies, we might well be entering a period of gestation in which the discipline seeks a new understanding of itself by turning to history: be this its history as a discipline, the history of theories of translation, the role that translation has played in book and publishing history, or a social-cultural history of the translator.

Were any of these histories to be written, two things would be clear in all of them: translation studies has thrived on a variety of approaches from a whole range disciplines, and self-doubt rather than ideologically founded triumphalism has been its *modus vivendi*. The question 'what is translation studies' has been a central concern; and many an attempt at answering this question has been made. At times the answer came in the form of clear definitions like those provided by James Holmes and André Lefevere (both in Holmes *et al.*, 1978). Then there was a period of less monolithic thinking, when the flexibility and interdisciplinarity of translation studies were seen as its major assets. This is reflected, for instance, in the title of Mary Snell-Hornby's, Franz Pöchhacker's and Klaus Kaindl's edited volume *Translation Studies: An Interdiscipline* (Snell-Hornby *et al.*, 1994), and their later *Translation as Intercultural Communication* (Snell-Hornby *et al.*, 1997). Sometimes, reflecting the speed of change in thinking about translation, the same researcher presented different views in quick succession. Thus Bassnett, whose *Translation Studies* (Bassnett, 1980) undoubtedly helped to rescue the discipline from oblivion, elevated its status even further in 1993 by suggesting that translation studies could solve the 'crisis' in comparative literature. Recently, however, Bassnett admitted that her view was then intentionally provocative:

Today, looking back at that proposition, it appears fundamentally flawed: translation studies has not developed very far at all over three decades and comparison remains at the heart of much translation studies scholarship. What I would say were I writing the book today is that neither comparative literature nor translation studies should be seen as a discipline: rather both are methods of approaching literature, ways of reading that are mutually beneficial. (Bassnett, 2006: 6)

Of course, such an argument is only possible from the perspective of a confident and established discipline. Nevertheless, there is an essential truth in Bassnett's statement: translation thrives in an interdisclipinary and transdisciplinary context. As a method, for instance, translation maintains a priori the dialogue between the inside and the outside, not only of disciplines, but of cultures, languages and histories. In other words, we practice translation each time we theorise connection.

So what of the practice of translation in relation to theory? Unlike in literary studies, where criticism and creative writing have, until very recently, only rarely been taught side by side in the same department, in translation studies it has been much more difficult to separate translation theory from translation practice. There is no point pretending that there has never been a conflict between translation and translating, but the gap between the two has never been vast because one simply cannot ignore translation practice while working in translation studies. There are moments, however, when practicing translators wonder why there is not a better interface between theory and practice. Emma Wagner, the education officer working for ITI who wrote a book on this subject, has been trying to initiate a more fruitful dialogue between the theorists and the practitioners. In her view, the gap has less to do with entrenched attitudes than different institutional set-ups:

> I suggest that we treat the two activities – academic translation studies and professional translation practice – as two separate industries, each with its own priorities and constraints, each with its own production line and targets. (Wagner, 2006: 48)

For Wagner it is important that something is done to break up the rigid institutional boundaries, so that translators and translation studies scholars can work more closely together. It remains to be seen whether and how soon this closer collaboration is going to take place.

This very concern about the relation between practice and theory may indicate something else, namely, that research in translation studies has reached a point when major exponential growth of new ideas will not continue at the same pace as in the last two decades. This may therefore be the right moment in time to pose questions about the application of the concepts that translation theory has developed, that is, the applicability of theory in practice. And here we might well find that theory when applied in practice comes up against 'obstacles' that prevent its 'translation' into a practical context. In a conversation on the relation between theory and practice, Gilles Deleuze made this point to Michel Foucault:

> from the moment a theory moves into its proper domain, it begins to encounter obstacles, walls, and blockages which require its relay by another type of discourse (it is through this other discourse that it eventually passes to a different domain). (Deleuze, 1977: 208)

To conceive of the relation between theory and practice as a 'set of relays' rather than a one-to-one, unidirectional application, not only indicates that this relation is necessarily 'partial and fragmentary'. It also indicates that 'theory is always local and related to a limited field', and as such 'does not totalise; it is an instrument for multiplication and multiplies itself' (Deleuze, 1977: 208). In other words, theory is always modified, or multiplied, by its encounter with practice insofar as it must make connections with other theorems, each modified in turn by their encounters with practice. This is not to say that all research in translation studies is, or should be, geared towards the practice of translating, since many of us are theorists who ask important questions as to what translation is and how it functions. If, however, we were to begin to think of theory and practice together, how each transforms the other, how practice is altered by theory, and how theory is transformed when it confronts practical issues, this might well present a juncture at which consolidation and intellectual digestion, of what has been accomplished in the discipline, can take place.

After a period of rapid growth of ideas, a consolidation of any discipline is only possible when there is a clear panoramic view of what has been achieved. In their book on research in translation studies Jenny Williams and Andrew Chesterman (2002) have used a useful term, 'a map', when talking about research areas within translation studies. The aim of this volume is precisely to provide a map to help a keen researcher to navigate within this multi-faceted discipline. We have asked distinguished experts in the field to give their account of what has been achieved in the most important areas of translation studies, and where the discipline may go in the future. We have also asked our contributors to look at those areas where translation interacts with other disciplines, and consider the outcomes of this interaction. As with every publication of this kind there will be questions about the choice of issues that we have decided to investigate, and the issues we have decided to exclude. We admit that one can wonder, for instance, why there is no chapter on either localisation or globalisation, or translation and new technologies, since these areas are clearly developing very fast and have a close link with applied translation. However, our aim has not been to chase the newest trends, but to create an opportunity to reflect on what has been achieved and consolidate the knowledge that has already been accumulated. So we have selected those aspects of translation that have been researched for a relatively long time, and have already attracted considerable attention from students of translation, researchers as well as practitioners. From our contacts with young researchers and postgraduate students we know that they need a sustained critical account of the discipline, one that is more fleshed out than the concise encyclopedia entry, and one that is more complex than the basic introductory textbook.

For this volume then, we have selected several major areas: culture, philosophy, linguistics, history, literature, gender, theatre/opera, media and politics – all of which have touched on translation greatly, and have been touched by it. As any reader will quickly notice, it is difficult, if not impossible to keep these areas completely apart. The authors and the editors are well aware that there are overlaps and cross references. However, the complexity of the issues discussed makes it impossible to mount artificial barriers in a discipline whose most characteristic features are cross-fertilisation and interdisciplinarity.

This interdisciplinarity is clearly highlighted in Chapter 1, when Susan Bassnett says that the cultural turn in translation studies 'was a massive intellectual phenomenon, and was by no means only happening in translation studies. Across the Humanities generally, cultural questions were assuming importance'. Bassnett's contribution to this volume highlights how major developments in translation studies, such as polysystems theory and the concept of textual grids, coincided with developments in literary/cultural theory and postcolonial studies. As a result, a student of translation should be as much interested in textual issues as in the study of how cultures construct their prevailing tastes and myths.

Interdisciplinarity and interdependence are also important motifs in Anthony Pym's chapter when he states that translation studies is a 'client discipline drawing on philosophical discourses, and indeed on many other intermediary disciplines as well'. Pym then proceeds to present three ways in which translation studies relates to philosophy. First, he demonstrates how philosophers have used translation as a metaphor. Then, he concentrates on translation scholars and practitioners who have used philosophical discourses to support their views. Finally, he discusses research on the translation of philosophical discourses. This systematic analysis uncovers a number of issues that previously have not been discussed in translation studies. The most conspicuous one being the 'client' character of translation studies in relation to philosophy, together with a tendency to elevate poets or theologians to what Pym calls 'philosopher-like' authority. He singles out Humboldt, Schleiermacher, Nietzsche, Benjamin and Sartre as examples of this kind of elevation, which has transformed their status from thinkers to philosophers. These names, Pym contends, are now commonly quoted in translation studies texts, and their theses on translation are often presented as a philosophical foundation on which contemporary translation theories are built. Here, however, Pym sounds a note of caution, asking us to draw on philosophy more selectively, and only when it is necessary to the complexity of the task.

Gunilla Anderman's contribution (Chapter 3) also talks about the asymmetrical relationship between two disciplines: that of translation and linguistics. Unlike Pym, though, Anderman avoids using the explicit label of translation studies as a 'client' discipline. Instead, she claims that 'the relationship between translation and linguistics may take two different forms. In the case of Nida and Catford it expresses itself in an attempt to formulate a linguistic theory of translation; but it may also take the less ambitious form of merely an ongoing interaction between the two, each drawing on the findings of the other whenever mutually beneficial'. The chapter gives a wide-ranging overview of this mutually beneficial and pragmatic relationship, concentrating on those points of contact or interaction between the two disciplines that have proven most fruitful since the 18th century. This includes the most recent developments in corpus linguistics, and the ongoing research on contrastive analysis and language universals.

If a historical framework was the guiding principle of Anderman's essay, history is the central issue of Lynne Long's chapter on the history of translation (Chapter 4). Long draws the reader's attention to the fact that studying translation history provides us with two types of insights. Firstly, we can see that 'translation principles cannot always be defined and adhered to like scientific formulae, but at times remain as flexible and as fickle as language itself'. Secondly, the historical context allows us to build a link between past thinking about translation and contemporary strategies of translation. Long sees the study of translation history as a process of navigation using a variety of specialist maps. The term 'map' is crucial here, since navigation often takes place across the choppy waters of politics, religion and cultural conflict. The complexities of this navigation are illustrated by examples ranging from the translation of religious text to the translation of Ibsen's plays. Like other contributors to this volume, Long also draws our attention to the fact that studying translation history involves forays into several related disciplines, which may be a 'daunting' task but is also an opportunity for collaborative projects.

Of all the tasks given, Theo Hermans (Chapter 5) was confronted perhaps with the most daunting one: establishing not only what literary translation involves and how it has been theorised, but also defining what literature is, how it relates to criticism and literary theory, and how translated literature is perceived within literary studies. As a result, Hermans' essay engages as much with translation as with theory, demonstrating how approaches to literary translation have been modified by major developments in literary theory, beginning with formalist approaches and ending with deconstruction and postcolonial studies. His approach allows us to see that theorising about literary translation involves debates at the micro and macro level of decision-making – from the translator's choice of phrases to his or her adoption of a particular ideological or ethical stance. Hermans' conclusion is optimistic: 'both literary translation and translation studies appear to possess enough pockets of fractious heterogeneity to resist what Derrida, in a different context, called the hegemony of the homogenous'.

One of the pockets that Hermans mentions is gender studies, which has viewed the history of translation as 'an arena of conflict', and which has foregrounded 'what is excluded as well as what is included' from discourses. Luise von Flotow's essay (Chapter 6) elaborates on these issues, but also takes the relationship between gender and translation further. She gives a historical account of the differences between what she calls a 'first' and a 'second paradigm' in gender studies. Whereas the early paradigm adhered to a stable notion of what it is to be a 'man' or a 'woman', since the 1990s such categories have been problematised and destabilised. Gender is no longer essentialised, as possessing intrinsic or fixed characteristics, but regarded as a fluid performance. Similarly, if we regard translation as a performance of a text, then this changes how we theorise the power relations between original and translation. As von Flotow puts it in her chapter: 'The point is that translators may choose to privilege some women authors, say, or emphasise their own understanding of gender issues in a text, yet these are selective, performative aspects of the translation and do not represent intrinsic qualities of the text'.

Selectivity and performance, albeit in a different way, are also essential ingredients of stage and screen translation. In Chapter 7, on theatre and opera translation Mary Snell-Hornby gives a detailed account of how a misunderstanding of the concept of 'faithfulness' has impacted negatively on theatre productions of translated texts. The chapter provides examples of a number of divergent approaches to translating and staging theatre texts. What we can learn from these examples, Snell-Hornby contends, is that, in order to be successful as performances, translations for the theatre and the opera require a collaborative approach, whereby the translator is part of the production team. This, according to Snell-Hornby, would constitute a 'holistic' approach to staging a foreign text.

Eithne O'Connell's chapter on screen translation (Chapter 8) inevitably brings into play the impact of technology on translation. Her historical overview of dubbing, subtitling and revoicing thus creates an excellent opportunity to reflect on the enormous impact of technology on translation in the course of the last decade. O'Connell, being well aware of the technological developments, is convinced, however, that research in screen translation should not be solely concerned with the study of technological advances 'to the detriment of the linguistic, pedagogical, cultural commercial and political issues which continue to lie at the heart of screen translation in its various forms.' Again, as several other authors in this volume have done, O'Connell stresses interdisciplinarity without which translation studies would not be able to function.

However, nowhere else has interdisciplinarity been more vital than in the study of translation in a political context. In the final chapter, Christina Schäffner makes this very clear when she explains the complex nature of political discourse:

> In an increasingly globalised world, processes of text production and reception are no longer confined to one language and one culture. This applies to practically all spheres of human interaction, and in particular to politics. The universality of political discourse has consequences for intercultural communication, and thus for translation. Political communication relies on translation, it is through translation (and also through interpreting) that information is made available to addressees beyond national borders.

In her essay Schäffner addresses both the general issue of a politics of translation and the pragmatic problem of how political texts are translated. There is no doubt that in the context of the current international climate, this chapter will be most topical. This topicality aside, the chapter also provides directions as to where new and significant research in translation studies may be heading in the next decade or so.

The essays included in this volume address a variety of issues that research in translation studies has brought to our attention in the last few decades. The authors have discussed translation within a great many different disciplinary contexts, each giving a critical account of what has already been accomplished in their particular field but also pointing towards potential future areas of research development. The picture that emerges from this volume is of a dynamic discipline which may not have clear boundaries, but which can provide invaluable insights precisely because of its ability to interact with other disciplines.

Chapter 1

Culture and Translation

SUSAN BASSNETT

Why did Translation Studies take a Cultural Turn?

A long time ago, in 1990 to be precise, André Lefevere and I were writing an introductory chapter to a collection of essays entitled *Translation, History and Culture* (Bassnett & Lefevere, 1990). We wanted to draw attention to changes that we believed were increasingly underpinning research in translation studies, changes that signalled a shift from a more formalist approach to translation to one that laid greater emphasis on extra-textual factors. The study of translation practice, we argued, had moved on and the focus of attention needed to be on broader issues of context, history and convention not just on debating the meaning of faithfulness in translation or what the term 'equivalence' might mean. The kind of questions being asked about translation were changing:

> Once upon a time the questions that were always being asked were 'How can translation be taught' and 'How can translation be studied?' Those who regarded themselves as translators were often contemptuous of any attempts to teach translation, while those who claimed to teach often did not translate and so had to resort to the old evaluative method of setting one translation alongside another and examining both in a formalist vacuum. Now, the questions have been changed. The object of study has been redefined; what is studied is text embedded within its network of both source and target cultural signs. (Bassnett & Lefevere, 1990: 11–12)

When we wrote that, we were mindful of a split between linguistic approaches to translation and literary ones, and we sought to challenge both as too narrow and prescriptive. Translation studies had been developing as a distinct discipline through the 1980s, employing methodologies that drew upon research in linguistics and comparative literature and we felt, along with many other people working in the field of translation, that the time had come for increased employment of the tools of cultural history and cultural studies. Looking back, our introduction appears both naive and simplistic, for translation studies developed so rapidly in the 1990s and now occupies such a solid place in the academy that there is no longer any need for special pleading. The arguments we sought to present – that translation plays a major role in shaping literary systems, that translation does not take place on a horizontal axis, that the translator is involved in complex power negotiations (mediating between cultures, as it were), that translation is always a rewriting of an original – have been taken much further by scholars such as Michael Cronin (1996; 2000), Edwin Gentzler (1993/2001), Lorna Hardwick (2000), Theo Hermans (1999b, 2006), Tejaswini Niranjana (1992), Douglas Robinson (2002), Sherry Simon (1996), Harish Trivedi (1993), Elsa Vieira (1999), Lawrence Venuti (1995; 1998b) and many others. Translation studies has become an accepted academic subject and books, journals and doctoral dissertations appear faster than one can read them all, and at the heart of most of the exciting new research are broad questions about ideology, ethics and culture.

Even in 1990 we were by no means the only translation scholars arguing the case for a cultural turn. The move to broaden the object of study beyond the immediate frame of the text had started long before, with the work of the Polysystems Group inspired by Itamar Even-Zohar (1978), Gideon Toury (1978) and James Holmes (1978). In Germany, Canada, Brazil, France and India, arguments similar to ours were being presented, albeit from different perspectives, as translators and translation scholars set about the task of redefining the importance of translation in literary history, tracing the genealogy of translation in their own individual cultural contexts, and exploring more fully the ideological implications of translation and the power relationships that are involved as a text is transferred from one context to another.

Polysystems theory was primarily concerned with literary translation, but other translation scholars whose work included the non-literary were pursuing parallel paths. The *skopos* theory, for example, developed by Hans Vermeer, Katharina Reiß (Reiß & Vermeer, 1984) and others, postulates that the objective or function of a translation determines the translation strategies to be employed. Hence the translator's subjective takes precedence, and the function that a translation is meant to fulfil in the target culture enables that translator to make certain choices. This is a far cry from source-focused theories of translation, and can also be said to reflect a cultural turn. Summarising translation studies in the 1980s and 1990s, Edwin Gentzler writes:

The two most important shifts in theoretical developments in translation theory over the past two decades have been (1) the shift from source-oriented theories to target-text-oriented theories and (2) the shift to include cultural factors as well as linguistic elements in the translation training models. Those advocating functionalist approaches have been pioneers in both areas. (Gentzler, 2001: 70)

What is obvious now, with hindsight, is that the cultural turn was a massive intellectual phenomenon, and was by no means only happening in translation studies. Across the humanities generally, cultural questions were assuming importance. Linguistics has undergone a cultural turn, with the rise of discourse analysis and, as Douglas Robinson (2002) has argued, a move away from constative towards performative linguistics. The growth of interest in corpus linguistics, pioneered by Mona Baker, is arguably another manifestation of a cultural shift in linguistics.

In literary studies, cultural questions took over long ago from formalist approaches to textual study. From post-structuralism onwards the tidal waves of new approaches to literature that swept through the last decades of the 20th century all had a cultural dimension: feminism, gender criticism, deconstruction, post-colonialism, hybridity theory. Literary studies adopted methods from cultural studies, blurring the lines between what had once been distinct fields of investigation. History too underwent a similar shift, with more emphasis on cultural and social history, and the expansion of what had once been marginal areas such as the history of medicine, the history of the family and the history of science. Cultural geography led to a renaissance of geography as a subject. As area studies grew in importance, modern language departments renamed themselves to emphasise the cultural approach. Classics discovered a new generation of students whose interest in the subject was fuelled by studying the relationship between ancient cultures and contemporary ones.

Lorna Hardwick, scholar of ancient Greek and author of a book on intercultural translation, suggests that the act of translating words also 'involves translating or transplanting into the receiving culture the cultural framework within which an ancient text is embedded' (Hardwick, 2000: 22). She makes bold claims for translation as an instrument of change, and in so doing alters the emphasis for today's student of classical languages. The task facing the translator of ancient texts, she argues, is to produce translations that go beyond the immediacy of the text and seek to articulate in some way (she uses the organic metaphor of 'transplantation', which derives from Shelley) the cultural framework within which that text is embedded. Moreover it is the very act of translation that enables contemporary readers to construct lost civilisations. Translation is the portal through which the past can be accessed.

The cultural turn in translation studies, then, can be seen as part of a cultural turn that was taking place in the humanities generally in the late 1980s and early 1990s, and has altered the shape of many traditional subjects. In translation studies, polysystems theory had prepared the ground for a cultural turn since, despite its formalist origins, the issues that came to occupy a prominent position related principally to questions of literary history and the fortune of translated texts in the receiving culture. As an example of parallel trends in the study of translation and the study of literature, we need only think of the way maps of literary history can be altered when a period is considered from an alternative point of reference.

Feminist criticism questioned the dominance of male writers in the literary canon and effectively forced a reassessment of how that canon had been constructed. In consequence, if we consider the 18th century from a post-feminist perspective, it no longer appears as a century dominated by male writers, but rather as the age when women began to make a major contribution to intellectual life. Similarly, if we look from a translation studies perspective at the 15th century in England – which used to be regarded as something of a wasteland, with little of any significance being produced after the death of Chaucer in 1400 – what we find is a period of intense translation activity of both secular and sacred texts. The feminist reassessment of the 18th century in terms of rethinking the canon and the re-evaluation of literary production in the 15th century in terms of the importance of the translations undertaken are but two examples of how new information can change our historical perspective. The works by women had simply become invisible, just as the importance of translation had been ignored. Reassessing these two periods of literary history involves rethinking our assumptions about what constitutes significant literature. In both cases, a parallel process of questioning established norms has taken place, and this process can be considered a definite cultural turn.

Central to polysystems theory as articulated by Even-Zohar was contestation of established literary canons. Even-Zohar argued that any model of a literary system should include translated literature, for translation was often the conduit through which innovation and change can be initiated: 'no observer of the history of any literature can avoid recognising as an important fact the impact of translations and their role in the synchrony and diachrony of a certain literature' (Even-Zohar, 1978: 15). Having stated his belief in the fundamental importance of the role of translations in a literary system, Even-Zohar then endeavoured to define the circumstances in which translations might assume particular importance.

He pointed out that, as literatures evolve, their need for translations fluctuates; hence a well-established literary system might translate less than one that is undergoing changes and upheaval. Newly evolving literatures would, according to Even-Zohar's theory, translate more texts, a hypothesis proven by translation scholars (e.g. Macura, 1990) working in northern or central European literatures, for example. Literatures, such as Czech or Finnish, that evolved in the 19th century in the context of both a linguistic revival and a political struggle for national independence were greatly aided by translation. In complete contrast, we have China, which for centuries translated very little since Chinese writers had no need of external influences. Today, however, there is a translation boom in China, linked to modernisation, Westernisation and China's entry into the global economy. English literature offers yet another example: translation activity started to slow down in the 18th century, after several centuries that had seen the introduction of new poetic forms (e.g. the sonnet and *ottava rima*), new ideas (e.g. political and social theory) and revolutionary shifts in religion with the coming of the Reformation and the great debates about Bible translation. By the late 18th century the need for innovation from outside had diminished, and the wealth of writers producing texts in English resulted in a diminishing of translation. This resulted in a decline in the status of translation, so that today translation into English is minimal and, as English continues to develop as a global lingua franca, there are no signs of translation regaining the importance it had in the age of Shakespeare or the age of Dryden.

Even-Zohar's (1978) proposition that cultures translate according to need seems self-evident today, but in its time it was an extremely important statement, for the implications of his theory of cultural change were enormous. The historical situation, he suggested, would determine the quantity and type of translations that might be undertaken, and the status of those translations would be greater or lesser according to the position of the receiving culture. So a work could be fundamentally important in the source culture, and could then be translated and have no impact at all in the receiving culture or, vice versa, a translation could alter the shape of the receiving literary system. The case of Jack London, a relatively minor American novelist who enjoys canonical status in Russia and other former Soviet countries, is an example of how translation can radically alter the fortunes of an individual writer. Another such case is provided by Clarice Lispector, the Brazilian novelist who was translated into French and English in the 1980s by very able translators. The translations came at a moment when the continent of South America was the object of fascination in European literary circles, and writers such as Borges, Garcia Marquez and Vargas Llosa were lionised. Lispector filled a particular need: she was female, Brazilian and beautifully translated, among others, by Giovanni Pontiero. As a result, her works were widely read and she came to occupy a more prominent position in Brazilian letters outside her own country than she had ever enjoyed at home in Brazil (see Lispector, 1992a, 1992b).

A further example of the cultural turn in translation studies has been the expansion of research into norms governing translation strategies and techniques. Gideon Toury (1978; 1995), Andrew Chesterman (1993) and Theo Hermans (1999b) in particular have sought to explore translational norms, in terms not only of textual conventions but also in terms of cultural expectations. Toury is explicit about the cultural importance of norms in translation:

> Translation activities should be regarded as having cultural signifi-
> cance. Consequently, 'translatorship' amounts first and foremost to
> being able to *play a social role*, i.e. to fulfil a function allotted by a commu-
> nity – to the activity, its practitioners, and/or their products – in a way
> which is deemed appropriate in its own terms of reference. The acquisi-
> tion of a set of norms for determining the suitability of that kind of
> behaviour and for manoeuvring between all the factors which may
> constrain it, is therefore a prerequisite for becoming a translator within a
> cultural environment. (Toury, 1978: 83)

More recently, there has been growing interest in examining norms of accountability operating in a particular context, as attention shifts again in translation studies towards greater emphasis on ethical issues in translation.

By the time Lefevere and I wrote our book, *Constructing Cultures* (Bassnett & Lefevere, 1998), we felt able to say simply that the house of translation now had many mansions. We recognised the enormous amount of work being put into all aspects of translation, into translator training and translation theory, and we recognised also the different emphases that the growing number of translation studies scholars placed on the multiple aspects of translation. In our introduction (Bassnett & Lefevere, 1998: 6), we suggested that the most tremendous change in the field of translation had not happened as more inter-fields or sub-fields (literary, anthropological, cultural, etc.) were added to the linguistic, but rather that the goal of work in the field had itself been widened:

> In the 1970s, translation was seen, as it undoubtedly is, as 'vital to the
> interaction between cultures'. What we have done is to take this state-
> ment and stand it on its head: if translation is, indeed, as everybody

believes vital to the interaction between cultures, why not take the next step and study translation, not just to train translators, but precisely to study cultural interaction. (Bassnett & Lefevere, 1998: 6)

We suggested that translation offers an ideal 'laboratory situation' for the study of cultural interaction, since a comparison of the original and the translated text will not only show the strategies employed by translators at certain moments, but will also reveal the different status of the two texts in their several literary systems. More broadly, it will expose the relationship between the two cultural systems in which those texts are embedded.

Cultural Capital and the Textual Grid

As methodological instruments for engaging in this process, we proposed two critical tools deriving from the work of Pierre Bourdieu (1994): the idea of cultural capital and the notion of the textual grid. Cultural capital can be loosely defined as that which is necessary for an individual to be seen to belong to the 'right circles' in society. When Kemal Ataturk proposed a state-inspired process of Westernisation that would bring Turkey closer to Europe, a programme of translation of major European literary works ensured that Turkish readers would have access to the cultural capital of the west. In *Constructing Cultures* (Bassnett & Lefevere, 1998) Lefevere discusses the changing status of Virgil's *Aeneid* as cultural capital, pointing out that educational systems are the primary means of controlling the creation and circulation of cultural capital. A decline in the study of a language such as Latin, for example, can have massive implications for the value attributed to Latin literature and equally massive implications for the role of translation, once that literature can be accessed by only a small minority of readers. The value of the classics as cultural capital has changed dramatically in a few decades.

The importance of the textual grid in the study and production of translations is equally, or perhaps even more significant. In formulating our notion of textual grids, we pointed out (Bassnett & Lefevere, 1998: 5) that some cultures (such as French, German and English) share a common textual grid that derives from the Christian and Greco-Roman traditions. Other cultures (such as Chinese and Japanese) share less with others. But the textual grids seem to exist in all cultures in ways that pre-exist language. The grids are constructs, they reflect patterns of expectations that have been interiorised by members of a given culture. We proposed 'that students of translation should pay more attention to them than they have in the past, whether they want to learn the technique of translating, or whether they want to analyse translations and the part they play in the evolution of cultures' (Bassnett & Lefevere, 1998: 5).

The idea of textual grids is a helpful one for the analysis of translation. In a later essay that developed his thinking around the idea of textual and conceptual grids, André Lefevere (1999: 76) asserted that problems in translating are caused 'at least as much by discrepancies in conceptual and textual grids as by discrepancies in languages'. The problems become particularly apparent when translation takes place between Western and non-Western cultures. Lefevere argues that Western cultures have constructed non-Western cultures by translating them into Western categories, a process that distorts and falsifies:

> This brings us, of course, straight to the most important problem in all translating and in all attempts at cross-cultural understanding: can culture A ever really understand culture B on that culture's (i.e. B's) own terms? Or do the grids always define the ways in which cultures will be able to understand each other? Are the grids, to put it in terms that may well be too strong, the prerequisite for all understanding or not? (Lefevere, 1999: 77)

Postcolonial translation theory is yet another example of how research in the field of translation has developed in parallel with research in literary and historical studies more generally. In India, Canada and Brazil, to name but three centres of postcolonial translation activity, questions have been asked about the unequal power relationships that pertain when a text is translated from, say, Tamil or Kannada into English, the language of the colonising power. The very act of translation itself has been seen by some, most notably Tejaswini Niranjana (1992), as an act of appropriation. Translation, Niranjana argues, is a collusive activity that participates in the fixing of colonised cultures into a mould fashioned by the superior power. Eric Cheyfitz (1991) similarly maintains that translation was a crucial component of European colonisation on the American continent. Cheyfitz and Niranjana focus attention on the inequality between literary and cultural systems which, in their view, transforms the activity of translation into an aggressive act. Theirs is an extreme position, since the logical result of such an argument would be silence, for if translation by a dominant culture can never be legitimate, then translation becomes a form of cultural theft, a dishonest act that should not take place. The only way for translation to become valid is for it to take place from the dominant into the less powerful language: hence translation from English into Québécois or from German into Scots becomes a political statement that asserts the rising status of the formerly-marginalised tongue.

Niranjana and Cheyfitz were writing in the early 1990s, at a time when the emphasis in post-colonial thinking about translation, inspired by Edward Said (1978), was on the inequality of power relationships, hence most of the early translators of non-Western texts were depicted as colonialist lapdogs. Such a position has been challenged as more is discovered about the history of translation. So, for example, a great deal of translation in India is between Indian languages, or from English into Indian languages, and any assessment of the Indian picture needs to take this fact into account. Nor can all the Orientalist translators be condemned out of hand. Many of those early Orientalists, such as Sir William Jones (1970), were motivated by a genuine passion for the works they translated, but the framework within which they wrote ensured that none of their translations entered the English mainstream. To understand that framework we need to take account not only of socio-political factors, but also aesthetic, stylistic, ethical and linguistic factors. The resistance of English literature to new and unfamiliar forms and genres in the 19th century meant that none of the Orientalist translators, regardless of competence, were able to produce texts that had much impact on the receiving literary system. Yet, bizarrely, one non-Western text in translation did succeed, and became the most successful translation in English literature: Edward Fitzgerald's (1859) version of the Persian *Rubaiyat of Omar Khayyam* can be considered a canonical English text. The questions to ask are not only why this poem should have succeeded with English readers, but also why so many other translations of non-Western texts should have failed; and to answer these questions we need to engage with the broader cultural context in which translating was taking place and to consider norms, reader expectations, what was happening in English poetry at precisely the moment when the translation appeared and what strategies the translators were using to reach their readers. It is also worth remembering that while 19th century English readers may have been resistant to poetry in translation, they devoured translated plays and novels, particularly by French and Russian writers. And even if we acknowledge the weaknesses of the work of Sir William Jones and his peers, how can we explain the curious phenomenon that leads English language readers today to buy enthusiastically the works of Indian writers who use English (Vikram Seth, Salman Rushdie or Arundhati Roy, for example), while leaving translations of excellent contemporary Indian writers languishing on the shelves? To attempt an understanding of this phenomenon we have to go more deeply into how taste is constructed in a culture, how publishers market their authors in accordance with those changing patterns of preference and how one culture invents its myth of another.

The power of cultural mythology is immense. If we take the example of China as manifested in translation, we find an intriguing dichotomy. On the one hand, we have Cathay, the imaginary China created by early translators such as Ezra Pound and Arthur Whaley through a style of poetic language that has itself become conventionalised. So strong is that convention that it even prevails in cinema, when Chinese films are dubbed into English. The myth of Cathay involves nostalgia, loss, passion and a high aesthetic sense, it is a fictional China from a distant, imaginary past created in a conventionalised poetic form, using an artificially-constructed language. Yet on the other hand, despite enormous Western interest in the new China today, there is little interest in contemporary Chinese literature. The tough, neo-realist Chinese novelists of today are not finding a responsive audience in the West. Is this because of Western post-modernist sensibilities, or is it because the new wave writers do not fit into the mythical China/Cathay created over a century ago by English and American poets? If this is indeed the case, then we need to understand how a mythical construct created through translation can acquire and retain so much power.

Much remains to be done in studying processes of cultural interchange and understanding more about how different cultures construct their image of writers and of texts. The theory of cultural capital and of textual grid systems can be useful here, and it is significant that one of the newer fields of research linked closely to translation studies should be drawing upon a range of different disciplines, from linguistics to anthropology, as it explores similar questions. I refer, of course, to the study of travel writing. For as a growing number of scholars point out, travel literature, like translation, offers readers access to a version of another culture, a construct of that other culture. The travel writer creates a version of another culture, producing what might be described as a form of translation, rendering the unknown and unfamiliar in terms that can be assimilated and understood by readers back home. The dominant model is one of domestication, making the unfamiliar accessible through a set of strategies that enable the reader to travel vicariously guided by the familiar. The travel writer operates in a hybrid space, a space in-between cultures, just as the translator operates in a space between languages, a dangerous transgressive space that is often referred to as 'no-man's land'.

In his brilliant book that explores travel writing and translation, Michael Cronin (2000: 150) reminds us that translators and travellers are both engaged in a dialogue with languages and with other cultures. He uses the terminology of nomadism to discuss the similarities between the traveller and the translator, both of whom are transforming otherness into an acceptable form for consumption by their target readers:

The translator and the interpreter, moving between disciplines, between the allusive language of general culture and the hermetic sublanguages of specialisms, are practitioners in a sense of the encyclopaedic culture of travel, of a *third culture* that is inclusive not only of the classic polarities of the humanities and science, but of many other areas of human enquiry. In an era of disciplinary parochialism, the third wo/man as translator or travel writer is valuable as a nomad bringing us the news from elsewhere. (Cronin, 2000: 150)

The travel writer and the translator are major elements in shaping the perspective one culture has of another, and it is interesting that so little research should have been undertaken to date on the relationship between travel and translation. That it has started and should be flourishing is an indication of how the cultural turn in translation has opened up greater possibilities. We are likely to see anthropology paying more attention to the problematics of translation, even as we see more ethnographic and anthropological methods being employed in the study of translation. Cronin's (2003) research has moved to considerations of translation and globalisation, and others are following.

There are still occasional dissenting voices who argue that translation, surely, is primarily about language, not culture, and that the proper business of translation studies is to focus on the linguistic aspects of the translation process. In response to such voices, I would answer that of course translation scholars must focus on language, for translation is, after all, about transferring a text from one language to another. But separating language from culture is like the old debate about which came first – the chicken or the egg. Language is embedded in culture, linguistic acts take place in a context and texts are created in a continuum not in a vacuum. A writer is a product of a particular time and a particular context, just as a translator is a product of another time and another context. Translation is about language, but translation is also about culture, for the two are inseparable. As Tymoczko and Gentzler (2002) point out in their introduction to a collection of essays on translation and power relations, translation is implicit in processes of cultural transformation and change.

The cultural turn in translation studies reflects the cultural turn in other disciplines, which is an inevitable result of the need for greater intercultural awareness in the world today. It is greatly to be welcomed, for it offers the best chance we have to understand more about the complexities of textual transfer, about what happens to texts as they move into new contexts and the rapidly changing patterns of cultural interaction in the world we inhabit.

Chapter 2

Philosophy and Translation

ANTHONY PYM

Translation Studies and Western Philosophy

The various disciplines in the humanities are related by chains of authority. Sociolinguistics, for example, historically refers to linguistics and to sociology for the authority of its founding concepts, just as linguistics in turn might refer to philology, or sociology might look back to history, to psychology or to political economics. These chains allow concepts to be borrowed and thus constantly displaced. They also allow authority to be projected back onto the discipline referred to, such that authority itself is also constantly displaced across our disciplines.

This frame enables us to idealise Western philosophy as a set of discourses that do *not* ostensibly borrow authority from external disciplines. It is, if you will, a place where terms and concepts would be elaborated and refined for use in other disciplines; it might supremely act in the service of others. Of course, philosophical discourses more realistically form a place where the authority circulates internally, as philosophers read and re-read philosophers, schools and traditions are formed, at the same time as a mode of authority can flow inward from whatever discipline appears to be advancing the frontiers of knowledge.

Our general frame also enables us to hypothesise that translation studies as a client discipline is drawing on philosophical discourses, and indeed on many other intermediary disciplines as well.

The discourses of philosophy might thus be related to translation studies in at least three ways:

(1) Philosophers of various kinds have used translation as a case study or metaphor for issues of more general application.
(2) Translation theorists and practitioners have referred to philosophical discourses for support and authority for their ideas.
(3) Philosophers, scholars and translators have commented on the translation of philosophical discourses.

Since authority would seem to flow more from philosophy to translation studies than the other way around, the political relations are very different in each of the above cases. Here we shall thus consider their evolutions independently, even though, in history, they operate side by side within the general epistemologies of the humanities.

Translation as an Example for Philosophy

Western philosophy has no traditional discourse on translation. Indeed, the term 'translation' is absent from most of the specialised encyclopedias and glossaries. The concept plays virtually no role in Greek philosophical discourse (as remarked by Robinson, 1992, 1997b: 225–238) and little would seem to have been done over the centuries to cover the lacuna. This more or less active exclusion might be attributed to a profound ethnocentricism, to the attitude that regards all foreign languages as 'barbarous' (from the Greek *barbaros*, foreign). The exclusion might be seen as running through Roman culture as well (the comments we have from Horace and Cicero concern dramatic poetry and oratory, not philosophy) and indeed through much of the medieval tradition. When Vermeer (1996), for example, takes the systems of a Ramon Llull or Thomas Aquinas and develops the translation theories those thinkers could have produced, the interpretative *tour de force* simply begs the question of why the medieval thinkers did *not* produce the translation theories. Robinson (1991, 1996) has attempted to trace the repression of translation from the days of Egyptian and Greek cultural transfers into Rome, then on through a repressive Christendom. Something similar can be found in Meschonnic (1999: 32–34) when he argues that Europe is the only continent whose culture was founded on translations (from Greek for its philosophy, from Hebrew for its religion) and that it has constantly *concealed* those translative origins by treating translations as if they were originals. Berman (1984: 59, 1985: 88, citing Schlegel) made much the same critique of Islamic cultures in which originals were supposedly destroyed once the translation had been completed: translation is something to be hidden, not theorised. Hence, perhaps, the traditional silence of the philosophers.

Great care, however, must be taken when painting entire cultures with such a wide brush. There are at least two further reasons that might explain the reticence.

First, for much of Western history, the production and dissemination of new ideas has been a politically dangerous activity; philosophers have not always been on the side of power. In some circumstances, it is convenient to present new texts as if they were translations from afar (i.e. as pseudo-translations), if only to protect the author. This might explain the suspiciously large numbers of philosophical translations for which no originals can be found – and not only in the Islamic tradition (see Badawi, 1968).

Second, the transmission of ideas for much of the Latin ages was dominated by a theological hierarchy of languages. At the top stood the languages of divine revelation (Hebrew, Greek, Arabic, Sanskrit for some), then the languages of enlightened mediation (notably Latin), and then the written vernaculars (English, French, German, etc.), with the spoken *patois* remaining excluded from consideration. This very powerful idea underlay numerous translators' discourses (humility tropes abound in the prefaces). It also informed numerous metaphors for translations as inferior products, given that the directionality was normally from prestigious to inferior languages. Since the hierarchy thus positioned translating itself as an inferiorising activity, the result was not worthy of dignified discussion. Should we really lament the absence of any great traditional 'philosophy of translation'? One might as well regret the historical lack of a 'philosophy of furniture' – found in Poe (2004) but nowhere else.

Only once the vernaculars had been re-evaluated with respect to Latin was it possible to dignify the translator's activity as an object of serious thought. This process began in 15th century Renaissance humanism, where Leonardo Bruni successfully insisted on elegance in translations. The dignification of translation then rode on the back of the rising European nationalisms, based on the idea of strong all-purpose languages between which something like equivalence was conceivable, well before the term itself was used. This general mode of thought reached a significant degree of completion in German Romanticism.

Wilhelm von Humbolt (1836) viewed all languages as being worked in the same way, moulding concepts into complementary world-views. This was a result of a sudden widening of the conceptual world, first through the enormous time scale of geology (cf. Foucault, 1966), then through the voyages of exploration. Humboldt was looking at languages such as Quechua and Basque, beyond the established translation networks, and at cultures, such as German, that were evidently in the process of historical development. The result was not only an upward re-evaluation of cultural difference (*counter to* the medieval hierarchies), but also an awareness of how translation could be used to refine and standardise developing target languages (*in keeping with* the hierarchies). This historical contradiction largely hid from view the logical possibility that, if languages had different worldviews, translation in any ideal sense must be impossible (this would be problematised by Walter Benjamin and 20th century linguistics).

In lieu of that problem, we find Humboldt, along with Schleiermacher and others, stressing the priorities of foreignising (*verfremdend*) over domesticating (*verdeutschend*) translation. This meant requiring that a translation read like a translation, and not like just another target-language text. Would the result just be a jumble of translations? For Schlegel, protection from that extreme involved searching for conceptual lines between 'strangeness' (*Fremdheit*) in a translation and what could be valued as 'the foreign' (*das Fremde*) (Berman, 1984: 246–7; 1992: 154). Such distinctions would theoretically allow translations to contribute to the development of German language and culture (for which some degree of ideal sameness was still required) at the same time as they marked translations as a separate kind of text, potentially apart from the truly national (others, notably Levý, would later pick up the idea of translations as a separate literary genre). Underlying this theorisation was not an exclusive concern with translation but a series of ideas about the future development of a very particular national culture.

The legacy of the German Romantic complex can be traced along two lines. The first would depend on the fundamental opposition to domesticating modes of translation. If domestication is the norm of a dominant, prestigious culture, the Germanic insistence on foreignisation can be idealised in ethical terms, as a mode of openness that welcomes rather than excludes the other. Translation theory thus becomes a way of talking about issues of cultural protectionism. The German Romantic dichotomy underlies Ortega y Gassett's *Miseria y esplendor de la traducción* (1937/2000), and the ethics of foreignisation has been well suited to a number of intellectuals situated within dominant cultures, for whom it has offered limited expiation. In French it is recuperated in Meschonnic's (1973/1999) single-minded insistence on rendering the rhythm of the original; it opened the way for Antoine Berman's (1984) thorough critique of ethnocentric textual practices. In English, the same mode of thought can be found in Venuti's (1995, 1998b) initial critique of 'fluency' in translation. In all these contexts, the various debates concern the effects of translations on *target* languages and cultures.

The second legacy of the German Romantics would be the general hermeneutic tradition that runs across all these contexts. Here the focus of arguments is the nature of the *source* text or author that is translated. As soon as one sets up dichotomies of translation, one must recognise that there is more than one way to translate. The status of the source text consequently becomes problematic. No text can give all the information necessary for its complete rendition; all texts are thus to some extent open to competing interpretations. The question then becomes how, and with what degree of confidence, one can presume to have understood that which is to be translated. That is a question at the root of phenomenology, running right through Husserl, Heidegger, Gadamer and Ricoeur.

Although the general problematic of translation is never far from the concerns of these thinkers, Martin Heidegger is the only one to have used translation as a mode of philosophical exposition and perhaps of thought. His particular interest in translation is not just in the plurality of interpretations, but in an ontology of language itself, in the very reasons why there are many languages, and more particularly in a curiously assumed relation of equality between German and classical Greek. In this, Heidegger, along with Walter Benjamin, drew on the fragmentary ideas of Hölderlin, a hitherto sidelined figure in German Romanticism (on the many relations between these figures, see Steiner, 1975). The central idea for Benjamin is that the original expression contains a plurality of meaning in its very form, in the same way as the Kabbalistic tradition construes meanings from the numbers represented by the characters of Hebrew script. To work on the original form, to bring out those hidden meanings, is the task of translation. In Benjamin's 1923 essay 'The Task of the Translator' (Benjamin, 1955), this is expressed as the idea that each language is itself a fragment of a larger whole, and that the translator is actually piecing together the parts of a divine meaning, broken in the fall from grace. The practical application of this is nevertheless difficult to discern in Benjamin's fairly uneventful translation of Baudelaire, for which the famous essay was originally an introduction.

Chau (1984) summarises the hermeneutic approach in terms of a few basic tenets. Since there is no truly objective understanding of a text, no translation can represent its source fully and all translations cannot but change the meaning of the source text. Further, following Gadamer, 'prejudices' are unavoidable and can be positive in all acts of interpretation. Chau claims that this general approach makes the translator at once humble and more responsible, taking part in the active creation of a translation rather than remaining a slave to illusions of necessary equivalence. Others might claim that the approach encourages the translator to transgress the ethics of fidelity or equivalence. Here, very clearly, the paths of the philosophers have diverged widely from the positivistic tenets of 20th century linguistic analysis.

As formulated, the hermeneutic approach reflects aspects of the 20th century loss of certainty. Indeed, its tenets reappear in many contemporary approaches, certainly in Derrida (who started as a reader of Husserl) but also, perhaps paradoxically, in the move to descriptive translation studies, where positivistic conceptions of empirical science have nevertheless revealed the vast plurality of translatory practices. On both these fronts, cultural relativism and historicism have taken over from claims to correct or complete interpretations. All these various strands have rejected the view that there is only one way to render any given source element; all have sought to understand how and why a translation is under-determined by its source.

A genealogically different view of translation was initiated by the American analytical philosopher Willard Quine (1959) with the publication of his essay 'Translation and Meaning'. Quine was concerned with the general problem that the one set of data can be accounted for by more than one theory, and that there is no way to decide between the theories. The hermeneutic tradition ultimately sought ethical, ontological or eschatological ways of solving that problem. Quine, however, was from a conservative analytical tradition that sought a technical, logical answer, drawing on behaviourism and following a path that could only lead to scepticism. His use of translation is clearly as a thought experiment, an illustration of a general epistemological principle (nevertheless known as the 'indeterminacy of translation').

Quine posits a situation of 'radical translation', where there has been no previous contact between the cultures concerned (he immediately admits that real life provides no such situations). A rabbit runs past, the native exclaims 'Gavagai!' and the linguist notes this term as meaning 'rabbit', or 'Lo, a rabbit!', or 'undetached rabbit-part', or 'there is a flea on the rabbit's left ear', and so on. Will subsequent investigation reveal the one true meaning of the term? Quine's analysis locates degrees of certainty for various kinds of propositions, but concludes that there can be no absolute determination of the translation: the meaning of 'Gavagai!' will never be translated with certainty.

Interestingly enough, Quine's indeterminacy thesis was published in the same volume (Brower, 1959a) as Roman Jakobson's (1959: 232) statement that 'the meaning of any linguistic sign is its translation into some further, alternative sign'. This might also be called the principle of semiosis, of meaning itself as a constant process of interpretation or translation. The idea can be traced back to the American thinker Peirce, sometimes regarded as the founder of semiotic approaches to translation (see Gorlée, 1994). Taken as such, the principle of semiosis should mean that translations do not transfer or reproduce meaning but are actively creating meanings. From the very beginning, this idea was present within the very discourse of those (including Peirce and Jakobson) whose prime search was for certainty, for a sure grounding of thought. At the time, however, the principle of semiosis was regarded as dissipation rather than liberation.

An intriguing though largely forgotten snapshot of the associated analytical approaches is the volume *Meaning and Translation*, edited by Guenther and Guenther-Reutter in 1978. Here we find a general assumption that the problems of translation are those of formal semantics, to be cured by heavy doses of propositional logic. The debates concern the extent to which social or contextual factors need be taken into consideration, whether meaning is in one's head or in social use, and the exact nature of translatability (a problem that was found but never solved by the tradition of the German Romantics). We find, for example, translation involved in Katz's principle of effability, which says that each proposition can be expressed by some sentence in any natural language – similar propositions can be found in Frege (1984), Tarski (1994) and Searle (1969). Katz (1978: 209–216) recognises the principle to be basically true but subject to 'performance limitations', notably the length of the resulting sentences. Since all real-world translations are subject to such limitations, Katz effectively moves the problem of translatability into the social or pragmatic domain, away from the concerns of philosophical semantics at that stage.

An associated area dealt with in the *Translation and Meaning* volume is the analysis of translational discourse as a mode of reported speech. Bigelow (1978) recognises that translators are doing something in between reported speech ('The author said, *"Ich bin müde"'*) and indirect speech ('The author said he was tired'). A translational mid-point ('The author said, "I am tired"') can be named as a partly Fregean hyperintensional operator, present in the proposition that 'X translates as Y'. This is a fine analysis of the discursive form of ideal equivalence. At that point, however, the philosopher can go no further without recognising the intervention of historical subjectivities (a translator *chooses* to render X as Y). Historical subjectivity was once again considered beyond the analytical philosophers' remit.

Something similar happens with W.D. Hart's (1970) little-remarked observation that translators cannot simultaneously preserve self-reference, truth-value and reference. This means that the sentence 'The first word of this very sentence has three letters' cannot be rendered word for word into French (where the first word would have two letters) without becoming untrue. There are several strategies for solving the problem (to refer to the English sentence, or to talk about two letters instead of three). Burge (1978) usefully sees this paradox as important for the rendering of dialogue, where the reader is not sure of what language is being referred to and truth-value cannot be maintained. For the formalist, however, the neatness of the analysis once again dissolves into questions of context and choice, together with the awareness that actual translation solutions are often between the alternatives mapped out in theory. Interestingly enough, the French thinker Maurice Blanchot (1949) had pointed out the half-way status of Hemingway's characters who, by speaking Spanish in English – inserting the occasional Spanish term and adopting Spanish syntax – created a 'shadow of distance' that could then be translated as such. For Blanchot, this meant that the text, prior to translation, was in more than one language, working an internal distance that obviously escaped the vision of formal semantics. But that was a Europe, a different world, lying in wait of Derrida.

The analytical philosophers were doing eminently useful philosophical work. They were taking very real problems, defining them in neat terms, and formulating some possible solutions. They could have been of real service to mainstream translation research. Unfortunately, with some exceptions (see Malmkjaer, 1998a: 9), their formulations have had minimal authority in translation theory, much to the detriment of the field. Why?

First, there has been little ongoing tradition within analytical philosophy itself, where translation has remained no more than an interesting test case. The fundamental debate raised by Quine has occasionally been picked up (cf. Kirk, 1986; Føllesdal, 2001) and has had applications in anthropological research (Feleppa, 1998). However, as a general epistemological principle, it has generally failed to transcend positions such as Chomsky's (1980: 15) pronouncement that the indeterminacy of translation is 'true and uninteresting'. As Katz (1978: 220) put it, if two translators give different renditions of the same sentence, and both renditions are equally acceptable, then they may disagree personally but there is strictly nothing for them to argue about. In the parlance of the day, there is no 'fact of the matter'.

Second, although the search for certainty could formulate precise problems, it could not offer any authoritative solutions. This kind of philosophy marked itself off as an ultimately regional field of inquiry, of service at some points but not willing to enter the world of action. There has been a more radical engagement with uncertainty, notably in the work of Donald Davidson, and this might be in tune with general trends away from ontological assumptions. Davidson refers to translation explicitly when defending the thesis that the attribution of a truth-value to another's utterance is inseparable from the assumed translatability of that utterance. If we believe the native's 'Gagavai!' has a referential (extensive) meaning, then we must assume that it is translatable into our language (Davidson, 1984: 194–195). This would effectively enlist translation in an argument against radical cultural relativism. However, in raising the philosophical stakes to the highest level, Davidson does little to prove any degree of actual translatability, nor does he offer much direction to anyone seeking to investigate actual translations.

Third, and more fatally, a vitriolic debate took place between John Searle and Jacques Derrida, mainly between 1983 and 1988 (see Derrida, 1988). Searle defended the existence of literal meaning, in the line of the kind of necessary beliefs that Davidson was working on. Derrida was arguing against any such stable ground for meaning, in the line of the critique of 'transcendental signifieds' that he had been denouncing in French since the late 1960s. Although not about translation as such, this debate did turn on problems of shared or non-shared cultural conventions, most immediately about how one should behave in academic debates. The result was only superficially a dividing line between English language and French philosophy (the former still nostalgic for certainty, the latter seeing any such beliefs as reactionary). It also became, in the English-speaking academy, a dividing line between linguistic and literary approaches to problems of alterity. Since that debate, many literary scholars have felt they no longer needed to read anything from the analytical tradition, as if the latter had simply all got it wrong. And remarkably few analytical philosophers make any reference to Derrida, as if he were only for lunatic fringes. Although the debate did not concern translation, its divisions have had profound effects on the authority of philosophical discourse in translation theory, as we shall see below.

Prior to his American debate, Derrida had had remarkably little to say about translation. In his most influential early work, *De la grammatologie* (1967), his approach was presented as a critique of traditional separations of form and meaning. Saussure, for example, could formulate the two-part sign (signifier and signified) only by excluding from his science the difference between spoken and written signifiers. For Derrida, the illusion of stable meaning can only come from such exclusions. The work of active thought (in this case, of grammatology, the science of the excluded writing) must be to restore those suppressed differences, and to make them work against stability. This was a critique eminently suited to the spirit of May 1968, albeit without expressed political allegiance. To anyone reading that work from the perspective of translation theory, the critique was also a theory of semiosis, of meaning as a constant process of interpretation and re-interpretation (Peirce's (1931–1958) theory of the interpretant is cited). In a word, it was a generalised theory of translation, not as a process conveying meaning but as constantly creating it.

We will pick up the later Derrida in the next two sections. But two aspects should be noted, here. First, to our knowledge, Derrida has never formulated that generalised theory of translation as such. He certainly mentions the issue in an early commentary on non-equivalence (Derrida, 1968) and in a much-cited reading of Walter Benjamin (Derrida, 1985).

Indeed, in that same reading he dismisses Jakobson because of a few absolute categories, but does little to integrate the notion of semiosis. Second, Derrida's actual commentaries on translations are more conservative and constructive than are those of the many translation theorists who would take their lead from him.

To understand why this might be so, we must try to see how the authority of philosophy has fared in the more precarious spheres of a fledgling intellectual discipline.

Philosophy as Authority for the Theorisation of Translation

The theorisation of translation, whether by translators or academics, has leant on philosophical discourses far more than philosophers have seriously considered translation. In this highly asymmetric relationship, difficult texts fall into the hands of readers from more generalist spheres. One suspects that the philosophers would not always identify with what has been done in their name.

The authority function is of long standing. Jerome, for example, has long been cited as an authority for fidelity to both form and sense, since he actually condoned both modes of translating (one for sacred texts, the other for the rest). More famous is the case of Horace, whose '*nec verbo verbum*' has repeatedly been used as an authoritative pronouncement both *for* literalism and (correctly, we believe) *against* it, down to quite recent dates (see García Yebra, 1994: 48–64). What is perhaps more surprising is the extent to which the theorisation of translation has elevated such figures (a theologian-translator, a poet) to philosopher-like authority, speaking with the wisdom of a distant past. One might attribute such levitation to the relative silence of properly philosophical discourses. Yet something similar still happens with figures such as Humboldt, Schleiermacher, Nietzsche, Benjamin and Sartre, who would certainly qualify as thinkers, theologians, translators and writers, but not always as philosophers in any professional sense. That is a status sometimes thrust upon them. In so doing, those who theorise translation too easily assume the consensus and possible coherence of philosophy. In many cases the authority has been created and projected by the translation theorists themselves.

A consequence of this 'boomerang' authority function is the fairly common practice of stringing together names that appear to be on one's side. Thinkers of various shades are cited because of the prestige they enjoy in the circles in which translation is being discussed. For instance, we find the American theorist Lawrence Venuti borrowing frames from the French Marxist Louis Althusser in 1986, revindicating Schleiermacher in 1991, bowing to Derrida and De Man in 1992, being Nietzschean in 1995 and working from Benjamin and Blanchot in 1995. Then in 1998, we find Venuti citing Lecercle's arguments that linguistics always leaves an untheorised 'remainder', a part of language that is not systematised. Venuti attaches this idea to Deleuze and Guattari's arguments for 'minority cultures', ideally created through translations that exploit linguistic remainders (see Venuti, 1998a, 1998b). Those references stimulate discussion on translation. Sometimes, however, they fare badly in the trip from philosophy, becoming falsely new and occasionally falling wide of the mark. The idea of the remainder, for example, can be found in earlier Marxist thinkers such as Lefebvre (1968: 24–45) or Pêcheux (1975: 20–82); as a critique of linguistics it completely misses whole developments like the sociolinguistics of variation (since Labov) or descriptive text linguistics (since van Dijk). Nor are the sweeping critiques strictly necessary: Venuti's greater virtues lie in bringing political and social contexts to literary translation in English, and in his close relation with both the practice and the practitioners. Although his earlier texts can be read as an intellectual defence of foreignising translation strategies, broadly in the hermeneutic tradition, his translation practice has also espoused 'fluent translating' when suited to the particular project (Venuti in Wilcock, 2000: xvii). One should thus perhaps not look for doctrinal philosophical thought, but for a constantly engaged translatorial practice. Nevertheless, the philosophical references give weight and good tone when read by people distant from European traditions, especially those already adverse to positivist linguistics (following the Searle–Derrida debate, if not for other reasons). Venuti the translator has thus managed to develop his own thought while simultaneously manipulating the prestige of the foreign. Note that this particular prestige function is enhanced by the distance of the source: by citing French and German names, reducing them to a few lines or paragraphs, Venuti can at once simplify their contribution and become their privileged interpreter, channelling their authority.

The translation theorist as privileged reader of philosophy is by no means limited to the American literary academy. In France, Antoine Berman (1984) developed arguments in favour of foreignisation by drawing out the ideas of selected German Romantics, unabashedly elevating Humboldt and Schleiermacher to the status of philosophers, and passing in silence marginal German thinkers such as Hegel (cf. Pym, 1997). Berman could thus construe 'foreignising' as a clearly Germanic tradition, to be opposed to the French tradition of the *belles infidèles*, leaving himself as the privileged point of contact. Berman was nevertheless able to turn his readings into a radical and stimulating project for an ethics of translation, based on the defence of otherness and the critique of ethnocentric textual practices. In the terminological and conceptual rigour of his project, one sees the imprint of Berman's academic training in philosophy. This is a tradition that also bears fruits in work by Jean-René Ladmiral (1979) – where meticulous attention is paid to the paradoxes of translation and its teaching – and in Alexis Nouss's (2001b) work on cultural *métissage*, which might be regarded as developing Berman's ethical project beyond the confines of translation.

Other cross-cultural references are not quite so open. Alfred Hirsch's editing of the collective volume *Übersetzung und Dekonstruktion* (1997) opens with a translation of an early essay by Derrida (using the concept of translation to conceptualise the role of philosophy within the academy). However, 'deconstruction' then turns out to be more or less everything that can be borrowed from Walter Benjamin (the points of contact are explicit in Hirsch, 1995), such that French thought on translation is actually shown to be German, and to have been so for quite some time. In this case the authority of foreign philosophical thought turns out to be a reminder of a 'forgotten code', something good that one had at home all along.

The authority of philosophy thus creates privileged readers and, through them, strangely coherent opposing traditions in the theorising of translation. Further translation theorists then tend to follow one tradition and simply not see the other. For example, a fine theoretical article on the non-binary options involved in translating dialogue (Lane-Mercer, 1997) refers to a whole French–American literary tradition simply by naming Berman and Venuti. However, the text makes no mention of how the same problems were dealt with in the Quinean tradition.

Something similar can be found in German in the development of translational action theory (from Holz-Mänttäri, 1984) and functionalist *Skopostheorie* (from Reiß & Vermeer, 1984). Holz-Mänttäri borrows initial general perspectives from the action theory of von Wright (1968), adding insights from both extensions of the action and functionalist social anthropology (citations from Humboldt and Malinowski). The basic idea for Vermeer, on the other hand, is that translating is an action carried out in order to achieve a purpose (*Skopos*). This purpose is highly variable (it may or may not involve equivalence to a source) and is negotiated with any number of social actors. Holz-Mänttäri stresses the complexity of these negotiations, the translator's social role as an expert, and the many modes of translational action (since her translators do far more than translate). Vermeer would give more weight to the client's commission and to the conceptual priorities involved. Despite their fairly complex terminological webs, both might claim to have 'dethroned the source text' (Vermeer, 1989), revealing that there are numerous other determinants on what translators do. Within German-language research, this has been enough to form a close-knit group of self-citing theorists, weaving the image of a theoretical revolution, an epistemological break with a millennial past of fidelities and equivalencies. The ideas of action theory, however, were by no means the exclusive preserve of this general translation theory. The notion of purpose-based action has had a philosophical language since Kant and is common enough in any sociological approach. It could lead to a focus on purposes, competencies and expertise theory, as it has done in German, but it also has several feet in linguistic pragmatics, deontics, system theory and new methodologies of empirical observation. These latter aspects have been better developed beyond *Skopostheorie*, yet in ways that remain in fundamental agreement with its founding principles.

One should not be surprised, then, when a more cognitive kind of action theory, coming from the pragmatics of Watzlawick *et al.* (1967) or even the ethics of Varela (1992), appears in alternative theorisations of translational action. For example, Monacelli and Punzo (2001) start from the paradoxes like the fact that a translation is at once equivalent and non-equivalent to its source, depending on the momentary perspective of the observer. Such relations can be mapped by fuzzy logic (cf. also Grant, 1999). What might be surprising, though, is that the origins of action theory, whatever its social, mathematical or psychological extensions, lie in analytical philosophy, in the tradition of Wittgenstein and Quine. That, at least, is where one must place the pioneering work of von Wright (1968) and Watzlawick *et al.* (1968).

So would the interest in action theory represent a late awakening to analytical philosophy? It seems more the case that the translation theorists concerned were turning to fragments of philosophical discourses, not in order to legitimise any systematic analytical approach, but as part of an attempt to solve isolated and often long-standing problems. Andrew Chesterman (1993), for example, cites the pragmatic branch of philosophical inquiry, again referring to von Wright, in order to define the notions of 'norms' and their implications for ethics. Yet Chesterman (1997) also borrows from Karl Popper on several occasions either to clarify concepts (as with the notion of 'three worlds') or to adapt specific ideas. In the field of ethics, for example, Popper observed that people agree more on what is bad than on what is good. Chesterman thus proposes that translation should have a similarly 'negative ethics', based on avoiding misunderstandings rather than on any ideal of complete equivalence.

Another use of philosophical discourse as a problem-solving tool would be Arnaud Laygues' readings of Buber, Marcel and Levinas (Laygues,

2001), none of whom discussed translation at length, but all of whom developed ideas that can help translators think about their human relations. When Martin Buber, for instance, regards I–you discourse as ethically more authentic than third-person discourse, Laygues proposes that the ethical translator should regard both text and reader as second persons, not as objects. When Emmanuel Levinas regards the other (the person who is non-I) as a face to which we have certain ethical obligations, Laygues proposes that the translator seek an adequate ethical relation with the other (text, author, reader) and only then be concerned with the deontology of professional action. In a similar vein, Melby (1995) has attempted to apply Levinas's insights on otherness to the general field of language technology. In all these cases, philosophical discourse is used as a source of stimulating analogies or necessary terminological precision, but not as a ready-made solution to all the problems of translation studies.

Thanks to such borrowings, the translation theories of the 1990s were increasingly concerned with ethical issues. This was partly a reaction against traditional concepts like fidelity and equivalence, which 20th century uncertainty had left without any conceptual grounding. Yet it was also a response to the empiricism that had motivated many parts of translation studies in the 1980s. Equivalence, for example, had become a fact of all translations for descriptive translation studies (cf. Toury, 1980), dissolving the concept to the extent that it could no longer state what translators should do; the scholar's task was merely to describe its variants, norms and possible laws. At the same time, equivalence had become no more than a restricted 'special case' for _Skopostheorie_, which sought to provide translators with alternative professional guidelines (cf. Pym, 1995). For what were becoming deconstructionist or postmodern approaches, however, notions like equivalence and fidelity were traditional essentialist illusions, unable to provide any guidelines at all. Barbara Johnson (1985) proposed 'taking fidelity philosophically', as might a cheated spouse. That loss of faith left a gap, allowing for a return to fundamental ethical issues, this time based on the texture of human relationships rather than on any empiricism of performance. Not gratuitously, this return to ethics has accompanied greater attention to dialogue interpreting, where more importance is intuitively given to people rather than to texts (see Pym, 2001).

If there is a particular way of using philosophical discourse at this level, it is frequently not for isolated problem solving. Some theorists take a whole system on board, seeking its ethical consequences in a more global sense. Here one might return to Walter Benjamin (1923) reflecting on his translations of Baudelaire through the worldview of Kabbalistic tradition (see Steiner, 1975). A more frequent point of departure is Jacques Derrida, whose texts since the late 1980s frequently work on and with translations. This later Derrida seems very aware that his work is not only being translated into American English, but is also being interpreted within American departments of Literary and Cultural Studies. He plays with this translational relationship, revamping Benjamin, writing for and to his American translators, and reading translations of literary texts, notably Shakespeare.

Derrida's main translational interest in this period is the plurality of the (apparent) source. The oft-cited phrase '*plus d'une langue*' expresses this plurality: it could be translated as 'more than one language' or as 'let us have no more of one language', and both readings are in the source. Derrida, however, does not seek to 'dethrone the source text', as Vermeer has claimed to have done and as many deconstructionists have believed. In a 1992 text we find Derrida asking how it is possible that a work such as *Romeo and Juliet* could make sense – any kind of sense – well beyond its original historical and cultural location. This apparent mode of translatability is called 'iterability', attributed not to anything semantic but to the literary institutionalisation of certain meaning effects (cf. Davis, 2001: 30–35). In this, Derrida necessarily recognises that literature is a system operating with ideals *other* than the constant process of deconstruction – this had been recognised much earlier (Derrida, 1967: 229) – as indeed might be operative ethical concepts like justice (Derrida, 1993: 147). The source text may thus be seen, not as a set of obligatory orders, nor as an entirely annulled monarch, but as a phantom, an image that organises without determining the range of translational variants. It returns, like the ghost of King Hamlet (Derrida, 1993: 42–3). Derrida takes care to distinguish this from a claim to translatability, the sameness of which would make strict alterity impossible and must thus necessarily be broken. He nevertheless implicitly pays homage to the great literary text, moreover situating himself in a reading position to grasp all translational variants, to judge French translations of Shakespeare, and to legitimate their pertinence to the source. That is, Derrida not only recognises the essentialist roles played by literary concepts, he plays the same humanist game himself.

Other deconstructionists, we have noted, have tended to be far more radical and sweeping in their theorising of translation. The Brazilian theorist Rosemary Arrojo has perhaps led the critique of translation as 'meaning transfer', as the enactment of necessary equivalencies, or indeed of any assumption of positional stability. We thus find her enlisting deconstruction and fellow travellers (psychoanalysis, postmodernity) not just against all assumptions of meaning transfer as such (Arrojo, 1993) but also against many feminist approaches to translation (Arrojo, 1994), against ideal symmetrical relations (Arrojo, 1997) and indeed against all forms of linguistic essentialism (Arrojo, 1996). Similar negativity can be found in Kaisa Koskinen (2000a), who ostensibly works from Derrida and Bauman in order to assess the ethics of the translation theorists Venuti and Pym. Her postmodern eschewal of any position that would seek to guide the individual's responsibility for their own actions forces her to reject not just idealist political causes but also searches for a professional subjectivity, derided as 'neo-tribalism' (Koskinen, 2000a: 78). Such critiques allow little response, not least because theorists such as Venuti and Pym tend to write at practical levels where notions like 'professionalism' are simply assumed: they are embodied in social entities such as professional associations. At those more applied levels of discourse, as in much of feminism or Marxism, the philosophical authority of postmodern ethics is not immediately recognised. There are often more pressing problems to solve.

At the opposite end of such conceptual conflicts, some translation theories have managed to flourish without reference to any philosophical authority at all. The *théorie du sens* developed by Danica Seleskovich in Paris claims that one translates 'sense', not words (Seleskovich, 1975; Seleskovich & Lederer, 1989). The exact nature of this 'sense', however, remains virtually untheorised. One finds a few early references to the French psychologist Piaget, but beyond that, a whole school of theorists and pedagogues has been based on the simple practical certitude that fragments of language make 'sense', and that 'sense' can thus be translated. This 'sense' might have been the 'literal meaning' defended by Searle; it might even be a necessary assumption of Gricean conversation, or of Davidson's truth-values. However, in the Parisian theory it requires no more than institutional justification: 'sense' is an idea that works for the training of translators, and no more need be said. The result is that, when polemicists from this school (perhaps Sergio Viaggio and Mariano García-Landa) seek philosophical debate on the issue, they are left with scarcely a leg to stand on. Their position was undermined by Quinean skepticism several generations ago; the division between sense and form was rubbed out by deconstruction; the terms of reference no longer find any philosophical frame.

Any advance in translation theory perhaps depends on greater awareness that most of the traditional arguments are now non-arguments. The strategies of minor power nevertheless lead the other way. Most schools or would-be schools of translation theory have needed to build a *Feindbild*, an image of the enemy. For Seleskovich and her followers, the enemy was anyone who said one should translate words, not sense (did any serious contemporary really believe that?). For *Skopostheorie*, the enemy was anyone who believed in equivalence as the only necessary goal of a translation (but surely it depends how they defined 'translation'?). For descriptive translation studies, the enemy was anyone who tried to tell translators how to translate, since that was prescriptivism (but can descriptions be entirely neutral?). For desconstructionists, it was anyone who believed in translation as 'meaning transfer' (but did anyone ever pretend you could pick up a meaning?).

Most of those enemies are actually quite difficult to find in translation theory, at least in the simplistic terms in which they have been attacked. And none of those binary oppositions is tenable in terms of contemporary philosophical discourse. It is for this reason, we suggest, that few philosophers would entirely identify with everything that translation theorists have done in their name.

Translating Philosophy

The early Derrida (1968: 9) claimed that 'with the problem of translation, we are dealing with nothing less than the problem of the passage to philosophy'. His immediate concern in that text was a translation of Plato, where the Greek term *pharmakon* could be rendered in French as either *remède* (cure) or *poison* (poison), but not both terms at the same time. The translation problem was thus one of respecting the particular terminology of philosophical discourse, or at least of the philosophy that shares its terms with other discourse genres. In noting the inadequacy of the existing translations in French, Derrida might be said to have achieved a more effective translation himself, albeit exceeding certain performance limitations. He did so because, obviously, a philosopher who uses a vernacular has a special interest in the translation of philosophy. Translation becomes a condition of philosophy's own iterability, placing its legacy in foreign hands (for the anxieties of Nietzsche on the subject, see Pym, 1998a). After centuries of neglect under a hierarchy of languages, translation might even become too important to be left to mere translation theorists.

The translation of philosophy (Plato will serve as our example) has been a concern of Western philosophy ever since the relation with the classical past became problematic. In 15th century Renaissance humanism, Leonardo Bruni insisted on elegance as a necessary feature of Plato translations, engaging in a watershed debate with the Spanish bishop Alonso de Cartagena, who defended a medieval translationese that was difficult to read, full of calques, and rarely mistakable as anything from the target culture. In that debate, Cartagena might be seen as defending foreignness, technical terms and linguistic plurality, in a way that many postmodernists would approve of. He was also arguing for translations that would keep pagan philosophy indelibly marked as being different from Christian doctrine. Unfortunately, that debate was historically won by Bruni. Plato found a translational voice as a stylist, a person; philosophy used the same words as other genres; pagan thought mixed with Judeo-Christian theology; discourse flowed from Greek to Latin to the vernaculars of Europe; Derrida's problem with *pharmakon* thus became thinkable.

That humanist tradition of translating philosophy is really what Derrida is playing with and against. It remained largely unchallenged until philosophy became at once secular and theological. The Protestant theologian Schleiermacher, for example, could pretend to be ideologically untroubled about translating Plato as a pagan; he was more concerned with philological otherness of the text. The thought of German Romanticism was on the level of form, language, identity, not of content as such. Schleiermacher's Plato was thus anything but elegant, with so many translator's notes that Ortega y Gassett (1937/2000), while largely agreeing with the foreignising strategy, took time out to decry it as 'ugly'.

An anti-personalist strand of German Romanticism can be followed through much of the hermeneutic tradition. More than any one else, Martin Heidegger used translation to illustrate the tortuous paths of interpretation, using translation as a mode of philosophical exposition, and perhaps of thought. This can be seen in his polemical retranslations of German philosophical terms from pre-Socratic Greek, in his constant reflections on the differences between languages, and in his insistence that translation (*Übersetzung*) is not just interpretation but also a handing-down, a question of legacy (*Überlieferung*), as key concepts draw on what was hidden in a prestigious anteriority (Heidegger, 1963: 395–396). Translation becomes a way of actually doing philosophy, as carrying on a lost tradition. In this, we find a possible inspiration for Derrida's concern with a term such as *pharmakon*, if not for the respect paid to iterability and the ghostly presence of the past. We might also divine the reason why these philosophers seem to prefer their own translations to anything produced by mere translators: Western philosophy, at a certain level, has become a series of conceptual translations of itself.

One might equally say that many contemporary philosophical discourses share an intimate concern about their own language being translational on some level. The result is commonly a heterogeneous text, which tends to become less so in translation (on English translations of Wittgenstein and Plato, cf. Venuti, 1998b: 106–119). One of the possible laws of all translation is that it tends to homogenise discourse. However, in the case of philosophy this may now be less so, since the authors speak with authority within the humanities: the American Derrida, for example, cannot be confused with the language of American philosophy. Indeed, translators and translation theorists tend to respect the philosophers far more than any philosopher ever had kind words to say about a translator.

Future Orientations: The Limits of Philosophy

The main problems in the relations between philosophy and translation should by now be fairly evident. Where philosophical authority is present, many translation theorists are needlessly partisan. And where it is absent, a rather quaint empiricism reigns, as in much of descriptive translation studies, or in corpus linguistics or think-aloud protocols, which rarely transcend positivist notions of science. The continental divisions of philosophical discourse itself have served us poorly in this respect. Half the world pretends to know immediately what is wrong with the other half. The result is not just a lack of dialogue, but serious misunderstandings.

Some of the most unfortunate errors concern the status of linguistic inquiry. For instance, it is not uncommon to find literary theorists (cf. Venuti, 1998b: 21–24) railing against something like Grice's maxims for conversation (do not tell lies, do not speak for too long, be relevant, etc.), since such things are culturally variable. And we can find quite a few normative articles where the same maxims are used to judge how well translators have performed, as if the maxims were laws for good texts. Both the theorists and the prescriptivists ignore or downplay the fact that Grice sees pragmatic meaning being produced by the *breaking* of these maxims. Not to see this is a serious loss. Within the analytical tradition, Grice is no doubt seeking something like semantic certitude, but what he has found is that people create meaning by breaking rules. So the rules are not laws; they are operative fictions that we use in order to communicate; and the breaking can lead to any number of nuances and ironies. This might provide a clue for the future status of the things people say and believe about translation.

One of the few theorists who have referred to both the analytical tradition and the hermeneutic–deconstructive complex is Andrew Benjamin, whose labyrinthine 1989 book *Translation and the Nature of Philosophy* has had remarkably little impact on the field. Like many others, Benjamin realises there is no philosophical grounding for translation as 'rational recovery' (the use of reason to recover the meanings of the source). Like many literary scholars he believes that, instead of semantics and the search for certainty, 'the emphasis must shift to the text itself and a concern with language' (Benjamin, 1989: 86). Yet Benjamin goes a little further, attempting to formulate what it is in language that is to be translated, or created in translation, and he does so in interactional terms: 'In the beginning was the site of conflict' (Benjamin, 1989: 108). So it is that site that is extended in translation.

That kind of reasoning might show a way forward, especially if conflict can be reconceptualised as neo-classical cooperation. The important point is that we move beyond the facile critiques of illusions. The sites of conflict (or cooperation) become places where ideas such as fidelity, equivalence, translatability, invisibility or professional ethics have functional organising roles (cf. on equivalence, Pym, 1995; on translatability, Pym & Turk, 1998; or on 'presumed sameness' Gutt, 1991, although Gutt's restrictive definition of 'direct translation' does lead to unnecessary normative consequences). Those roles can indeed be grasped in terms of the analytical tradition. This kind of non-believing return might even be postmodern, as if the terms mattered.

One remaining problem is the role and responsibility of the individual translator. Ammann (1994), citing the authority of existentialism, claims that translation studies has consistently tried to exclude the individual by developing categories of equivalence or binary dichotomies. That is true enough. We might go further: if any science is of the general, any scientific kind of translation studies must exclude the purely individual. So is our only option then to use philosophy to denounce the impositions of theory, and thereby liberate or empower the individual by pretending that they make their own decisions? That position would seem to stymie our desire to recognise operational fictions.

There are several possible solutions here. One of them, argued by Chesterman (1999), is to claim that translation studies need not directly tell translators what to do; it can carry out empirical scientific research in order to predict what is likely to happen if translators adopt option A, B or C in a given situation. This carries empiricism to a logical consequence, without necessarily assuming that the theorist's terms of analysis are ideologically neutral or devoid of borrowed authority.

Another possible solution is to use sociological discourse to conceptualise modes of individuality that are constantly conditioned by social relations, without being reduced to them. Here we might pick up the concept of 'habitus' formulated by Bourdieu (cf. Simeoni, 1998) and attempt to make it compatible with the notion of translation norms developed by Toury (1995). This, however, is merely to name a 'site of conflict' within the object of study, without actually solving the conflict and without relating it to the position of the theorist.

At the same time, one might similarly follow Bourdieu in accepting that the human sciences are not simply of 'the general'; they are based on social relations in which both theorists and practitioners participate, often within the same person. There would thus be considerable individuality involved, with philosophical authority ultimately giving way to sociological reflection on our own positions and interests. Translation theorists, as mediators between philosophical discourses and translational practices, are actively involved in a constant dialogue, in which we must learn from both sides. Seen in this light, the problem of translation studies is probably not that it has to read more philosophy, but that it should pay more dialectic attention to what *translators* do and say. A guideline for this might run as follows:

> Translating can be seen as a problem-solving activity in which a source element may be rendered by one or more elements in the target language. If translators have only one available option, there is no more to be said; no philosophy is needed. When, however, they have two or three options, translation is worth talking about, ideally between translators, who thus start theorising. And when, as occasionally occurs, there are numerous options available and no clear theory about how to reduce that complexity, the cause for discussion reaches levels where philosophical discourse may be turned to, for ideas about the options, although rarely for the translational solutions. This can be seen in most of the theories and approaches we have dealt with here: philosophical discourses tend to be appealed to, or intervene, with respect to problems where more than three or four alternatives are available. To develop words appropriate to those alternatives might be the role of philosophy such as we have seen it; to adapt and propose them might be one of the roles of Translation Studies.

What the philosophical discourses thereby miss, of course, are the logics of the more everyday activities, the many techniques by which translators themselves constantly reduce complexity. Those are the operational fictions that we need to grasp. And to do so, we should perhaps learn to think more bottom-up, from the actual practices, rather than top-down, from the great conceptual systems, if ever the ends are to meet.

Linguistics and Translation

GUNILLA ANDERMAN

Throughout the ages, translation as well as linguistics, the formal study of language, have attracted comments and speculation. The need for practising translators is acknowledged as early as the Old Testament where, in the Book of Daniel 1:4, reference is made to the need for mastery of 'the tongue of the Chaldeans' for use in 'the king's palace'. And since time immemorial the nature and origin of human language has invited speculation. As late as the 17th century one view held that the primitive language of mankind was Chinese, which was spoken by Noah and his family in the Ark and survived the flood (Aitchison, 1996: 4). It was to take until the latter half of the 18th century before linguistics, then known as philology, started to emerge as a discipline in its own right; for translation studies to become an independent academic subject with established interdisciplinary links to other fields of study including linguistics was to take close to the dawn of a new millennium.

In 1786, the first step was taken, nudging the study of language closer towards becoming a discipline in its own right. In a paper presented to the Royal Asiatic Society in Calcutta, Sir William Jones (1746–1794) of the East India Company declared that no philologist could examine the Sanskrit, Greek and Latin languages without believing them to have sprung from some common, Indo-European source which perhaps no longer existed (Jones, 1970). Comparative and historical linguistics now became the focus of the attention of philologists, and, by the possession of distinctive, shared characteristics, languages were successively grouped together genealogically into families. While the similarity of cognates such as 'hand' in English, *Hand* in German and *hand* in Dutch, Danish, Norwegian and Swedish points to a related Germanic group of languages, French *main*, Spanish *mano* and Italian *mano* constitute some of the languages belonging to the Romance language family while *ryka*, *rêka* and *ruka* in Russian, Polish and Czech respectively suggest membership of the Slavonic group of languages. The implications for translation arising from the groundbreaking work of philologists of the 19th century in grouping together into families the Indo-European languages as we know them today were aptly illustrated a century later by the observation made by translation theorists Vinay and Darbelnet that 'literal translation is a unique solution [...] It is most commonly found in translations between closely related languages (e.g. French/Italian)' (Vinay & Darbelnet, 1995: 34).

Following the discovery of the common historical origin of the Indo-European languages, the interest of linguists began to focus on the historical development of languages to the extent that, during the latter half of the 19th century, a reaction was beginning to be felt to the preoccupation with the past and the rigorous analytical methods employed in linguistic analysis, which at times were less than rigorous. In particular, criticism was voiced by the Junggrammatiker, a group of German linguists centred round the University of Leipzig in the 1870s. The legacy left by these scholars, known in English as the 'neo-grammarians', remains in currency today: a concern with the spoken language as an object of examination coupled with an insistence on statable principles and a theory capable of formulation as a prerequisite to empirically-based linguistic investigation.

The focus on a more systematic approach to the study of language attracted the attention of linguists from other countries including the Swiss scholar Ferdinand de Saussure (1857–1913), who, following studies in Leipzig and Berlin returned to Switzerland to lecture at the University of Geneva. 'The father of modern linguistics', de Saussure stressed the importance of a *synchronic approach*, the study of language at a given point in time, not related to its past, which is the pursuit of historical or *diachronic* linguistics. Also of importance to de Saussure's theoretical framework was the distinction between *langue*, the underlying set of rules of a language and *parole*, the actual use made of language by individual speakers. This distinction is still not granted sufficient importance in translation theory, where serious attention has only recently started to be given to vernacular and dialect translation. Another key concept introduced by de Saussure was *the sign*, which he invested with two parts, the *signifier* and the *signified* (1916/1983). While the former is a mental image of the physical sound made when saying for instance 'dog' in English, the latter is a mental concept or representation of dogs in the real world. The relationship between the signifier and the signified was, according to de Saussure, an arbitrary social construct, a potential problem for the translator as signs do not signify in isolation. Although 'dog' in English translates into Spanish as *perro*, the two words carry different sets of associations or connotations. In English, animals like humans have 'legs', 'backs' and 'necks'. In Spanish, on the other hand, human legs are known as *piernas*, their backs as *espaldas* and their necks as *cuellos* while animal legs are referred to as *patas*, their backs as *lomos* and their necks as *pescuezos*. These observations tell a different story of the place of animals in Hispanic culture from that of the dog as beloved pet and man's best friend in English-speaking parts of the world.

The first half of the 20th century also saw links established between translation and anthropologically-based linguistics. Through the Empire, English speakers had been brought into contact with a world beyond Europe and with speakers of vastly different languages. Through his field-work centred on the life of the Trobriand islanders of New Guinea in the southwest Pacific, Bronislaw Malinowski (1884–1942), holder of the first Chair of Anthropology at the University of London, was empirically confronted with the limits of translation. With no English terms available for concepts crucial to his description of the culture and religion of the islanders, Malinowski was left no choice but to become '[i]n the history of English linguistics [...] the first scholar to deal with the systematic use of translation in the statement of meaning in ethnographic texts' (Firth, 1968: 76). Previously undocumented languages also attracted the attention of linguists in the United States, where interest focused on the Native American languages. Rapidly facing extinction, these became the object of study of such linguists as Franz Boas (1858–1942) and Edward Sapir (1884–1939), both born in Europe and trained in neo-grammarian methodology. The observations of Sapir, and in turn Benjamin Whorf (1897–1944), found an expression in what has become known as the Sapir/Whorf hypothesis which, with its emphasis on disparity in world view between speakers of vastly different languages (Whorf, 1956), makes translation a near impossibility in its more extreme, 'stronger' interpretation. In its 'weaker' version, on the other hand, it does little more than confirm the experience of every practising translator that languages differ not so much with respect to what it is possible to say in them as to the degree of difficulty with which it can be said.

The European heritage of the neogrammarian insistence on rigour in methodology was at the time reinforced in the USA by the influence of behaviourist, mechanistic psychology on linguistics, which found its leading exponent in Leonard Bloomfield (1887–1949). With its strong emphasis on methodology and concern with the structure of language to the exclusion of meaning, Bloomfield's *Language* (1933) dominated the study of linguistics during the 1930s and 1940s, confining the scope of linguistic analysis of American 'structuralists' to only the structure and rules of the language investigated.

Early views on the link between translation and linguistics are found in an often- quoted paper by the Czech-born American structuralist Roman

Jakobson. In 'On linguistic aspects of translation', Jakobson (1959/2000) points to three different kinds of translation. While *interlingual* translation entails the transfer of content as well as of form from one language to another, *intralingual* translation entails the process of rewording in one and the same language for purposes of clarification. The third kind is *intersemiotic* translation, which is the method employed when a written text is transferred to another medium such as film or music. Acknowledging the need for the latter two types of translation, Roman Jakobson presciently anticipated recently-debated issues and developments in present-day translation studies. In an article in the *Independent* of 15 November 2001, Susan Bassnett provoked a lively debate with her proposal that, in order to maintain the interest of present-day school children, Shakespeare is in need of rewording (in other words, intralingual 'translation') into modern English. And, as the need for expertise in audio-visual translation rockets between English and other lesser-used European languages for use in film and television, intersemiotic translation is becoming the subject of avid attention.

The behaviourist stronghold on American linguistics came to a hotly debated end in the middle of the 20th century when the work of Noam Chomsky challenged the undisputed reign of leading behaviourist exponent B.F. Skinner (1904–1990) and the emphasis shifted to conditioning as the sole explanation of verbal behaviour. The interest of linguists now shifted to the study of the intuitive knowledge that speakers possess about their language; instead of highlighting the differences between languages attention turned to a search for the properties that they might share.

The 1940s had seen the first systematic attempts at developing automated translation, and the problems now occupying the interest of linguists were already familiar to scientists engaged in the process of trying to overcome the obstacles inherent in the advancement of machine translation. One such problem to be solved in non-human translation was the difficulty posed by syntactic ambiguity. Depending on whether 'the turkey' is the subject or object of 'eat', the sentence 'The turkey is ready to eat' may be interpreted either as 'The turkey is ready to eat something' or 'Someone is ready to eat the turkey'. In the former case, the application of a 'transformation' (a set of operations that at the time formed part of Chomsky's theoretical framework) has moved the object of the underlying 'core' or 'kernel' sentence into sentence initial position resulting in one, ambiguous surface structure representation. Venturing beneath the surface structure and focusing on speakers' *competence*, the internalised set of rules that speakers have about their language (which are often at variance with their *performance*), the search was now on for underlying universals. These are more easily detectable in the early language of children, prior to the acquisition of the transformations subsequently learnt by speakers in order to gain syntactic and grammatical mastery of their language (Chomsky, 1957, 1965).

In spite of the far-reaching claims of his transformational–generative (TG) grammar, Chomsky (1965: 30) was less than optimistic about its implications for translation: 'The existence of deep-seated formal universals ... does not, for example, imply that there must be some reasonable procedure for translating between languages'. Nevertheless, the tenets of Chomsky's thinking offered an opportunity for a theory of translation to be given a linguistic framework and to be provided with a 'scientific' foundation. At the time, this demand was increasingly placed on the social sciences, as evidenced by the titles of two early works by linguist and anthropologist Eugene Nida, in which the principles of TG grammar are applied to translation: *Towards a Science of Translating* (Nida, 1964) and, co-authored with C. Taber, *The Theory and Practice of Translating* (Nida & Taber, 1969).

Prior to the transfer of the text from source to receptor language (Nida's designated term for what is more commonly known as target language), two types of grammatical analysis are applied, grammatical and lexical. Drawing on Chomsky's framework as a mechanism to find solutions to the translation problems encountered by Bible translators for whom he acted as a consultant, Nida uses the concept of transformations and kernel sentences in order to account for the need for syntactic divergence from the source text in translation. If, for instance, a language uses nouns only to denote concrete objects, the transfer into another language of nouns denoting events would require the application of 'back-transformations' in order to arrive at the kernel sentences to be used in translation. A biblical phrase such as 'the creation of the world' from Ephesians 1:4 would therefore need to be 'transformed' into 'God created the world' in order for the original English noun phrase to be translated (Nida, 1969: 83).

For the solution of problems of translation on the lexical level, one of Nida's immediate concerns is the difficulty of interpretation frequently encountered in Bible translation. In order to determine correctly the meaning of a word in the source text, whether it is synonymous with another word having a different *connotative* rather than *denotative* or referential meaning, Nida subjects it to *componential analysis*. Following the analysis the transfer of the text is undertaken; this process enables Nida to make use of a concept such as 'synthesis of components' that, to use a contemporary European example, transforms 'sister and brother' in English into *'Geschwister'* in translation into German. Nida also discusses the addition of explanatory information, in present-day parlance the technique of *explicitation* (Klaudy, 1998: 83) – as in the case of expanding the reference to Vilnius in a text written in Lithuanian into 'Vilnius, the capital of Lithuania' in translation into English for ease of reader comprehension.

Critical voices raised against Nida's proposed model have fastened on the seemingly disparate step-like progression of the journey from source to receptor language, which is less likely to reflect the work of practising translators than an overall more closely synchronised approach. Nevertheless, Nida's linguistic training and his data (collected from long experience as a practising translator), in combination with his attempt to formalise his findings within a linguistic framework set the course for translation theorists to further advance the interrelationship between translation and linguistics in the years to come.

While Chomsky's approach to the formal study of language reflected his cognitively-based interest, in the UK Malinowski's legacy set English linguistics on a different course. As developed by J.R. Firth (1890–1960), Malinowski's concept of 'context of culture' was turned into 'meaning as function in context' and, as further advanced by the 'neo-Firthian' Michael Halliday, the notion became a full-scale linguistic theory, known as *Scale and Category Grammar* or *Systemic Grammar*. In a Hallidayan theoretical framework, the notion of context is viewed as the function of language operating on a number of different levels. According to Halliday, a problem such as syntactic ambiguity finds an explanation in the notion of rank shift, as in: 'The man came from the police station'. In one reading the adverbial (from the police station) ranks as 'group' answering the question 'Where did the man come from?' In another interpretation, however, it has been 'shifted' from the rank of 'clause' (who was employed at the police station) and in its contracted form becomes a mirror image of the unshifted adverbial, ranking as 'group'.

As in the United States, the emergence of a new linguistic theory that attracted a following among linguists was quickly followed by attempts to apply its theoretical framework to translation. In *A Linguistic Theory of Translation*, J.C. Catford (1965) drew on Halliday's linguistic framework and applied it to translation, including the notion of shift to account for the departure from formal correspondence that takes place when the original text is translated into the target language. While in English the sentence 'John loves Mary' may be sequentially described as subject, predicator and adjunct (SPA), in translation into Gaelic, it corresponds to the structure PSCA. '*Tha gradh aig Iain air Mairi*' is 'love at John on Mary' where C stands for 'complement'. This in turn yields the translation equivalence: English: SPA, Gaelic: PSCA (Catford, 1965: 77).

The notion of *equivalence* was of paramount importance, not only to

Catford, but also to other early translation theorists attempting to formulate a linguistically-based theory of translation. In Nida the concept was accounted for by giving *formal correspondence* second place in importance to *dynamic equivalence*, achieved if the impact of the translation produced the appropriate response from the receptor in the target language. Catford's theoretical framework carefully eschewed Nida's somewhat cavalier treatment of a concept of crucial importance to the development of automated translation, and Catford's shifts bear real similarity to notions of complex transfer in *machine translation* (MT), where formal correspondence continues to hold pride of place (Kenny, 1998: 78).

In addition to Nida and Catford, there was no shortage of attempts by other translation theorists in the 1950s and 1960s to define the concept of equivalence and its place in translation theory. In their detailed, contrastive analysis of English and French, Vinay and Darbelnet (1958/1977) proposed a set of procedures for the translator to use in order to account for the need for 'indirect' translation involving instances when equivalence in the target language cannot be established. One such procedure, *'chassé-croisé'*, turns 'Blériot flew across the Channel' into *'Blériot traversa la Manche en avion'* (Vinay & Darbelnet, 1958/1977: 105). While in English, motion and manner are both contained in the verb 'flew', in translation into French the two features cannot be expressed through the use of one verb. Instead the notion of 'motion' is conveyed through the verb *traversa* (crossed) and that of 'manner' expressed separately, in *'en avion'* (by plane).

Drawing a distinction between a number of different equivalence types, the approach to the problem of accounting for the lack of equivalence between source and target text in translation that is favoured by German translation theorist Werner Koller (1972/1979) implicitly acknowledged that the notion is not an undifferentiated one. While *connotative equivalence* entails a choice between synonymous expressions, *text-normative equivalence* concerns the usage norms for a given text type, *pragmatic equivalence* involves the receiver to whom the translation is directed and *formal equivalence* concerns formal-aesthetic features such as word play (1989).

In the framework used by Peter Newmark (1981), equivalence came in for yet another form of treatment; to account for departures from formal correspondence between source and target text, Peter Newmark introduced the concepts of *semantic* and *communicative* translation. While the French *'Défense de marcher sur la gazon'* in semantic translation into English yields 'Walking on the turf is forbidden', in communicative translation it is normally rendered as the more familiar 'Keep off the grass'. Similarly, in translation from German *'Frisch angestrichen'* reads in semantic translation into English as 'Recently painted' while in communicative translation it turns into the more easily recognisable 'Wet paint!' (Newmark, 1981).

Although varying in the use of terminology and approach, the notion of equivalence and departure from close correspondence between source and target text remained an issue of prime concern to early translation theorists. This can be explained in part by the importance of the notion in the development of automated translation, and in part by the firmly established role of translation as a means of language learning and teaching in a wider, European educational context.

At the end of the 18th century, the grammar translation method had been devised for use in secondary school teaching in Prussia (Howatt, 1984: 131), based on the principles employed for the teaching of Greek and Latin. In the study of the classical languages, translation had always formed an important part, ranking high in popularity as a teaching exercise. As spoken varieties of Latin and Greek no longer existed, the sole focus was on the written mode of language, and the role of translation was frequently that of examining in writing the acquisition of vocabulary learnt by memorising from wordlists new lexical items in the target language, together with their 'equivalents' in the source language. When, in the mid-19th century, the study of modern languages was first introduced as a serious pursuit, the high prestige in which Greek and Latin were held caused the teaching pattern to be replicated. The emphasis was on the written language, and grammar was learnt by means of translation into and out of the foreign language. Translation, as a result, came to be associated with the process of testing the knowledge of grammar and vocabulary in the foreign language and the 'equivalents' found in dictionaries and vocabulary lists were viewed as constituting the authoritatively correct answers. Based on the model of a course in French by Johann Valentin Meidinger (1756–1822), the first so-called grammar–translation course appeared in English in 1793, devised by Johann Christian Fick (1763–1821) (Meidenger, 1783; Howatt, 1984; Malmkjaer, 1998b). In 1858, a system of public examinations was introduced, monitored by the universities of Oxford and Cambridge, this further sanctioned the method that was to remain the prevailing approach to foreign language teaching in Europe from the late 18th century until the 1960s. As large numbers of immigrants started to arrive in the USA from all over Europe, more conversational methods were required and, in his directives issued to teachers steeped in the principles of the 'natural method', Maximilian Berlitz (1852–1921) firmly ruled out the use of translation in language teaching (Malmkjaer, 1998b: 4). The deathblow to the grammar–translation method was further reinforced by the need, during World War II, for United States servicemen to rapidly acquire spoken command of foreign languages, which helped to trigger sweeping changes in language-teaching methodology.

The approach to translation in an educational context, whereby words and grammatical structures in the source language were replaced with their 'correct' equivalents in the target language, did not fail to leave its mark on the generations of translators regularly subjected to the process. Translators continued to translate the way they had been taught to translate. In the case of translation from French, familiarity in Europe with the language and culture of France often facilitated the work of the translator while, in translation from other languages, lack of equivalence was accounted for through the use of detailed footnotes. This was, for example, the practice of Ibsen translator William Archer (1856–1924) in translation from Norwegian.

Commenting on translations of another 19th century European dramatist, playwright Tom Stoppard notes that early English translations of Chekhov's *The Seagull* reveal what he terms almost 'a philosophy' towards translation. 'They are as scrupulous as ledgers: everything on the Russian side of the line is accounted for on the English side, sentence by sentence, and the sentences themselves [...] faithfully carry over nouns, verbs and qualifiers' (Stoppard, 1997: vi).

In addition to the misrepresentations of the source text that may arise from such an over-religious adherence to Stoppard's 'ledger principle', the approach may also make the translator more susceptible to the allure of 'false friends'. In English where historical factors led to an influx of French loanwords into the lexicon, the 'philosophy' of the grammar–translation method has been of little help to the translator in steering clear of the pitfalls in rendering for instance *prétendre* ('intend') and *luxure* ('magnificence') into English as 'pretend' and 'luxury' as has been noted in English Sartre translations of the 1950s (Reed, 2000: 1237).

In addition to the part that it played in language teaching methodology, translation fulfilled yet another function for modern European linguists following in the footsteps of de Saussure. Unlike the UK and the USA, for many smaller nations in Europe knowledge of more than one language constitutes a lifeline with the outside world and contrastive studies of modern languages have traditionally been a pursuit of scholarly interest. In 1926, Vilém Mathesius (1882–1946), together with Roman Jakobson and Nikolai Trubetskoy and others, founded the Prague Linguistic Circle whose publications, in particular *Travaux du Cercle linguistique de Prague*, belonged to the most important writings on linguistics of the epoch. Unlike the American structuralists, the approach of the Prague School was characterised by a three-level concept of syntax: every sentence was viewed as having a grammatical structure, a semantic structure and a structure of sentence organisation. Through contrastive analysis, often taking the form of translation, differences were pinpointed in what was termed *functional sentence perspective* (FSP). Take for example the translation between German and English of the sentence *Das meine ich* ('That mean I'). The first constituent of the sentence receives stress in German and is less likely to be replicated as 'That I mean'; instead, a cleft construction of the type 'That's what I mean' often takes the place of the stressed German constituent in translation into English (Kirkwood, 1969: 96).

Through systematic studies concerned with the textual dimensions of contrastive problems between languages as revealed through the use of translation, Prague School linguists succeeded in unearthing consistent differences between European languages. This provided the practising translator with a background against which translation problems might be viewed and options for suitable solutions sought. These options may in turn be analysed from the viewpoint of evaluation of translations, as in the more recent work by Brno-born linguist Jan Firbas. In a study of four different translations from Russian into Dutch, English, French and German of the opening paragraph of Boris Pasternak's *Dr Zhivago*, the application of the concept of FSP allows Firbas to assess the faithfulness of the translations in relation to the communicative purpose of the original (Firbas, 1999).

The relationship between translation and linguistics may take two different forms: in the case of Nida and Catford it expresses itself in an attempt to formulate a linguistic theory of translation. However, it may also take the less ambitious form of just an ongoing interaction between the two, each drawing on the findings of the other whenever this is mutually beneficial. For linguistics, such interaction might entail the use of translation as a form of contrastive analysis as in the work by linguists following the Prague School tradition. The gains on the part of translation theorists on the other hand have often been the findings resulting from the research undertaken by linguists engaged in the study of language above the level of the word and the sentence.

The study of the factors affecting the overall organisation of the text above sentence level increasingly attracted the attention of linguists during the 1970s and 1980s. While early application of linguistic findings to translation drew its influence from the field of *stylistics* (Enkvist, 1978), later impetus was provided by *discourse analysis* (Hatim & Mason, 1990). Again, as the focus of the interest of linguists began to centre on *text linguistics*, translation theorists closely followed in their footsteps, looking for new models of description. In a paper delivered at the 1981 conference of the

Association International de Linguistique Appliqué titled 'Translation, interpreting and text linguistics', Albrecht Neubert pointed to the importance of paying close attention to the textual features inherent in the source text. 'It is a different text. It is couched in a different world of discourse' (Neubert, 1981: 132). Hence the translator needs to be sensitive to the type of discourse that target language readers are likely to expect under similar communicative circumstances, often revealed through a comparison with _parallel_ texts. Parallel texts form the background texts with which translations often do not compare favourably; as its parallel text in French the British Highway Code has for comparison _'le code de la route'_ and in German, _'die Strassenverkehrsordnung'_ (Neubert, 1981: 135).

Following the legacy of the previous century and its scientifically-based approach to the study of language, the 1970s–1980s saw a number of German translation theorists apply text linguistics-based theories to translation. A major, early influence, Katharina Reiß' work on text types uses as her starting point Bühler's (1934) three functions of the linguistic sign, the informative, the expressive and the operative, to which, presciently, an audio-medial type is added, where verbal sparseness is of the essence. While primarily 'informative' texts such as reports and operating manuals need to be translated in plain prose with, if necessary, explanations in the form of expansions, a basically 'expressive' text such as a poem or a play requires a greater degree of identification between translator and originator. In the case of remaining types, operative texts such as those used in advertising, call for an 'adaptive' translation while the translator of audio-medial texts needs only to supplement what is already expressed by another medium (Reiß 1976; 1977).

A Hallidayan approach involving three macro-functions of language accounting for content (ideational), the relationship between speaker and addressee (interpersonal) and the cohesive links necessary for text cohesion (textual) also enabled Juliane House to put forward one of the first models for evaluating translation quality, focusing on a retrospective comparison of source and target texts of German/English translations (House, 1977, 1981). The importance of the function of the translated text is further emphasised by Hans Vermeer, who views translation as action to which an aim must always be ascribed or, to use the Greek word _'skopos'_. According to Vermeer's _skopos theory_, a translation is inevitably undertaken for a purpose laid down by a client or the translators themselves, and is always accompanied, implicitly or explicitly, by a set of specifications as to how the source text should be translated whether it needs to be translated faithfully, paraphrased or completely re-edited (Vermeer, 1983, 1989). The growing demand from industry during the last couple of decades for professional translation is also reflected in the curriculum design of European translation training programmes. In the *translational action model* put forward by Holz-Mänttäri, highly specialised translation commissions point to the need for attention to be paid to the different roles of the participants in the translational action. The translator may require information with respect to text type and advice from subject area experts as well as knowledge about the users and ultimate uses of the translated text (Holz-Mänttäri, 1984). The *functionalist approach* is further emphasised by Christiane Nord (1988, 1991, 1997), who also points to the importance in a programme of translators' training of the 'translation brief', the problems resulting from the function assigned to the translation and the importance of close analysis of the source text.

Just as the study of language may be extended beyond the level of the sentence to include the overall organisation of the text, it may be widened even further to take into account extra-linguistic factors. In the 1970s, research projects began to appear that were concerned with the influence of social variables on language use. In the USA, William Labov (1972b) first investigated the speech patterns of the inhabitants of Martha's Vineyard, off the coast of New England, then turned his attention to a very different kind of community. Through a study of the variation in speakers' use of the linguistic variable [r], he was able to point to a prestige-linked relation between speech and social class amongst New Yorkers (Labov, 1972a). The Labovian method of structured interviews was also used in a pioneering study in the UK undertaken by Peter Trudgill, in which he examined the interaction between language and social structure in his native town of Norwich (Trudgill, 1974). Sociolinguistics-based studies were increasingly attracting the interest of linguists, and a number of systematic research projects were initiated with the aim of revealing the causes underlying language variation and the interaction between language and variables such as geographical origin and social class membership of speakers.

Henry Sweet (1845–1912), the first British linguist to pursue a scholarly interest in spoken English, studied German philological methods at the University of Heidelberg before returning to England to enter Balliol College, Oxford. While still an undergraduate, Sweet edited King Alfred's translation of the *Cura Pastoralis* for the Early English Text Society, his commentary laying the foundation of Old English dialectology. In 1877, Sweet's interest in spoken language found an expression in the publication of *A Handbook of Phonetics*; this was followed in 1890 by *A Primer of Spoken English*, the first scientifically-based description of educated London speech, received pronunciation (RP). Bernard Shaw, who knew Sweet personally and regarded him a man of genius, writes in the Preface to

Pygmalion, of his 'Satanic contempt for all academic dignitaries and persons in general who thought more of Greek than phonetics'. Sweet, sharing a number of characteristics with Professor Higgins in Shaw's play, was a member of the Reform Movement of the late 19th century which stressed the primacy of speech, and the priority of oral classroom methodology, running counter to the grammar–translation method (Howatt, 1984; Malmkjaer, 1998b).

Having studied under Henry Sweet, Daniel Jones (1881–1967) further advanced the study of speech sounds, rising to become the head of the first Department of Phonetics in Great Britain in 1912. Influential in spreading the use of the International Phonetic Alphabet (IPA), throughout the world, his efforts provided the mechanism for the use of transcription of speech sounds. However, the distinction between written/spoken and standard/dialect is frequently not reflected in translation and awareness amongst translation theorists of the problems involved in vernacular and dialect translation has been slow in coming. While social class-linked dialects are likely to be found in most urban environments, facilitating the transfer of a vernacular such as Eliza Doolittle's cockney in _Pygmalion_ into other languages, the work of European dialect writers has frequently fared less well in translation into English. Part of the work written in Sicilian dialect by Italian writer Luigi Pirandello (1867–1936), the 1934 recipient of the Nobel Prize for Literature, still remains unavailable in English translation. Also largely ignored in English translation is the 1912 Nobel Prize laureate Gerhart Hauptmann (1862–1946). Written in north-east German dialect, his masterpiece, _The Weavers_ has only recently been translated by Bill Findlay into Scots in a translation where the relationship of standard English/Scots parallels that of German/Silesian. Together with his sometime co-translator, Canadian-based Martin Bowman, Findlay has also succeeded in finding an English voice for the Quebéc playwright Michel Tremblay who writes in _joual,_ so called after the pronunciation of the word 'cheval' amongst the speakers in the district of east-end Montreal. Again Scots may be viewed as existing in relation to standard English as _joual_ does to international French. Translating in the opposite direction, from Scots into Quebécois, the use of non-standard French has also enabled Martin Bowman and Montreal playwright Wajdi Mouawad to adapt Irvine Welsh's novel _Trainspotting_ for the French-speaking stage (Bowman, 2000). In addition, it has proved successful as a medium in transferring the work of American writers such as Tennessee Williams and Edward Albee onto the French-speaking stage as well as the muscular dialect use of Brecht's _Mother Courage_ and Jean's sociolect in Strindberg's _Miss Julie,_ a means of overcoming the linguistic void in the normative system of French literature with which the translation of sociolects into French has to contend (Brisset, 2000). On other occasions, the prescriptive norms imposed by the Académie Française and the Bulletin Officiel, which rule out the use of dialects in works of literature, have seen the distinctive New York voice of Holden Caulfield in J.D. Salinger's *The Catcher in the Rye* disappear in translation into standard French (Mailhac, 2000) or the northern English dialect in *Kes* by Barry Hines replaced by a French sociolect (Fawcett, 1998: 120). In the absence of socially as well as geographically determined options, the translator may as a last resort decide on the use of an ideolect, the linguistic system favoured by individual speakers. In for instance the case of the translation into Swedish of *Educating Rita* by Liverpool playwright Willy Russell, the failure to find a match for Rita's scouse in an appropriate dialect or sociolect resulted in the eponymous protagonist being given a colourful ideolect, a language all of her own making.

In addition to studying language as determined by social and geographical factors, linguists have also begun to investigate other factors influencing its use. Now a discipline in its own right, the field of *pragmatics* is receiving increasing attention among linguists interested in examining the purposes for which sentences are used and the real-world conditions under which they are appropriately uttered. In an attempt to describe translation in terms of a general theory of human communication, Gutt (1991) uses as his basic premise the ability of humans to infer what is meant through the principle of *relevance*. In addition to the descriptive use of language, which is restricted to entities in the real world, the interpretative use of language also entails references to thoughts and mental processes. Translation, according to Gutt, is an instance of interpretative use, constrained by the principle of relevance; the translation 'should be expressed in such a manner that it yields the intended interpretation without putting the audience to unnecessary processing effort' (Gutt, 1991: 101–02). However, in addition to the attempt to incorporate translation into a general theory as suggested by Gutt, who used as his framework Sperber and Wilson's *Relevance Communication and Cognition* (1986), there is also, as in other branches of linguistics, the possibility of translation theorists drawing on the insights provided by linguists working in the field of pragmatics and when relevant, applying them to translation. Problems may, for instance, arise when *speech acts* are transferred in translation: situations such as when we make a complaint or a request, offer an apology or give a compliment. While the sole purpose of a conversation is, in a summary of Grice's maxims (1975), to 'be brief', 'tell the truth', 'be relevant' and 'be clear', the intervening need for urbanity often makes necessary further, culture-bound embellishment. When making complaints and requests, speakers of some languages are likely to voice their discontent more directly than do English speakers, as has been shown in the case of German speakers (House & Kasper, 1981). As indirectness in English is a favoured politeness marker, the question 'Would anyone like another cup of coffee?' put by an English hostess to her guests as a social evening is drawing to an end may be less of a question than a request that the visitors take their leave. In translation into a language using other kinds of politeness markers the question may, however, be interpreted at face value, achieving the opposite effect to that intended, which in turn places the translator in the position of having to consider the need for adjustments in translation. Awareness of the existence of such differences between languages is of particular importance in the translation of dialogue, which often lacks the clues needed for the interpretation of utterances that are more easily found in narrative text. Another speech act that may require some consideration in translation is that of apologising, as the formulas used to repair a situation caused by the violation of social norms may also differ between languages. In English, as in many other languages, the apology speech act normally starts with the use of a performative verb such as 'Please, forgive me' or 'Excuse me', and some form of explanation often follows (Brown & Levinson, 1987). It is not uncommon for an English speaker, late for an appointment, to offer as an apology 'Please forgive me, but the traffic was just terrible'. If, however, a language traditionally requires only an explanation in order to meet the demands of politenes – as appears to be the case in Russian and Hebrew (Ohlstain, 1983) – speakers of such a language may find their apologies somewhat begrudgingly accepted if, when arriving late for a meeting in the English-speaking world, they use only the second part of the formula and simply announce 'The traffic was terrible'.

Another, recent but fast-growing field of linguistics that has already provided translation theorists with valuable information, is that of *corpus linguistics*. The study of language on the basis of text corpora can be traced back to around 1960 with the launch of the Survey of English Usage (SEU) at London University and the advent of computers which made it possible to store large amounts of material. The first machine-readable corpus compiled at Brown University in the early 1960s was soon followed by others such as the London–Oslo/Bergen (LOB) Corpus. Capitalising on the combined strengths of the Brown and SEU corpora, starting in 1975, Jan Svartvik and his colleagues at Lund University in Sweden, rendered the unscripted spoken texts of the SEU corpus machine-readable. This resulted in the London–Lund Corpus (LLC), an unmatched resource for the study of spoken English. While the Brown Corpus and the LOB Corpus may have seemed vast at the time, their size has been easily surpassed as massive amounts of machine-readable texts have become available as a by-product of modern electronic communication systems.

Since its beginning in the 1960s, the corpus as a source of systematically retrievable data, and as a test bed for hypotheses, has become widely used by linguists, resulting in findings that include some with obvious implications for translation. Using a corpus consisting of 75 novels published 1967–1977, half of which were novels originally written in Swedish and half were translations, Martin Gellerstam of the University of Gothenburg has systematically compared original texts with texts in translation. His early 1986 study as well as later ones (Gellerstam, 1996, 2005) point squarely to the influence in translation of the source on the target text and also revealed previously-unobserved cross-linguistic differences between the two languages involved in the translation process. Another early corpus study of the influence of English on lexical selection in Danish confirmed Gellerstam's findings, showing that modality, typically expressed in many Germanic languages through the use of modal particles (such as '*jo*' and '*vel*' in Danish), was greatly underrepresented in texts in translation. In their place instead appeared English-influenced modal verb constructions such as 'I presume' or 'I suppose', often resulting in a marked awkwardness of style (Jakobsen, 1986). More recently, translation corpora have investigated the fate of another kind of particle in translation, so-called discourse particles such as 'oh', 'well' and 'now', which tend to express emotional attitudes and contribute towards the coherence of the utterance. In translation into other languages, these discourse particles are frequently rendered in a multitude of different ways and the availability of translation corpora now makes possible a study of the semantic and contextual reasons underlying the translator's choice as shown by Aijmer (forthcoming) drawing on an English/Swedish Parallel Corpus. Other language pairs for which parallel corpora have been compiled include English/French, English/Italian, English/Norwegian and English/German.

Not only are translation theorists close on the heels of linguists as new fields of inquiry such as pragmatics and corpus linguistics become the focus of new research interest, well-established notions in linguistics are also frequently revisited and introduced anew to provide translation theory with conceptual tools. In the late 1970s, Gideon Toury introduced the concept of *norms* in order to account for the translation options favoured by translators at a particular time in a given socio-cultural setting (Toury, 1978, 1980). A set of three translations into Hebrew of Ernest Hemingway's *A Story of Three Killers* showed that readers possessed an intuitive awareness of their chronological order, the result of the different translations being the product of prevailing norms at a particular time (Toury, 1999). Toury's concept of norms has been viewed as representing an interlevel between 'competence and performance in Noam Chomsky's terms' or *'langue* and *parole* in Ferdinand de Saussure's terms' which makes it possible according to Mona Baker 'to investigate what is typical rather than simply what is or what can be' (Baker, 1998: 164). Another development in translation theory reminiscent of what at one time represented a departure from earlier product-orientated approaches to linguistic investigation, is found in the 'think-aloud' method, which shares with Chomskyan linguistics the emphasis on introspection and reliance on speakers' intuitive knowledge about their language. The approach first came to attention in the 1980s when experimental methods drawn from psychology began to be used in order to investigate the translator's mind during the process of translating. Translators were invited to verbalise their thoughts as they were translating and the recorded *think-aloud-protocols* (TAPs) were then studied with the aim of revealing how translators go about their task (Jääskeläiner, 1998).

From the time linguistically-based observations on translation ceased to be ad hoc and anecdotal, linguistics has provided an impetus to translation theorists to apply their findings to translation. When, in 1963, Joseph Greenberg made public his findings that, although the vast majority of languages may have several variant word orders, they all have a single dominant one, his observations became a clarion call to linguists who now began to classify languages according to type. As a result, over the years findings resulting from research in *typology* have succeeded in complementing the knowledge about languages previously made available by genealogical classification. As the result of continued work in typology, Vinay and Darbelnet's procedure triggered by the need for *'chassé-croisé'* in translation between English and French, is now known to be a transposition that needs to be applied not only between English and French but equally applies to Spanish, Italian and to all languages belonging to the Romance family (Talmy, 1985: 62).

Early linguistically-based work in translation theory has also been further developed in order to meet new sets of interests and circumstances. As English grows more and more comfortable in its role as the global language and the lingua franca of Europe, the attention of translation theorists is increasingly being directed towards its impact on other European languages. As a result, the linguistic framework previously employed by Juliane House for the assessment of translation quality has recently been adjusted to apply to an investigation of the influence of English via translation and text production on German, French and Spanish (House, 2003).

In a review of Chomsky's (2000) *New Horizons in the Study of Language and Mind*, the lack of advancement in the search for the innate set of the rules of Universal Grammar (UG) was ascribed to the fact that 'the sheer complexity of the different rule systems for the different languages was hard to square with the idea that they are really all variations on a single underlying set of rules of UG' (Searle, 2002). In their search for universals, translation theorists of the 21st century have now begun to tread where linguists trod before. On the basis of contrastive analyses of translations and their source texts, a number of features considered common to all languages now clamour for the status of universals. With a linguistic feature such as 'distinctive distribution of lexical items' amongst potential candidates (Sara Laviosa-Braithwaite, 1998: 288), translation theorists would seem to have their work cut out for the foreseeable future. In their search for universals, the task facing early typologists of tackling the problem posed by the complexity of polysynthetic languages was made less unmanageable by their familiarity with Native American languages. The challenge facing contemporary translation theorists by Inuit, another such language where *sikursuarsiurpugut* translates into English as 'we-sail-through-the-big-ice' can only be described as formidable.

As the American linguist Dwight Bolinger observes:

> Translation may be viewed amorphously as the rendition of a text from one language to another. This is translation from the standpoint of *la parole*: the text, the act of speech or writing is the thing. Or it may be viewed as a systematic comparison of two languages: this is translation from the standpoint of *la langue*. (Bolinger, 1965/66: 130)

Given this inherent interrelationship between translation and linguistics, linguistics seems set to continue to provide translation theorists with new research avenues to explore for further advancement of translation studies while, in the contrastive study of languages, translation will also have a role to play in helping linguists in their search for shared features and similarities between languages.

Chapter 4

History and Translation

LYNNE LONG

> *Indeed, one might even assert that, without translation, there is no*
> *history of the world. Consider the rise of certain civilisations: the Roman*
> *world, the Italian, French, English, German, and Russian, and*
> *contemplate the role of translation in the development of those cultures.*
> Ouyang (1993: 27)

What Exactly is Translation History?

Translation history is sometimes presented solely as the history of translation theory, but this leaves large areas of territory unexplored and unaccounted for. Ideally it combines the history of translation theory with the study of literary and social trends in which translation has played a direct or catalytic part. It is the story of interchange between languages and between cultures and as such has implications for the study of both language and culture. It pays attention to the observations made by those who were involved in translation processes and by people whose brief it was to comment on the finished product or the context of the translation activity. Closely allied to literary history, translation history can describe changes in literary trends, account for the regeneration of a culture, trace changes in politics or ideology and explain the expansion and transfer of thought and knowledge in a particular era. It may also be used as a tool to open up the study of similar texts across cultures, or of the same text through time. It is surprisingly relevant to many areas of literary study, and absolutely central to some.

It goes without saying that each culture will have its own particular translation history according to the historical and political events that have shaped it. What we should be discussing here perhaps are translation histo-*ries*, since the term in the singular suggests that there is a fixed sequence of events from which we can draw universally applicable conclusions, and this is not the case. There are of course periods in history featuring translation that are common to many cultures. The expansion of the Roman empire, for example, the Ottoman empire, the invention of printing or the

Reformation all had impact on most areas of Europe and its translation activities. Other continents will have experienced other invasions, other advances in technologies, other religions. Events like these are always good points of departure for research, but their effect on an individual culture varies according to the local context. The problem is to find a way through the maze of historical material and emerge triumphant with specific information relating to case studies in translation. Before attempting to navigate the way, it might be a good idea to ask what exactly is the purpose in studying translation history.

How Important is Translation History?

The study of translation history reminds us that translation is a human activity that has been going on since language began to evolve and may be affected by all kinds of external events, as unexpected as they are uncontrollable. It shows us, if we did not already know, that translation principles cannot always be defined and adhered to like scientific formulae, but at times remain as flexible and as fickle as language itself. Placing translated texts into their historical contexts helps define and account for the policies employed by past translators and so gives at least a point of departure for developing strategies. Through history we encounter examples of the darker possibilities of translation, of the opportunities for distortion or manipulation of text, of the translations undertaken with hostile intent. Looking at the history of translation theory gives bases for comparison and demonstrates whether translators are making progress or simply repeating the same mistakes. It also helps to assess whether modern theorists are saying something new or simply repeating the same ideas in different language.

The study of prefaces or postscripts of a past age may reveal the translators' attitudes towards both translation and the translated text. The 1582 preface to the Rheims translation of the Bible, to take one example, reveals that some translations are performed with the utmost reluctance (Pollard, 1911: 301). Alexander Ross's preface to his translation of the Qur'an from the French version in 1649 informs the reader that there is such a thing as hostile translation, a translation performed for the purpose of challenging the text rather than promoting it (Arberry, 1955: 8). Through the study of translators' commentaries it can be demonstrated that there is sometimes a discrepancy between the intention of the translator and the realisation of that intention, a subliminal shift in ideology of which the translator is unaware. (See Belitt (1978) on his translation of *Neruda's Fulgor y Muerte de Joachim Murieta* and then read the translation.) In other words, translators do not always do what they say they are doing or, indeed, what they think they are doing.

Case studies viewed historically can reveal so much about strategies and conventions. It is possible to trace the progress of the Phaedra story, for example, from Euripides' *Hippolytus*, via Seneca's Latin *Phaedra*, Racine's *Phèdre* to Edmund Smith's English translation of Racine, to continue through J.C. Knight, John Cairncross and Robert Lowell's versions of the same and to conclude by looking at Ted Hughes' translation, the modern version of Paul Schmidt and the controversial play by Sarah Kane. The history of Phaedra in translation teaches how translation conforms (or not) to the dramatic and cultural conventions of the target language. It addresses adaptation as a form of translation, shows how subtlety in choice of words can change a character, gives strategies for coping with verse forms that do not exist in the target language, and also illustrates the difference between translating for performance and producing a text in the target language.

It may come to us as something of a shock to realise that many of the texts that we treat as English originals are in fact translations, some from other languages, some from older forms of English, some from both. The Bible, *The Iliad, Beowulf*, the works of Dante, Chaucer, Cervantes, Ibsen, Tolstoy, Hugo, Goethe, Neruda are just a few examples. How many people watching a production of *Ghosts* or *The Cherry Orchard* or *The House of Bernada Alba* are truly aware of the translation implications surrounding what they see and hear? How many readers of the Bible are conscious of the significance of the translation history of what they read? Being aware of translation issues in literary studies sharpens the skills required for textual analysis and, depending on the depth of research, may encourage consultation of the original or at least other translations of the same text.

It is important to make the connection between technological developments in history such as the invention of paper or the introduction of printing, and developments in society such as the increase in literacy and the rise in the use of the vernacular. History may equip society to deal better with innovations that affect modern perspectives. It raises awareness, for example, that the use of computer technology may affect the way that people work with texts in the same way that the invention of printing changed the 15th century perception of the written word. The possibilities for corpus research are now greater than ever before, and the advances in machine translation have become more realistic now that so much information can be stored in such small packages. But as yet there is some way to go before the human element can be completely withdrawn from the translation process. Translation experience should at least help us to recognise the advantages and disadvantages of press button conversion from language to language when clicking on *translate this page.*

How can we Navigate Translation History?

Negotiating translation history is rather like navigating with various specialist maps. Individually they give different features of the cultural, linguistic, political, historical, religious, technological, literary landscape, but there is too much information to make a single map of them. Consequently, it is necessary to separate out some relevant aspects of each in order to draw a specialist translation history map. Interdisciplinary research is essential, since most sources are interrelated and may be approached from several directions, but gradually a picture of the target area should emerge. There are some general accounts of translation history, mostly theory (Bassnett, 1980/2002; Kelly, 1979; Munday, 2001) but perhaps the most ambitious project is the proposed compendium of translation history envisaged by the International Federation of Translators (Delisle & Woodsworth, 1995: 1). Some points of departure from which the journey might begin are listed below. The suggested methodology could be applied to any culture; the examples are taken from my research and are obviously somewhat limited by space. A keyword search on the online library catalogue using any of the areas below should produce some volumes to initiate research. The bibliographies and textual references will lead to more information.

Language issues

This area includes the history of language, the rise of the vernacular, education and translation as a tool for learning a foreign language. General books about alphabets and scripts (Jean, 1992), or about language (Bryson, 1990; Potter, 1950) will provide interesting background, since a good place to begin the study of translation history is with some research into linguistic history. Individual language systems have their own story of derivation and influence, and these will often detail the major changes of linguistic direction including changes in alphabet, orthography or syntax. The influence of Norman French on English language and literature after the conquest of England in 1066, or the impact of 1st and 2nd century translations of Buddhist works on the syntax, vocabulary and phonology of the Chinese language, are both examples of key areas from which a study of translation history might develop.

Tracing the history of a language from its ancient to its modern forms includes looking at translation principles. Latin to modern Italian, Anglo-

Saxon through Middle English to modern English involves the study of syntax, meaning, vocabulary, register, tone and changes in linguistic fashions. Thus the phenomenon of texts being translated within a single language – of intralingual translation – is encountered. Studies on language are more likely to be available in the language they describe, however many language-teaching books contain a short history of the language or an introduction outlining the main influences. For the English language there are many histories (e.g. Baugh & Cable, 1994; Crystal, 2004), and Burnley (1992) provides a source book of the different developments of English, with translations where appropriate.

Most European countries used Latin as their intellectual means of communication until well into the 16th century. Some writers considered their native language as inferior or better suited to certain types of text; some, like Dante Alighieri (1263–1321) in Italy, Geoffrey Chaucer (1342–1400) in England and Martin Luther (1483–1546) in Germany, actively promoted its use. Dante's *de Vulgari Eloquentia* has been translated and edited by several scholars (Botterill, 1996; Shapiro, 1990) and is a good source of information about historical attitudes to the use of vernacular languages in the Middle Ages.

One way of validating the vernacular was to write in it, another was to translate classical texts into it. Chaucer himself translated the *de Philosophae Consolatione* of Boethius (480–524) out of Latin into the English of his day using short explanatory phrases within the text when he felt they were needed (Benson, 1987). There was a strong tradition surrounding Boethius and his philosophical treatise was translated into medieval French, medieval German, old and middle English (Kaylor, 1992). Martin Luther's translation of the Bible into German had a substantial influence on the development of German language and Luther himself had a good deal to say about the kind of language he used in terms of syntax, register and tone. His *Sendbrief von Dolmetschen* translated as *An Open Letter on Translating* (Bachmann, 1960; Robinson, 1997b: 84) sets out his methods and strategies and is an excellent source of his translation theory.

As confidence in the vernacular increased, so its use created a need for translations of important Latin and Greek classical texts. Having these texts in the vernacular gave it status and encouraged the growth of national literatures. Using the vernacular became and still is one of the signs of development in the growth of national identity. A study of the vernacular Finnish epic *Kalevala* reveals its oral origins and its role in establishing a national literature following the dominance of Swedish as the official language of Finland (Bassnett & Lefevere, 1998). Its translation into German, Russian, English, French and Japanese underlines its status as world literature

(Delisle & Woodsworth, 1995: 123). The development of the nation state in Europe at various times in history has involved raising the status of the vernacular and prioritising language and literature as a mark of identity in the same way that minority languages (such as Breton in France, Euscadi in the Basque country, Welsh in Britain or Catalan in Spain) today assert regional identities.

The use of classical language sources (Greek, Roman, Chinese, Sanskrit) as models had repercussions in the educational systems used in previous centuries. Translation was and still is used as a tool for language learning and is often the first experience of a foreign tongue. The way translation is experienced through its learning function often shapes the perception (or misperception) of translation issues. In this way the history of education in Europe sometimes complements the history of translation, or at least the way translation has been used to gain access to other cultures. The translation-intensive method of teaching Greek and Latin, inherited from the Renaissance grammar schools, survives, albeit in a less vigorous form, into the 21st century. The way translation is perceived in the language learning situation often colours attitudes towards the translation process and towards translation theory. The linguistic element will always be the basis of language transfer, however literary translation necessarily includes consideration of the cultural aspects in language and appreciation of what has come to be called 'the cultural turn' in translation studies.

Literary issues

This area includes literary history, history of translation theory and the work of individual translators. Just as the history of language extends understanding of the issues surrounding translation, the history of literature illustrates some of the most important effects of its use. There are few literatures untouched during their development by translation as a literary activity (see Beer & Lloyd-Jones, 1995; Ellis, 2001), and some are, or have been in the past, almost totally dependent on translation for the regeneration of a suppressed or declining home literature (see Even-Zohar's article 'The Position of Translated Literature within the Literary Polysystem' in Venuti, 2000). The early history of the literature of Turkey, for example, covers a cultural overlap of three prestigious languages, Persian, Turkish and Arabic. Modernisation and the National Literature Movement of the 19th and 20th centuries required the introduction of a great number of translated works for the specific purpose of developing Turkish writing. Indian literatures engage with the translation of traditional works such as classical poetry, folk tales, the epic *Mahabharata*, or parts of it, from a common cultural core into the many languages of the country as well as into European languages (Trivedi, 1993; Williams, 1991). The development and diffusion of emergent African literatures remains dependent on inter-translation between lingua franca and source language on one level and on writing the oral traditions on another. Histories of literature may provide some of the information required.

Since the ancient classics were first translated, they have projected a considerable influence on most European if not world literatures, as well as being used as historical sources. Research into translations of the classics may be an interesting project for the translation historian. Diachronic study of the translations of Homer's Greek epics into English for example necessarily involves a review of translation issues in general and those relating to Homer in particular (Lathrop, 1967; Underwood, 1998). The bibliographies of such volumes afford useful links to other books about aspects of translation history.

In terms of translation history, Marcus Tullius Cicero (106–43 BC) and Quintus Horatius Flaccus (65–8 BC) were not only Latin writers (and in the case of Horace an influential poet), but also had observations to make on many things, the art of translation included, and so are counted among the very earliest recorded theorists. Cicero's *de Optimo Genere Oratorum* and Horace's *de Arte Poetica* are often quoted as early models of translation theory. Cicero writes that when translating the Greek orators into Latin, 'I did not hold it necessary to render word for word but I preserved the general style and force of the language' (Hubbell, 1949: 365; Robinson, 1997b: 9). Horace, writing about literary translation, also discourages the literal approach: 'nor should you be so faithful a translator, careful to render word for word' (Brink, 1971: 601; Robinson, 1997b: 15). Both texts are available on the Internet as part of the Perseus project at www.perseus.tufts.edu and have been translated into most European languages at varying times in history.

Generally speaking there seem to be two main types of writing on translation theory. The first is a response by writers such as Cicero and Horace, whose particular experience of translating has inspired analysis of practice in theoretical terms, or whose translation has provoked reaction that the translator feels obliged to defend. It often consists of a discussion of specific processes and strategies. The second type is more philosophical and includes speculation on the nature and effect of translation in general terms. Access to writings about later translation theory is conveniently provided in historical anthologies (Schulte & Biguenet, 1992), 20th century readers (Venuti, 2000) and collections of translation theory (Gentzler, 1993/2000). The writings of earlier theorists are a little more difficult to track down. There is a useful source book with brief extracts and bibliographical references (Lefevere, 1992c) and a general survey (Amos, 1920/1973), but for a more detailed case study it is necessary to read through the complete works of, say, Luther or Jerome or Augustine of Hippo in order to discover all they said about the theory of translation. But let us return to the classical models.

Literature was not only translated from the rich sources provided by the ancient world; national literature was also modelled on the Greek and Roman forms. The epic genre, for instance, 'translates' many of the features of the classical style in aspects such as the invocation of various muses or references to deities. Translation and imitation of the Greek and Latin classics have always played a large part in the development of European literatures, and most world literatures have classical models to which they frequently refer.

Literary forms successful and innovative in one language often get translated into another. After the epic, the sonnet is another good example of this phenomenon, starting life in Italy in the 14th century, mainly through Petrarch, and arriving in English literature through the translations of Thomas Wyatt (Mason, 1959) and others in the 16th century. Its progress and the translation process are well documented in studies of English Renaissance poetry in general or of Petrarch and Wyatt in particular. Other verse forms, such as the Spanish *copla* (Brenan, 1951/1962: 373) or Japanese *haiku*, have similar manifestations in other languages. Then there are the examples of forms that will not translate, such as the Persian verses, the *Ruba'iyat of Omar Khayyam*, famously or notoriously recreated in English by the Victorian Edward Fitzgerald (see Lefevere, 1992c: 32) and later by collaboration between a Persian scholar and a poet (Avery & Heath-Stubbs, 1979). The form has no parallel, but the content has been successfully transferred from one culture to another through the skill and inventiveness of the rewriter/translators. Historical outlines on individual literatures are easy to find and provide general information about the areas most interesting and relevant to the student of translation studies. The research then becomes more specific with the identification of individual authors and precise literary movements.

The study of what we call 'world-class' writers, or classics, and the publication of their works in their own and other languages also produces interesting translation history case studies. What has been translated of Dante, Goethe, Shakespeare, Ibsen, Chekhov, Molière, Wang Chien, Tolstoy? How was it received into the target culture? What position does it occupy in the literary polysystem of the target language? The plays of Henrik Ibsen, for example, have been translated into many world languages, sometimes directly from Norwegian, sometimes from the

English translations. Bryan (1984: 413) contains a list of translations. In China Ibsen's plays had a considerable influence on both dramatic form and social thinking in the early part of the 20th century. As well as books detailing his influence on other literatures through translation, there are web sites giving information on his life and work, as well as reviews on the translations of the plays. Entering Ibsen's name into one of the popular search engines on the computer produces thousands of references. These of course need to be refined in order to be useful as a research tool, and one needs a good deal of patience to sift through the material, nevertheless they provide a good starting point. Paradoxically, information overload today seems to be as serious an issue in historical research as the scarcity of information used to be in the age when computers where not widely used as research tools.

Shakespeare has been translated into most languages and within the host culture there is often a tradition of the way translations are made. The story of Shakespeare's assimilation into the French literary canon in the 18th and 19th century for example is one of challenge and tension (Delisle & Woodsworth, 1995: 76). The plays translate well into the target language conventions of some cultures; in others they are more successful if adapted in plot and characters. Historical attitudes towards translated texts from a particular source may stem from political relations between countries. See Trivedi (1993: 29) for a discussion of the reception of Shakespeare in colonial India. More recent history might include the intersemiotic adaptations into film, which have ranged from faithful representation in language, setting and period to major reconstructions drawing on modern cultural and Hollywood referents.

Quite often a figure of considerable literary stature in a culture will also be a translator and as a consequence something of a translation theorist. William Caxton (c1422–1491), who was responsible for setting up the first printing press in England, was more of an entrepreneur who provided material for his press by translating. The prologues and epilogues to his translations, especially the prologue to *Eneydos* (Crotch, 1956; Robinson, 1997b: 61), provide an insight into the state of the English language at the time and into the translator's dilemma with regard to register and choice of vocabulary. John Dryden (1631–1700) and Ezra Pound (1885–1972) to name but two of many, were literary figures in their own right, translated as part of their literary activity and wrote about translation. There are many instances, too many to include here, of writers, poets and playwrights being involved in both literal and creative productions from other language sources and writing about their translation experiences.

Religious and philosophical issues

This area deals with the translation that arose from the spread of philosophical and religious systems from one culture to another. Evangelisation,
exegesis or curiosity required the translation of Buddhist texts first from
Sanskrit into Chinese and later into Japanese and English, produced a Latin
version of the Qur'an from Arabic and, later, European vernacular
versions, and necessitated the Bible's translation from various Greek and
Latin texts into one Latin version and eventually into European vernaculars. In fact, the spread of philosophies and religions probably accounts for
more translation activity in the first two millennia CE than any other single
factor and certainly accounts for the most discussion about translation.

The history of the Christian church tells the story of people such as
Jerome (c342–420), Augustine of Hippo (354–430), the Wycliffite group
(1390s), Martin Luther (1483–1546), William Tyndale (c1494–1536) and the
King James Bible translators (1611), who were all involved in both translation and in the defence and analysis of translated texts (Long, 2001). Jerome
was commissioned by Pope Damasus to edit the collected Latin texts of the
New Testament into one official version and he later completed a transla-
tion/editing of the Old Testament. His letter to his friend Pammachius *On
the Best Method of Translating* (Schaff & Wace, 1979: 113; Robinson, 1997b: 23;
Venuti, 2000: 21), describes the kind of criticism levelled at him while at the
same time defending some of his translation decisions. Augustine, his
contemporary and another of his correspondents, wrote about signs and
the difficulty of translating unknown or ambiguous signs in the Scriptures
(Gavigan, 1966).

Martin Luther's influence through Bible translation has already been
mentioned and there were others. Jan Hus (1372–1415), for example, translated the Bible into his native Czech and was later executed for heresy
(Delisle & Woodsworth, 1995: 140). Hus's project is said to have encouraged Wyclif to organise his followers into a Bible translation enterprise in
English. The preface to the second Wycliffite version of the 1390s, reputedly
written by John Purvey, demonstrates the technical difficulties experienced
by early translators (Hudson, 1988: 67) but does not mention the physical
persecution to which many were subject. Initially, translation was often
considered to be nothing more than the means of access to the text (this in
itself was a problem because access to sacred texts was not deemed appropriate for everyone). It grew, however, into a major consideration as the
implications for exegesis and, through perceived mistranslation, heresy,
became clear. Bible translation has been and continues to be an area of
translation studies that produces most enthusiastic debate. It is not too

much to claim that it has been the basis of a 20th century revival in interest in translation studies in the US through the work of Eugene Nida (1947, 1964). The present day debate continues in the area of what has come to be called 'gender neutral' or 'gender inclusive translation' (Carson, 1988; Poythress & Gruden, 2000; Strauss, 1998). It must be remembered that those who come to sacred text translation often do so through intense religious conviction. Consequently the translation issues involved come to take on a more vital significance. It is interesting in this context to note that in the Western tradition the earliest record of a translation experience is probably the story of the tower of Babel in the Old Testament (Genesis 11:1–9) and this narrative has often been taken as a metaphor for translation itself (see Derrida's *'Des Tours de Babel'*, 1985; Steiner, 1975). Images of the Tower of Babel are regularly used as a pictorial indication of translation activity or as a logo for a translation studies department or translation company.

Translations of sacred texts often include a brief outline of their translation history in the preface; see for example the preface to the King James Bible (Pollard, 1911: 301; Rhodes & Lupas, 1997) or A.J. Arberry's introduction to his translation of the Qur'an (Arberry, 1955: 25). The Bible has a number of volumes devoted exclusively to its translation history (Bruce, 1961; Long, 2001; Wheeler Robinson, 1940), for Buddhism and Hindu scriptures the information in the histories is less specifically related to translation, and there is much scope for further research in this area. The work of individual translators of the Qur'an, such as Robert Retenensis in the 12th century or George Sale in the 18th, is often referred to *passim* in larger volumes (Schacht & Bosworth, 1974: 98, 39). Translators of Hindu, Buddhist, Islamic, Jewish and Christian holy texts are discussed in *Translators through History* (Delisle & Woodsworth, 1995: Chapter 6), where there are also suggestions for further reading. For a more comprehensive coverage of the translation of all kinds of sacred texts see Long (2005). The translation schools discussed in the next section also have connections with the history of translating religious and philosophical texts.

Scientific interchange

This area includes translation activity concerned with the acquisition and expansion of knowledge. It can occur on quite a small scale in fairly local projects (the collecting of recipes and remedies for example), or it may encompass larger areas of medicine, astronomy, mathematics or natural sciences. For the history of scientific translations from Arabic culture, *The Legacy of Islam* (Schacht & Bosworth, 1974) is an excellent starting point and gives many leads for further study. *The Cambridge History of Iran* (Frye, 1975) is also a good source book with a considerable amount of information about the translation schools set up in Iran. Throughout the Middle Ages, at various times and usually under clerical or royal patronage, groups of translators devoted themselves to making important texts available to their fellow intellectuals. These 'translation schools' as they have come to be known existed at Cluny (Schacht & Bosworth, 1974: 98), Toledo (Pym, 2000: 34) and Seville (Delisle & Woodsworth, 1995: 141). The school at Alcala, or Complutum as it was known in Latin, was where Cardinal Ximenes and his team produced a polyglot Bible shortly after Erasmus published his Latin/ Greek New Testament in 1515 (Long, 2001: 124).

Individual translators such as Etienne Dolet (1508–46) (see Delisle & Woodsworth, 1995: 141) and Nicholas Culpepper (1616–64) (see Kelly, 1979: 86) embarked on crusades to counter what they thought of as appropriation of texts or, in Dolet's case, as the interpretation of texts by those in authority. Dolet's translations deliberately challenged the conservative Catholicism of the French authorities and he was burnt at the stake in 1546 for a too-free translation of Plato that was considered heresy. Culpepper made himself unpopular with his peers with a critical translation of the *Pharmocopoeia* in 1649, making it available to the layperson by translating it into English from Latin. Culpepper's aim was to demystify the medical and scientific information that was being withheld from ordinary people by retaining the use of Latin in medical and scientific documents.

Translation for the purpose of acquiring knowledge also affects language when new vocabulary accompanies new ideas. Most languages have loan words and expressions, and some, Japanese for example, have a large proportion so well assimilated that after a certain length of time it is difficult to identify them (Bryson, 1990: 178). The connection of translation with knowledge and of knowledge with power leads us into the final area of translation history, that of exploration and conquest.

Exploration and conquest

In the 16th and 17th centuries in Europe, exploration and conquest produced colonies where language became part of the power base of the conqueror, and the act of travelling itself promoted cultural and linguistic interchange. There are few countries that have not been occupied at some point in their history by a foreign power, and that act of occupation invariably generates translation activity and a struggle for supremacy between languages as well as people.

One of the best-documented records of early modern conquest is the *Historia general de las cosas de Nueva Espana* by ethnographer and Franciscan friar Bernadino de Sahagun (translated by Anderson & Dibble, 1950). The final book of the *Historia*, which is the account of the actual conquest, was revised by the author in 1585, and there has been both interesting comparison of the two versions and speculation about his motives for doing so (see Cline, 1988: 93). The history itself was written in parallel Spanish and Nahuatl and was intended as a language-learning tool as well as an informative text. The idea was for the Franciscans to learn Nahuatl for the purpose of evangelisation and conquest. Once conquest was achieved, Spanish became the language of government and eventually by the 19th century, replaced Nahuatl in all written texts (see Lockhart, 1991: 22).

It is interesting to see how the language of a coloniser, once imposed on a colony, takes on through time a distinctive, hybrid form that distances it from its parent language. Castilian Spanish differs from that spoken in the Latin American countries, French in France from French in Algeria, Canada or Cameroon, English from Scots or American English; there are dozens of other examples. This feature of difference stops short of preventing cultural interchange, so that former colony Brazil provides drama, poetry, novels and TV programmes for the now less-active ex-coloniser Portugal. Tracing the history of post-colonial literature involves looking at translation not simply as linguistic transfer but as cultural interchange (Bassnett & Trivedi, 1999: 2) and as a way of asserting power. By extension, travel writing and immigrant literature become part of the study as 'translations' of culture that are themselves often translated or as dialogues between the colonised and the coloniser.

Endnote

The relative newness of the subject of translation studies and its interdisciplinary nature means that research into the history of translation is still in the early stages and somewhat patchy. This means that there is much work to be done but also that there is considerable scope for the enthusiastic researcher to make a contribution to the field. Defining the area of study is the first problem; after that there is much reading to be done around the subject to pick up any possible leads. If the brief was to investigate Erasmus's contribution to translation studies, for example, one might well begin with a biography or two about him and then proceed to his own writings. Alternatively, the indexes of books detailing the history of the time would be a good starting point to see what passing references are made about Erasmus. Some books may even have chapters referring to his work or parts of his work, or detailing his connections with Thomas More or Henry VIII, or the Humanist movement, or the philological notes of Lorenzo de Valla.

To take another example, if the project were to see how the Chilean poet Pablo Neruda came to be translated into English, one might begin with the English translations of his work, reading the prefaces, looking for other work by the same translator. With luck one might discover that the translators of *Las Alturas de Macchu Picchu* have written a book about the translation process (Felstiner, 1981), and that the translator of *Fulgor y Muerte de Joachim Murieta* (Bellit, 1978) has published a collection of his own translation prefaces.

Quite often there are university research centres, for Latin American studies, or Caribbean studies, or Medieval studies covering particular areas, whose publications, either in book form, as papers published in journals, on the Web or as the proceedings of conferences may be useful. Specific articles in related journals can be useful for narrowing down the search area or complementing what has already been established.

Finally, one needs to remember that, in order to research in translation history successfully, one needs to dip into a number of related disciplines and study parallel situations in other contexts. History, modern languages, linguistics, theology, education, philosophy or classics are areas that need to be explored from a comparative perspective. This may be a daunting task, but it is also an excellent opportunity for collaborative projects, which should positively distinguish translation studies from other disciplines in the humanities.

Chapter 5
Literary Translation

THEO HERMANS

Rat Poison to Ted Hughes

What, if anything, is distinctive about literary translation? Few would doubt their intuitive sense that there is a difference between Ted Hughes' rendering of a play by Aeschylus and the English-language label on the packet of white powder in a Greek supermarket identifying the stuff in it, for the tourist's sake and good health, as sugar, salt, detergent or rat poison. But how are they different? Interestingly, Emma Wagner, a translation manager with the European Commission who mentions the Ted Hughes versus rat poison example in a discussion with a translation theorist, refers to the two kinds of translation as the top and bottom ends of the range, respectively (Chesterman & Wagner, 2002: 5). Not only is there felt to be a difference between literary and other forms of translation, but value enters the picture as well.

The standard view is that literary translation represents a distinctive kind of translating because it is concerned with a distinctive kind of text. The theory of text types, which seeks to classify texts according to their functions and features, duly places literary texts in a class of their own. The fact however that text typologies do not agree on what to contrast literary texts with – technical, pragmatic, ordinary? – suggests that what distinguishes literary from other texts may not be entirely obvious. And if there is no agreement on what makes literature distinctive, it may be equally hard to decide on what grounds literary translation should be awarded its own niche. In her *Translation Criticism*, first published in German in 1971 and now also in English, Katharina Reiß reviews various attempts to distinguish different kinds of translation. A.V. Fedorov, Otto Kade, J.B. Casagrande and Georges Mounin, among others, all include literary translation as a separate kind, but their criteria for doing so remain unclear or seem haphazard (Reiß, 2000: 7–23).

In recent years a number of general reference works on translation have appeared. Can they shed light on what makes literary translation special?

The *Dictionary of Translation Studies* (Shuttleworth & Cowie, 1997) has entries for 'literal translation', 'free translation' and the like but not 'literary translation'. Its entry on 'aesthetic–poetic translation' turns out, with linguistic, ethnographic and pragmatic translation, to form part of J.B. Casagrande's fourfold and somewhat random list of translation types. The more encyclopedic reference works give out equally mixed signals. Writing on 'Literary translation: Research issues' in the *Routledge Encyclopedia of Translation Studies* (Baker, 1998), José Lambert considers the definition of 'literary' and the collocation 'literary translation' but does not reach conclusions. Its companion piece 'Literary translation: Practices' by Peter Bush side-steps the issue by declaring: 'Literary translation is the work of literary translators' and stressing the skill and worth of the latter. The German *Handbuch Translation* distinguishes only very broad text types: informative, appellative and expressive, the typology devised by Karl Bühler in the 1930s (Bühler, 1934). Under 'primarily expressive' texts, narrative, drama and poetry make an appearance along with film, comic strips and the Bible, but 'literary translation' as such is not featured (Snell-Hornby *et al.*, 1998).

There are now also a couple of reference works devoted specifically to literary translation into English. They must distinguish literary from 'other' translation; but how? In the preface to her two-volume *Encyclopedia of Literary Translation into English*, editor Olive Classe (2000) merely notes that she has followed general usage. Just as translation commonly refers to interlingual translation, and 'literature' and 'literary' tend to imply 'aesthetic purpose, together with a degree of durability and the presence of intended stylistic effects', so 'literary translation' is read as conventionally distinguished from 'technical translation' (Classe, 2000: viii). Peter France's *Oxford Guide to Literature in English Translation* makes a more determined effort. It speaks of literary translations as translations 'designed to be read as literature' and cites with approval Gideon Toury's distinction between 'literary translation' and the 'translation of literary texts', the latter, non-literary form of translation being described as 'informational' (France, 2000: xxi). Toury's distinction rests on his view, derived from Yury Lotman and, beyond him, Roman Jakobson and the Russian Formalists, that literature is characterised by the presence of a secondary, literary code superimposed on a stratum of unmarked language (Toury, 1980: 36–7). A formal definition of this kind no longer has currency in literary studies and anyway sits uncomfortably with the intentional aspect of accepting as literary any translation *designed* to be read as literature.

The search for a definition of literary translation leads nowhere. To students of literature this will not come as a surprise. They gave up trying to define literature some time ago. Today definitions of literature tend to be functional and contingent rather than formal or ontological. Let me use two introductory but influential textbooks to illustrate the point. Terry Eagleton's (1983) *Literary Theory* opens with a chapter 'Introduction: What is Literature?' which argues that literature is best defined as 'a highly valued kind of writing' and goes on to stress the social and ideological conditioning of values and value judgements. Jonathan Culler's (1997) *Literary Theory: A Very Short Introduction* adopts a two-pronged approach. The designation 'literature' serves as 'an institutional label', now denoting 'a speech act or textual event that elicits certain kinds of attention' (Culler, 1997: 27). However, for historical reasons attention of the literary kind has been focused on texts displaying certain features, notably such things as the foregrounding of language, the interdependence of different levels of linguistic organisation, the separation from the practical context of utter- ance, and the perception of texts as both aesthetic objects and intertextual or self-reflexive constructs (Culler, 1997: 28–35). The label and the features tend to correlate, so that the recognition of formal traits will trigger the institutionally appropriate kind of attention and vice versa. A conceptually sustainable way of modelling literary translation may then be based on prototype theory (following Halverson, 1999). In this view the prototypical literary translation is one perceived, and perhaps also intended, as a literary text, and hence as possessing literary features and qualities; around prototypical texts a host of other texts of more or less questionable member- ship will cluster, allowing the system to evolve in time.

For all that, Culler also notes that not much attention has been paid to the issue of the definition of literature in the last 25 years; what has attracted interest, he argues, is literature as a historical and ideological category, and its social and political functioning (Culler: 1997: 36). Broadly speaking, this has also been the development with respect to the study of translation, and of literary translation in particular. Questions of definition and demarca- tion have given way to functional approaches that have been increasingly preoccupied with the roles assigned to and the uses made of translation by a variety of actors in varying contexts. In the case of the study of literary translation, however, another institutional issue had to be settled first. It concerned the acceptance, by the literary studies community, of transla- tions as legitimate objects of study in the first place. Indeed comparative literature, the branch of literary study one might have expected to cham- pion translation as an instrument of cultural transmission and negotiation, was decidedly slow to wake up to its relevance.

The changing attitude may be gauged from the three successive 'Reports on Professional Standards' issued in 1965, 1975 and 1993 by the American

Comparative Literature Association or ACLA (Bernheimer, 1995). The first report stressed the need for 'some access to all the original languages involved' and drew a stern line between teaching 'foreign literature in translation' and comparative literature proper. Students of the latter were urged to read original works wherever possible and to rely on translation only as a last resort and for 'remote languages' (Bernheimer, 1995: 23). The 1975 report still called on teachers to work with original texts, not only for the benefit of those with a command of the relevant languages, but in order to 'make the remaining students aware of the incompleteness of their own reading experience' (Bernheimer, 1995: 35). The 1993 report strikes a different note. Not only is there the conciliatory statement that 'the old hostilities toward translation should be mitigated', but translation is now held up as 'a paradigm for larger problems of understanding and interpretation across different discursive traditions' (Bernheimer, 1995: 44). Coincidentally, Susan Bassnett's (1993) *Comparative Literature: a Critical Introduction* came out in the same year as the final ACLA report. Bassnett argued that traditional comparative literature was now well and truly dead and the new impulses were coming from cultural studies, gender and postcolonial studies, and translation studies. Rather than suggesting that the old hostilities towards translation be mitigated, she proposed translation studies as 'the principal discipline from now on, with comparative literature as a valued but subsidiary subject area' (Bassnett, 1993: 161). The provocation did not go down well in comparative literature circles. Nevertheless, introductions to comparative literature today pay attention to translation (e.g. Zima, 1992; Tötösy de Zepetnek, 1998).

Several things brought about the change in attitude signalled in the ACLA reports. Globalisation was one. As knowledge of Latin and Greek waned, comparative literary studies in the West found themselves in a postcolonial world full of potentially valuable texts in what the 1965 ACLA report could still refer to as 'remote languages'. Hermeneutics may well have been another. As early as the 1960s Hans-Georg Gadamer (1977: 98) observed that '[h]ermeneutics operates wherever what is said is not immediately intelligible.' The operation takes place in the first instance within the same tradition, when the accidents of time and change have erected obstacles to the transmission of linguistic meaning, but applies *a fortiori* across languages and cultures. Negotiating these barriers requires translation. Hence, as Gadamer (1977: 19) put it, '[f]rom the structure of translation was indicated the general problem of making what is alien our own'. How this process works in practice within one and the same linguistic and cultural tradition was illustrated in the opening chapter of George Steiner's (1975/1998) *After Babel*. Demonstrating the kind of deciphering needed to make sense, in contemporary English, of the language of English writers from Shakespeare to Noel Coward, the chapter was suitably entitled 'Understanding as Translation.' In his *What is Comparative Literature?* Steiner (1995: 11) went on to insist on what he called 'the primacy of the matter of translation' for all cross-cultural study. From a purely institutional point of view the fact that André Lefevere's *Translating Literature: Practice and Theory in a Comparative Literature Context* (1992b) was published under the aegis of the Modern Language Association of America was no less significant.

There are similarities between the emergence of translation studies as an academic discipline and the recognition accorded to literary translation by comparatists. The study of translation generally had to emancipate itself from its ancillary status with respect to translation criticism and translator training so as to be able to approach translation as a phenomenon worthy of attention in its own right. In a parallel movement the study of literary translation had to legitimise itself in the context of comparative literature by pointing to the significance of translations, not just as vicarious objects standing in for originals as best they can, but as significant counters in the symbolic economy and carriers of ideas, attitudes and values.

Comprehending Translating

In the Anglo-Saxon world the traditional academic approach to literary translation went via the practical workshop, often supported by exercises in close reading as popularised by the New Critics of the 1930s and 1940s (Gentzler, 2001: 5–43). The mutually beneficial combination of practical translation and criticism is summarised in Marilyn Gaddis Rose's (1997: 13) *Translation and Literary Criticism*: 'What translating does is to help us get inside literature'. For D.S. Carne-Ross, who became the editor of one of the first English-language journals devoted to literary translation (*Delos: A Journal On & Of Translation*, Austin, Texas, 1967–70), translation was 'essentially an instrument of criticism'. Carne-Ross added that '[t]rue translation is much more a commentary on the original than a substitute for it' (in Arrowsmith & Shattuck, 1961: 6). The statement highlights the alliance between translation and criticism while firmly assigning translation its place in relation to original writing.

Apart from serving as a workout and/or skills acquisition course for translators, the workshop employs translation as a means of probing the meaning of complex texts. Translating and understanding are two sides of the same coin. One of the leading New Critics, I.A. Richards, not only took a close interest in semantics but argued in the essay 'Toward a theory of translating', later renamed 'Toward a theory of comprehending' (Richards, 1955), that in principle it is possible, though exasperatingly difficult, to reach an adequate understanding of a unique text through a careful mapping of all its denotative and connotative dimensions.

Hands-on experience of translating is the workshop's main strength. In addition, the concept invites reflection on the process of translating, on the aims and contexts of the exercise, and on other people's achievements. Broadly speaking, two lines emanate from the workshop concept. One consists of testimonies by practising translators, the other of translation criticism and, eventually, history.

The former line can boast some grand names of translator-writers, among them, in the 20th century, Ezra Pound and Vladimir Nabokov. Book-length testimonies in English include Ben Belitt (1978), Burton Raffel (1971, 1988), John Felstiner (1981), Suzanne Jill Levine (1991), Susanne de Lotbinière-Harwood (1991), Douglas Hofstadter (1997), Robert Wechsler (1998), Clive Scott (2000) and Jin Di (2003). Collections like those compiled by Biguenet & Schulte (1989), Warren (1989), Weissbort (1989) and Boase-Beier & Holman (1999) feature shorter statements. The expositions fit old patterns. Much of the historical discourse on translation shows translators rationalising their own practice, more often than not in self defence. Some testimonies are more combative than others and slide from legitimising a particular mode of translating to legislating for all translation; Nabokov's vitriolic attacks on all styles of translating except his own are a case in point (Nabokov, 1955). Mostly, however, the shoptalk is concerned with concrete particulars; it is detailed, retrospective, introspective and experiential. As diagrams of the communication model hold theoreticians in their thrall, Clive Scott (2000: 248–9), for example, questions the received academic wisdom that translation is driven by communicative intent. Instead, he insists that reading and translating are intensely personal acts of self-discovery and self-expression. Robert Bly's (1983) eight stages of translation, as exemplified by poetry, adopt the form of a masterclass. Having (1) scribbled a literal version, the translator (2) establishes the poem's overal meaning, (3) rewrites the crib in an acceptable linguistic form and adjusts the text to (4) a particular idiom and to (5) the poem's mood and (6) it's sound pattern, before (7) checking the draft with native speakers and (8) preparing the final version. Typically, however, Bly's account makes no mention of working conditions or of the social functioning of literary texts. Indeed many translators who would be part of literature's symbolic economy also buy into its public agenda of privileging artistic integrity over either economic or ideological considerations. The exceptions tend to be those who have followed academe's growing interest in the social conditioning and effects of literature; this applies to gender-conscious and postcolonial translators and to their fellow travellers (de Lotbinière-Harwood, 1991; Spivak, 1993; Venuti, 1995).

The historical prominence of translators' discourses about their art and craft lives on in the tendency, evident in several branches of translation studies, to approach translation from the translator's point of view. Jiří Levý's influential article (1967) on translating as constant decision-making, for example, depicts the process from the translator's angle, as does Gideon Toury's account of the operation of translation norms, which builds directly on Levý (Toury, 1995: 53–69). In the hermeneutic camp, George Steiner's so-called fourfold motion of initiative trust, invasive aggression, tentative incorporation and eventual restitution (Steiner, 1975/1998: 312ff.) seeks to portray the successive mental stages of the translator at work. In the same way Antoine Berman's call (1992) for an ethics of centrifugal rather than ethnocentric translation is primarily an appeal to translators to allow the foreignness of the foreign text to remain visible.

The other line emanating from the translation workshop found one of its earliest and finest illustrations in Reuben Brower's essay 'Seven Agamemnons':

> When a writer sets out to translate – say, the *Agamemnon* – what happens? Much, naturally, that we can never hope to analyze. But what we can see quite clearly is that he makes the poetry of the past into poetry of his particular present. Translations are the most obvious examples of works which, in Valéry's words, are 'as it were created by their public.' (Brower, 1959b: 173)

The detailed comparison of texts, the workshop's strongest suit, here extends from aligning original and translation to inspecting serial translations. With this move from the pair to the series, the goal of the exercise also shifted from judgemental criticism to the historical embedding of texts. Brower's essay broke new ground in exploring seven English versions of Aeschylus' *Agamemnon* produced over several hundred years and reading each in relation to the dominant poetics of its time. The study of translation, for Brower, yielded insight into changing concepts of literature. The chronologically plotted renderings of a single original 'show in the baldest form the assumptions about poetry shared by readers and poets' (Brower, 1959b: 175).

Brower's essay accords translations symptomatic value: because they conspicuously reflect a period style, they supply the researcher with a handy key to the larger picture. Rewarding as this view of translation was at a time when serious attention to literary translations needed justification in academic circles, it reinforced the perception of translation as merely reflecting prevailing conventions. Why translation should be so passive, Brower did not explain. More recent researchers have attempted explanations, and they have involved much broader categories. André Lefevere downplayed the importance of linguistic aspects of translation and highlighted instead the role of poetics and of ideological factors and institutional control. Recognising that translation means importing texts (containing potentially subversive elements) from outside a particular sphere, Lefevere stressed the desire of those in power to regulate translation. Because they mostly succeed, most translation offers 'an unfailing barometer of literary fashions' (Lefevere, 1991: 129). Arguing from a gender position, Lori Chamberlain (1992: 66–7) has claimed that translation is over-regulated because 'it threatens to erase the difference between production and reproduction which is essential to the establishment of power'. By analogy with Michel Foucault's (1986) 'author function', Myriam Díaz-Diocaretz (1985) and Karin Littau (1997) have brought up the notion of a 'translator function' to identify the ideological figure that restricts the dispersal of meaning and locks translation in both a legal system and a hierarchical symbolic order that privileges original work over secondary work.

Whether these explanations of the place and role of translation seem persuasive or not, they show that the debate has moved on. In the same way, the issue of the role of translation as merely conforming to prevailing period tastes or as an active shaping force has been redefined. As early as 1920 T.S. Eliot recognised translation's potential 'vitalising effect', as he put it in 'Euripides and Professor Murray' – in *The Sacred Wood* (Eliot, 1969). Itamar Even-Zohar's polysystem theory would provide a theoretical framework for this potential. Revitalising Russian Formalist ideas, the model envisaged literature as permanent tug of war between conservative and innovatory forces, with translation joining now one and now the other side, either consolidating or undermining established modes of discourse (Even-Zohar, 1990). In this way translation was written into the broader scheme of things, along with other hitherto-neglected forms such as popular fiction or children's literature. The scheme of things grew even broader in the 1990s when translation came to be seen as helping to shape cultural identities. The selection of texts for translation and the way in which individual translations construct representations of foreign cultural products (and, metonymically, of foreign cultures as such) would now be read as offering a window on cultural self-definition. This is because domestic values inform both the process of inclusion and exclusion and the choice of a particular mode of representation (Hermans, 1999a: 58ff; Tymoczko, 1998; Venuti, 1998b: 67ff.).

The workshop approach to literary translation held practice and observation in a precarious balance. However, as the above paragraphs indicate, ideas about translation have developed rapidly as translation studies gained momentum roughly from the 1980s onwards. As a result, new perspectives, approaches and concerns have come to the fore, more or less in step with the evolution of literary theory. In what follows I will discuss the main developments in the study of literary translation, grouping them for convenience under three headings: linguistics, functionalism and interventionism.

Linguistic Signatures

If Reuben Brower reckoned in 1959 there was much in translation 'that we can never hope to analyse' (Brower, 1959a), linguistic approaches have sought to supply tools to scrutinise the textual make-up of both literary and non-literary translations. The application of linguistic models to the analysis of literary texts had its heyday in 1960s and 1970s, under the impulse of structuralism and transformational grammar (see e.g. Fowler, 1971; Ihwe, 1971–2). The momentum was not subsequently maintained, except in research on style. Linguistic approaches to translation seemed destined for a similar fate, but in recent years have bounced back with renewed vigour.

Early linguistically-inspired studies of literary translation concentrated on the semanticisation of form and on literary form as deviant usage. Richard de Beaugrande (1978) suggested ways in which translators might achieve 'equivalence' by seeking to match in the translation the original's ratio of deviation versus standard usage. The approach slotted comfortably into the theory of text types deriving from Karl Bühler, as mentioned above. Bühler (1934) recognised three main functions of language (to represent, to express and to appeal) and distinguished three text types according to the dominance of one of these functions. Although text-type theory largely bypassed literature, Katharina Reiß classified literature as 'form-focused text' (Reiß, 2000/1971: 31ff). In the same way, text linguistics and pragmatics, which reacted against the decontextualised treatment of language characteristic of structuralism and transformational grammar, turned their attention mostly to non-literary texts.

More recently, however, two lines of linguistic enquiry, corpus studies and critical linguistics, have been making significant inroads into the study of literary translation. Corpus studies interrogate computer-readable texts in a variety of ways, with the intention of tracing patterns and common features across large amounts of data (Baker, 1995; Laviosa, 1998; Kenny, 2001). For the machine to be able to respond, the questions fired at the corpus need to be formal and exact, and therefore linguistic in nature. One tendency of corpus-based translation studies has been to search for universals. For the time being, this exercise is compromised by the fact that the available translation corpora cover only a limited number of languages, lack a historical dimension and have no way of identifying whether the features encountered are exclusive to translation. Another line of enquiry, closer to traditional literary interests, has turned to stylistic investigation (Baker, 2000). Just as statistical data on individual usage enabled researchers to identify the author (Joe Klein) behind *Primary Colors*, the anonymously published insider novel about Bill Clinton's path from Arkansas to the US presidency, so corpus-based translation studies can pinpoint translators' personal voices across a range of apparently very different translations. The question of the coexistence of different subject positions in translated texts had been around in literary translation studies for some time (Folkart, 1991; Pym, 1992; Hermans, 1996; Schiavi, 1996). While a Bakhtinian emphasis on dialogism and heteroglossia might provide a suitable frame for their discussion, corpus-based studies were able to ask – and answer – much more precise questions, to extend their searches and come up with interesting correlations. For example, Mona Baker (2000) found that, for all their much-vaunted ability to wrap themselves around the style of their authors, translators leave their individual linguistic signature on texts belonging to very different genres and originally written in different languages. Today corpus-based translation studies are in full expansion across a broad spectrum of texts and languages. They work best when a sufficient volume of words can be scanned in and tagged; prose rather than poetry would seem to be their natural habitat.

Critical linguistics builds on pragmatics and discourse analysis, both of which made themselves felt in the study of translation in the 1980s. Indeed as early as 1986 Mary Snell-Hornby announced a 'pragmatic turn' in translation studies, prefiguring the spate of 'cultural' and other turns that would be declared later. In contrast to both structural and transformational models of language, M.A.K. Halliday's functional grammar views language as a social semiotic and has become an effective tool to delve into the way in which ideology is inscribed in the language we produce. Roger Fowler's (1981) *Literature as Social Discourse* demonstrated the relevance of this branch of linguistics for literary criticism. Among the earliest applications of Hallidayan concepts in literary translation studies was Kitty van Leuven-Zwart's model (1989–90) for the analysis of shifts in translated narrative fiction. Van Leuven-Zwart sought to map semantic shifts logged at the microlevel of original and translated texts onto the macrolevel of narrative structure. To make this transition, she projected the various micro-shifts resulting from her analyses on Halliday's three so-called metafunctions: the ideational (i.e. roughly the way of presenting information), the interpersonal (which establishes the speaker–hearer relation) and the textual (the thematic organisation of a text). From this she came up with discursive profiles that could show differences in point of view, agency, modality and such like across entire texts.

In recent years Jeremy Munday (2002) has proposed combining the Hallidayan model with the potential unleashed by corpus studies to explore linguistic differences between originals and translations and relate them to social and ideological contexts. The three metafunctions are again the essential tools. The precision of linguistic concepts, together with the blanket coverage afforded by computerised searches, allows a type of investigation that is new, detailed and replicable, without seeking to sideline judicious interpretation.

Functioning Contexts

Functionalist ways of tackling the study of translation began to be mooted in the 1970s and 1980s out of dissatisfaction with the predominantly prescriptive and decontextualised approaches holding sway at the time. Two particular schools of thought emerged, skopos theory and descriptivism. Skopos theory ('*skopos*' is Greek for 'aim' or 'goal'), which flourished in Germany, is explicitly functionalist in that it views translating as goal-directed action (Nord, 1997). It makes much of the intended functions and likely effects of translations in comparison with the functions and effects of their originals, stressing that as a rule the two communication situations are not parallel. Different translations may be needed to suit different kinds of readers, as indeed Theodore Savory (1957: 58–59) had pointed out 20 years earlier. The translator is meant to assess similarities and differences and act accordingly, bearing in mind the interests and expectations of all concerned. To the extent that institutional constraints and audience expectations figure prominently in the model, skopos theory falls in with literary reception studies. If it has had only limited impact on the study of literary translation, this is chiefly because audience expectations are notoriously hard to define in literature.

Descriptive work has focused less on the actual behaviour of translators than on the outcomes of their actions and decisions, less on process than on product. The textual orientation chimes with literary pedigree of most descriptivists. As with other functionalist approaches, the aim is not so

much description as understanding and explanation, even though (especially in the early days) descriptivism flaunted its empirical streak in order
to distance itself from the prescriptivism of the applied approaches and of
translation criticism. The leading descriptivist questions are historical:
who translates what, when, how, for whom, in what context, with what
effect, and why? The last question requires delving into the motivation
behind the choices made by translators and other actors. How to interpret
translators' actions? The answer was found in the concept of a 'translation
norm'. If we know the prevailing norm of translation, we can assess
whether individual translators' behaviour accords with it, and speculate
about their reasons for compliance or defiance. More likely than not, these
reasons will bear some meaningful relation to the individual's position in a
social environment, as an agent in a network of material and symbolic
power relations. With this, translation has lost its philological innocence.

The set of norms relevant to translation at a certain time amounts to a
translation poetics. It determines what will be deemed acceptable as translation in a given culture. Ways of processing texts that fail to meet the
criteria regarded as pertinent to translation in a given community may
result in the product being called paraphrase, imitation or pastiche, but not
translation. In this sense norms police the boundaries of what a culture
regards as 'legitimate' translation. Moreover, norms embody social and
ideological values. The implication is that translation is not an immanent
but a relative concept, culturally constructed and therefore historically
contingent. By following lines of thought of this kind, descriptivism
reached some fairly radical conclusions. At the same time, it dovetailed
with literary research on conventions, historical poetics and interpretive
communities (see e.g. Fish, 1980; Mailloux, 1982). And just as literary
studies grew sceptical about grand historical narratives and discovered the
micro-stories of New Historicism, descriptivists have relished the detail of
individual case studies.

While descriptivism helped to legitimise translation as a serious object
of literary study, much of the historical work on literary translation fits the
descriptive paradigm without being indebted to it. Nevertheless, descriptive researchers have invested much determined effort in literary translation, from comparative methodology (Holmes, 1978; Van Leuven-Zwart,
1989–90; Koster, 2000) and wordplay (Delabastita, 1993, 1997) to translation
as a catalyst of cultural and political change (Lambert & Hyun, 1995;
Lambert & Lefevere, 1993; Tymoczko, 1999). In the process, a substantial
range of aspects, modes and functions of translation in different contexts
was documented, mostly with respect to canonical Western literature. The
history of Western thought about translation received attention from

André Lefevere (1977), Lieven D'hulst (1990) and others, and bespeaks an ongoing interest, as testified by several international anthologies (Robinson, 1997b/2001; Lafarga, 1996; López García, 1996; Vega, 1994). The roll-call of canonical historical thinkers featured in each one of these readers, incidentally, consists of Cicero, St Jerome, Luther, Vives, Du Bellay, Dryden, Goethe, Schleiermacher, Wilhelm von Humboldt, Mme de Staël and Matthew Arnold. The literary presence is strong.

Descriptivism built on Formalist and Structuralist principles. From an early preoccupation with a taxonomy of shifts between originals and translations (Popovič, 1976, updated in Tötösy, 1998, 221ff.) it graduated to polysystem theory and to Gideon Toury's emphasis on empiricism and strict methodology (Toury, 1995). The attempt to account for translators' choices led first to concepts such as norms and patronage (Lefevere, 1992a) and then, as awareness of the need to bring context into view increased, to a 'cultural turn' (Bassnett & Lefevere, 1990). A large amount of detailed historical-descriptive research on literary translation was carried out in the 1980s and 1990s in Göttingen. This was mostly on translations into German but also on such topics as genre, narrative technique and translation anthologies (Essmann, 1992, 1998; Kittel, 1992, 1995, 1998; Kittel & Frank, 1991; Kullmann, 1995; Schultze, 1987). By the 1990s, as descriptivism was being urged into a more self-critical direction (Hermans, 1999b), other, ideologically more committed approaches were making their mark.

Problematic Others

If the collection *The Manipulation of Literature* (Hermans, 1985b) introduced the descriptive paradigm to Anglophone researchers, it is sobering to reflect that Jacques Derrida's altogether more daring '*Des tours de Babel*' appeared in the same year (Derrida, 1985). While descriptivism was cultivating its structuralist lineage, post-structuralism passed it by.

Perhaps post-structuralism is best seen in this context as a persistent questioning of taken-for-granted assumptions about translation. It raises doubts about the very possibility of translation by calling attention to such things as the instability of meaning, the materiality of language and the performance enacted by multilingual texts. By highlighting the double bind of translation as simultaneously necessary and impossible it also shows up the illusory nature of the attempt to dominate translation by theorising it from outside. Just as post-structuralism remains wary of the distinction between original writing and criticism, it distrusts the division between object-level and meta-level. Derrida's '*Des tours de Babel*' presents itself as a translation – sympathetic, perverse and oblique – of Walter

Benjamin's *The Task of the Translator* of 1923 (published in English in 1970). At once literary and philosophical, post-structuralist writing about translation partakes creatively of translating (Davis, 2001).

The post-structuralist levelling of the groundwork proved productive. Its critique of representation was taken up with a particular emphasis by the two main critical currents of the 1990s, gender and post-colonial theory. Both, in literary as well as in translation studies, have been concerned with the archive, with identity, with commitment and with ethics.

The history of translation has been viewed as an arena of conflict by gender-oriented and post-colonial researchers. They focus on what is excluded as well as on what is included in and for translation, on the hidden as well the declared agendas, the larger power structures underpinning particular events and acts. Following the example of gender studies in literature, translation scholars have dissected the social and educational systems that allowed some women to translate but not to write original work, or at least not in their own names, and to translate certain books and not others. Postcolonial researchers have reconsidered the West's image of other parts of the globe in the light of Edward Said's *Orientalism* (1978) and analysed translation as an instrument of domination and of information control: the metaphors speak of complicity and resistance rather than enrichment, of appropriation rather than transmission or transfer. If for the descriptivists the loss of philological innocence was a staging post, here it is the starting point.

Neither gender studies nor post-colonial studies distinguish absolutely between literary and other forms of discourse. All discourses are seen as contributing to the construction of identities and communities. This brings into play the researcher's own person, and the place of his or her discourse. Gender as well as post-colonial researchers emphatically speak from minority positions. The first group speaks as part of a non-masculine community under constant pressure from a predominantly masculine world; the other speaks as part of communities living under the historical aftermath of colonialism, the everyday reality of neocolonialism, or the exercise of other power differentials. The specifically literary forms they have been most involved with are *écriture féminine* and hybrid writing. Both forms challenge translation in that they evoke particular kinds of experience and self-consciously turn the standard medium of expression against itself. *Écriture féminine* invents its own body language outside the reach of male-dominated discourse. In the culturally-hybrid writing of post-colonial authors, the memory of other tongues is always inscribed, whether as the multilingual legacy of colonialism or through the migrant's lost speech. As profoundly displaced forms of writing, they establish not single but complex, polymorphous, uprooted identities. (See Chamberlain, 1992; Von Flotow, 1997 and Simon, 1996 for introductory texts on gender and translation; Bassnett & Trivedi, 1999; Cheyfitz, 1991; Niranjana, 1992; Kothari, 2003 and Tymoczko, 1999, among others, on postcolonial approaches.)

If the translation of such ideologically committed texts pushes the translator's own allegiance to the fore, so does their analysis. The metalanguage of translation cannot shake itself free of translation. As a result, ethical considerations have come to be applied both to translating and to its academic study. One illustration of this is provided by the work of Antoine Berman and Lawrence Venuti. Berman sought to counter what he termed the ethnocentric deformation of 'naturalising' translation by a dogged attachment to the letter, to the detriment of the restitution of surface meaning. Such refractory translating, he argued, refashioned the receptor language and made it more receptive to 'the Foreign as Foreign', an ethically desirable goal (Berman in Venuti, 2000: 285–6). Lawrence Venuti is currently the main advocate of this approach in English. While he concedes that all understanding is necessarily positioned and therefore 'domesticating', he remains keen to practise 'minoritising' forms of translation, forms that privilege substandard, marginalised, unorthodox, volatile and sedimented registers, everything, in short, that makes language teeming and heterogeneous. Venuti regards such translating as politically beneficial as well as ethically responsible, despite some paradoxes. It assists global English in appropriating the world's cultural goods even as it works to diversify its expressive stock. It commends a wayward mode of translation in polished academic newspeak. It exhorts economically vulnerable translators from within secure university walls. It is a very literary, almost quixotic undertaking. Even so, it raises fundamental concerns not just about translation but also about discourses about translation.

The interventionist strategies of gender and postcolonial approaches oblige those studying translation to reflect on their own positions, presuppositions, agendas and methodologies. That does not mean the different schools of thought in translation studies are moving closer together. No doubt the interventionist tendencies could learn from critical linguistics how to pinpoint value and ideology in texts with greater accuracy. The descriptivist search for renewal matches the self-reflexive moment in both critical linguistics and the interventionist camp. But the global context of current academic research, like that of contemporary literature, fosters diversity as well as uniformity. For the moment at least, both literary translation and translation studies appear to possess enough pockets of fractious heterogeneity to resist what Derrida, in a different context, called the hegemony of the homogeneous. It is a comforting prospect.

Chapter 6
Gender and Translation

LUISE VON FLOTOW

From Identities to Pluralities

Transcultural and translingual developments in the women's movement and its various offshoots since the 1970s have implicated translation
in every aspect of text production and reception, and have enormously
expanded the thinking about and research on translation and gender.
Diverse research initiatives have investigated the role played by translation
in transmitting new socio-political ideas focused on gender and their
literary expression across cultural boundaries; the roles played by women
translators in the present and the past, their reception and influence have
been studied; the importance of and the dangers involved in translating
women's writing in an era of universalist notions about women, and the
challenges involved in facing and recognising great differences between
women have been discussed at length. Women's representation in language, through language, and across languages, and women's participation
in this work of representation have underlain the entire period since the
early 1970s. More recently, ideas about gender instability have added new
dimensions to the discussions, and undermined the categories 'man' and
'woman' on which earlier debates were founded. Queer as well as gay and
lesbian studies, concerned with other gender identities and in particular
with individual choice in these matters, have taken debates into other,
though not necessarily new, areas. In the Anglo-American realm especially,
the focus on gender over the last part of the 20th century has powerfully
affected translation, and been powerfully reflected by translation.

In this chapter I will re-trace the first gender paradigm, the paradigm
that was shaped by the women's movement, feminist thinking, and feminist activism, and that strongly affected translation and translation studies.
After briefly reviewing a number of early publications, I will explore the
work that has been done in the field since those first articles and books[1]
appeared. In the second part of the chapter, my focus will be on the destabi-
lisation of the term gender, on what I have called the second paradigm (von

Flotow, 1999), which took hold in the early 1990s and is beginning to be reflected in translation studies, criticism and theory. Both paradigms reflect the interest in identity that became so important in post-1960s North America, and which, in Canada, was exacerbated by the French/English and American/Canadian divides. While these issues seem to have garnered enormous interest and exposure in the Anglo-American realm, they are widespread – European, Latin American, and increasingly, Arabic and Asian cultures are also taking an interest.

The first paradigm reflects the conventional assumption that there are groups of people in each society/culture that can be identified as women or men, and who, because of this identification and self-identification, are perceived and treated differently, with the group called women usually located in a subordinate position. To date most publications bringing together gender issues and translation have subscribed to this first paradigm – the notion of gender as a set of characteristics and behaviours imposed by society, as a construct that forms an individual and according to which that individual identifies. As Simone de Beauvoir's dictum '*on ne naît pas femme, on le devient*' ('one is not born a woman, one becomes one') (Beauvoir, 1949) so neatly implies, gender has been seen to imprint the dominant cultural expectations upon the male-sexed or female-sexed individual. Work in translation studies carried out under this first paradigm tends to subscribe to ideas derived from feminist theories and practices and thus focuses on women as a special minority group within 'patriarchal' society that has been subject to usually biased treatment, including the area of translation as well.

The second paradigm derives from the relatively new idea that the diversity of sexual orientation and gender, class distinction, ethnicity, race and other socio-political factors is so great that it is impossible, or unwise, or meaningless to identify anyone as primarily male or female, since so many other factors come into play. Still in development, this paradigm has been spawning work that focuses on gender as a discursive and contingent act, and on its performative aspects. The idea that a translation, too, is a performance causes a certain tentative overlap between gender and translation in this second paradigm, where gender issues are often aligned with gay and lesbian identities and interests, and the translation analyses tend to deal with works in which traditional ideas about two genders are called into question. The notion of performativity seems to have led translation researchers to focus largely on the role played by theatricality and linguistic markers in dialogue that signify 'gayness' (Harvey, 1998: 305). Just as in the theatre each performance is a passing phenomenon, so translation under this paradigm is viewed as a contingent, performative act. The *first para-*

digm, in contrast, is based on more fixed notions about gender identity, which are limiting and restrictive, yet can be overcome or subverted, and the work is typically revisionist. It posits a powerfully assertive translator, exploring the (mis)representation of women authors in translation, the invisibility of women translators, and the patriarchal aspects of translation theories.

First Paradigm, with Follow-up and Backlash

Because of the powerful influence of language in applying and enforcing a society's notions about gender, gender expectations and gendered behaviour, and in producing, creating and manipulating texts in translation, the two areas of study developed a productive overlap from the late 1970s onward. Feminist critiques of the so-called mainstream 'patriarchal' language that imposes gender restrictions through language, and feminist ideas about women's agency, activism, creativity and production soon countered traditional ideas about translation as a typically feminine activity of passive, yet often devious, repetition, re-production or mere procreation rather than creative production. Probably the most voluble and influential proponent behind the idea of feminist translation as production of meaning has been Barbara Godard, a translator of experimental feminist writing from Quebec and a professor of Canadian literature. Godard uses the term 'womanhandling' to describe feminist approaches to translation and considers that feminist translators should 'flaunt' their presence and agency in the text, making themselves and their work visible, and thereby reversing the age-old order of translators' and women's public and literary/scholarly invisibility (Godard, 1990).

While Godard's approach has been oriented toward creativity and visibility, thus revising the traditional quietist stance of the translator, various other forms of revisionism have also been highly visible in work on gender and translation. The title of Susanne de Lotbinière-Harwood's (1991) *Re-belle et infidèle* signals an attack on established notions that connect translation with a patriarchal view of women, as implied in the expression '*les belles infidèles*'. The term was, and still is, used to describe translations done in 17th and 18th century France that 'improved' the foreign text in translation, making it more beautiful, until it corresponded to aesthetic notions of the time. *Re-belle et infidèle* challenges the implicit misogyny of this saying, showing how such translation practices have occulted women's interests, ideas and presence in texts, and demonstrating how powerful a critically informed attitude on the part of the woman translator, and translation more generally, can be.

Sherry Simon's *Gender in Translation. Cultural Identity and the Politics of Transmission* (1996) also focuses on the interface between gender and translation, citing the famous dictum by John Florio (1603) that 'because they are necessarily 'defective', all translations are 'reputed females' as the opening. In a historical revision of translations, Simon then discusses influential, though largely ignored, women translators and their histories of working with male writers. She presents women's/feminists' versions of the Bible, and studies the difficulties involved in translating the polysemous neologisms of 'French feminism' as well as the more general problems involved in translating women's writing across cultures. Espousing the current idea that translation *produces* knowledge and meaning and not just repetitions, and examining this idea in terms of women's struggle for political, social and scholarly influence, Simon's (1996) work problematises fidelity both in translation and human relations. Her work places this problem squarely within the climate of intellectual indeterminacy and relativism that developed in the last decades of the 20th century, due in part to women's/feminists' contentious struggle over language and meaning as well as women's roles.

Flotow's (1997) *Translation and Gender: Translating in the 'Era of Feminism'* (1997) makes a further clear connection between feminist politics and translation. It shows how cultural politics deriving from the women's movement and feminism have affected writing and translation, how translations examined from a feminist perspective may be seen to require revision and re-translation, and how feminist theories and translation theory come together to counteract what one critic has called the 'androcentric slide into gender as trope in the postmodern translation theory' (Chance, 1998: 183), i.e. the gendered tropes of translation, such as *'les belles infidèles'*, that continue to proliferate.

Much of this work has been supported by an important theoretical/historical text entitled 'Gender and the metaphorics of translation' by Lori Chamberlain (1992). Chamberlain examines how theoretical and philosophical questions about language, mythologies, ancient 'authoritative' texts and the symbolic intent and impact of gendered metaphors of translation are linked to and reflect the power relations within heterosexual unions that regulate marriage, reproduction and especially the control over offspring through the control of women's sexuality. Chamberlain's contention is that the ancient and ongoing derogatory link between women and translation, which has been expressed in countless metaphors used to describe translation over the centuries, has to do with a struggle for power and authority between the sexes that results directly from men's fears about women's sexual infidelity.

Chamberlain's work continues to incite theoretical approaches, among them an important recent piece, 'Pandora's tongues' (2000) by Karin Littau, which reviews and contrasts the two main myths in Western thinking upon which translation hinges: the mythic tale of the tower of Babel and that of Pandora. Littau sets out to re-appropriate Pandora's story for feminist translation theory, and locates the source of the traditional view of Pandora 'releasing linguistic chaos' in 'phallocentric anxieties about Woman, both as regards language – the mother tongue, and as regards her gender – female sexuality' (Littau, 2000: 22). She then develops a complex argument around the psychoanalytic work of Luce Irigaray that posits women's sexual and psychological multiplicity to argue against the search for one 'true' meaning in translation that has underlain translation theories based on Babel, traditional psychoanalytic sexual anxieties and the mythic, messianic notions about a 'return' to one language. Multiplicity in meaning and in textual and visual representations of meaning, and especially in the 'seriality of translation' is connected here to plenitude, to the cornucopia that Pandora is sometimes pictured with, and to a deconstructive revision of gender symbolics. Both Chamberlain and Littau provide theoretical approaches that go beyond the earlier revisionism and re-writing of translation history with regard to gender, and stimulate more speculative work on the myths and symbols that underlie Western culture and play into the work of representation and rewriting that is translation.

However, a very important body of work that addresses theory, mythology and symbolics began to appear a good ten years before Chamberlain's article: the earliest feminist revisionist translation interests were focused on Bible translation. Simon (1996: 111–33) makes clear that Bible translation has always been a political activity that produces text for a specific community or readership and, hence, *adapts* the text for that particular purpose. There is no absolute, original biblical truth, though there are many claims to truth. Feminist translation approaches have also sought to re-interpret and rewrite the Bible differently in order to reflect the new understanding of women's positions in society. They have sought to minimise the masculine bias in the language (Haugerud, 1977), proposed a more 'inclusive' language not only for the biblical materials but also for the services and ceremonies of Christian churches (*The Inclusive Language Lectionary*, 1983), and provided new translations of key passages from the original Hebrew (Korsak, 1992). This work is always prefaced and accompanied by explanations and discussions of the intricacies of the language and the meaning that were being wrestled with. Moreover, the purpose is generally stated as making the biblical messages accessible and meaningful to women in the contemporary social and intellectual climate, as the title of

Haugerud's (1997) translation of four books of the New Testament implies: *The Word for Us*. On the one hand, the idea of writing a contemporary text, for a reading public that is learning from and responding to the upheavals caused by the women's movement and feminist thinking, has been important throughout these Bible translations. On the other, contemporary feminist thought has opened translators' eyes to new ways of interpreting old, ingrained meaning; since translations are initiated and carried out in a certain context and for certain reasons, any political and cultural changes in this context will allow new ways of understanding. Von Flotow's (2000) article on two differently 'literal' English versions of the Creation myth (Genesis 2: 18–22), translated from Hebrew and published in 1876 by Julia Evelina Smith and in 1992 by Mary Phil Korsak, presents this problematic of perception and context and its impact on the final text.

A combination of gender interests, translation and historical research and revisionism has been the most productive of new knowledge. A large and growing body of work in several different languages has unearthed and assessed the work of women translators throughout history, and the most recent publication is a series of portraits of women translators, *Portraits de traductrices* (Delisle, 2002). The translation and presentation of a large number of thus-far untranslated women authors has been undertaken (Kadish & Massardier-Kenney, 1994; Schwartz & Flotow, 2006), and many individual articles have examined existing translations of important authors in light of new feminist research and approaches. This labour of re-examination and often subsequent re-translation has spread well beyond the Anglo-American sphere with a productive working group focused on German and located in Austria (Grbic & Wolf, 2002; Messner & Wolf, 2001), further research interests developing in Spain (Godayol Nogué, 2000) and in other parts of Europe.

Other research initiatives have been triggered by the problems encountered in translating contemporary, often experimental, feminist writing across cultures, or simply in translating between very different cultures, especially once the realisation set in that feminist ideas and politics are culturally (and even subculturally) specific, and their impact is contingent upon social class, education, mobility and many other factors. Critics Gayatri Spivak (1993), Christine Delphy (1995) and Beverley Allen (1999) have all written about thoughtlessly imperialist aspects of certain approaches in Anglo-American feminisms which are based on the undifferentiated notion that translation is a harmless, even benevolent, form of communication and that feminist ideas are transcultural. These critics show that translations can serve those who commission them by uncritically appropriating the texts of the other cultures (see Delphy (1995), on the appropriation of 'French feminist' texts), by translating away from the original culture and imposing certain hegemonic versions on the translated texts (see Spivak (1993) on texts from developing countries in Western translation), or simply by disregarding the important cultural differences between closely related cultures (see Allen, on the translation of Italian feminist writings).

The revisionist work inspired by new perceptions of and positions on gender has proven enormously fruitful, both in terms of producing different knowledge and in shaking up conventional perceptions of translation that have for many years assumed that a translation produces a near-equivalent, though always weaker, version of the source text, and can usually be read and accepted in place of the foreign text. This attitude had not only rendered translators' work and intellectual achievements invisible, but also allowed them to dissemble their interventions in the text. The critical voices of feminist, and other, translation critics of the past decades have now led to the increasing visibility and responsibility of the translator and the entire translation process – publishers, editors, translation patrons, reviewers and readers included.

In one predictably conservative and politically touchy area, this opening of the translation process is, however, suffering a backlash: in 'gender-neutral' or 'inclusive' translations of the Bible. The 'gender-neutral' translation recently produced for evangelicals (the most conservative, fundamentalist Christians) – the *NLV, New Living Translation* – set off an enormous storm of controversy (Marlowe, 2001). Prepared and published in two versions in England, one version had 'gender-neutral' language and ostensibly used the translation technique of 'dynamic equivalence', derived from Eugene Nida, also an evangelist Bible translator. It met with enormous resistance from evangelical organisations in the United States. Similarly, the Vatican has recently cracked down on 'gender-neutral' liturgy. Having undermined and delayed developments in the English liturgy in this regard over the course of the 1990s, the Vatican is now trying to put an end to the attempts by the International Commission on English in the Liturgy (a group responsible for translations of biblical materials, the production of lectionaries and other Church instruments for English-speaking Catholics in 26 countries) to integrate gender-sensitive language into these texts. As a recent commentator has said:

> Jesus may once again invite Peter and other apostles to be 'fishers of men' instead of 'fishers of people', and the Nicene Creed may say 'the Son of God was made man,' instead of the Son of God 'became truly human'. (*Ottawa Citizen*, 2002: January 20)

The Vatican document condemning the 'faulty translations' produced over the past 25 years in English-speaking countries is entitled *Liturgiam Authenticam*, and claims that there is nothing in the Church's sacred texts that would allow prejudice or discrimination on the basis of gender or race. Everything depends on the 'right interpretation' which is the responsibility of the catechist or the homilist – not the translator, or the translating committee. What the Vatican calls for is very simple: 'liturgical books marked by sound doctrine, which are exact in wording, free from all ideological influence'. The Vatican's English press release on the document has a special section entitled *Gender*. I cite that passage here in full:

> Many languages have nouns and pronouns capable of referring to both the masculine and the feminine in a single term. The abandonment of these terms under pressure of criticism on ideological or other grounds is not always wise or necessary nor is it an inevitable part of linguistic development. Traditional collective terms should be retained in instances where their loss would compromise a clear notion of man as a unitary, inclusive and corporate yet truly personal figure, as expressed, for example, by the Hebrew term *adam*, the Greek *anthropos* or the Latin *homo*. Similarly, the expression of such inclusivity may not be achieved by a quasi-mechanical change in grammatical number, or by the creation of pairs of masculine and feminine terms.[2]

> The traditional grammatical gender of the persons of the Trinity should be maintained. Expressions such as *Filius hominis* (Son of Man) and *Patres* (fathers) are to be translated with exactitude wherever found in biblical or liturgical texts. The feminine pronoun must be retained in referring to the Church. Kinship terms and the grammatical gender of angels, demons and pagan deities should be translated, and their gender retained, in light of the usage of the original text and of the traditional usage of the modern language in question (N/ccdds/documents/rc_con_ccdds_doc_20010 507_ liturgiam-authenticam, May 2002).

These two paragraphs seem to order the reinstatement of many of the most conventional aspects of biblical language that were beginning to change under pressure from feminist thinkers and translators: the generic male term to refer to all humans; the 'traditional grammatical gender' of the Trinity which masculinises every member of this group from God to the Holy Ghost; and traditionally-gendered terms for the Church, angels, demons, *et al*. The issue of 'filius hominis' and 'patres' are concrete examples of this masculinist language of the Church, which rewriters such as Haugerud (1971) and the committee responsible for *The Inclusive Language Lectionary* (1985) sought to diminish. In their view, the sex/gender of Jesus is inconsequential, God's gender cannot be known, and the power vested in the 'Patres/Fathers' has historically filtered down to and been mistakenly appropriated by normal, everyday men of Christian societies – to the detriment of women. These concerns are evidently being swept aside in the name of 'a clear notion of man as a unitary, inclusive and corporate yet truly personal figure'.

While there may be a backlash from the Vatican, the scholarly sphere continues to burgeon with research and publications that derive from the first paradigm in gender and translation. An international conference at the Université de Montréal on women translators of the Middle Ages and the Renaissance (September 2002), another conference at the Universidad de Valencia on 'Gender and translation' (October 2002), two recent publications in German (Wood & Messner, 2000, 2001), as well as numerous MA and PhD theses – in English, French and other European languages – are concrete signs of such activity. Through its revisionist historical approaches and reconfiguration of translation as a creative, powerful, influential act in any context this is re-interpreting women's activities, visibility and influence in the field.

Other areas such as theatre and film translation and the translation of songs and libretti, all dealing with texts that arguably reach a much wider audience, are just beginning to be scrutinised in this vein. Klaus Kaindl's (1991) work on the romanticisation of women's roles in opera through the translation of opera libretti (in this case into German) is an early piece that examines the effect of 19th century German mores on the translation of Bizet's Carmen – her transformation from a sexually powerful street urchin to a coy and sentimental young lady. Similarly, recent work on the translations of musicals (cf. the unpublished manuscript on the German version of *La Cage aux folles* by Jürgen Weißert, Vienna, 2001, and on English translations of 1920s Berlin cabaret texts by Ryan Fraser, Ottawa, 2001), as well as on particular aspects of dialogue in theatre texts (Harvey, 2000; Limbeck, 1999) examine the constant of conservative, censorious tendencies in translating for the stage, where colloquialisms and double-meanings with regard to sexuality abound, and are systematically toned down or erased.

Second Paradigm: Gender Instability and Translation

The contemporary focus on theatre/stage and media translation accompanies the equally contemporary trend to view gender as a theatrical representation, as a performance, or as a 'performative' activity in which the individual discursively and often parodically struts his or her particular gender affiliation. Gender as performance, as an act that adults can choose to perform, counters the assumption of a seamless, stable identity imposed or acquired from childhood. Based on the much-discussed *Gender Trouble* (1990) by Judith Butler and other work in queer studies, the notion has highlighted one of the great weaknesses of early Anglo-American feminist theorising and current 'UN-style feminist universalism' (Spivak, 1996: 253) – i.e. that the term 'woman' is stable – across history, cultures, ideologies, and can be used as a basis or a category from which to engage in abstractions or political theorising. Much has been written on this topic (see David Gauntlett on 'Judith Butler', www.theory.org.uk) and translation studies has felt the impact.

One of the first to connect gender instability and translation was Carol Maier. Indeed, she and Françoise Massardier-Kenney claim that translation is wonderfully suited to reveal such instability:

> Recent work [...] subjects the terms 'feminism' and 'woman' themselves to what could be likened to exercises in translation, in which those terms are shown to be unstable points of departure for either theory or practice. Such questioning has made evident – and to a degree perhaps possible only through the practice of translation – the extent to which gender definitions are neither universal nor absolute manifestations of inherent differences but relatively local, constantly changing constructions contingent on multiple historical and cultural factors. (Maier & Massardier-Kenney, 1996: 230)

It has probably always been clear *to translators* that translation reveals such differences. By and large, however, translation has sought to minimise difference, and translation in the 'era of feminism' has focused on differences between the two first paradigm genders, tending to occult those between women. Now, in the wake of queer theory, gender instabilities and post-colonial critiques by authors such as Spivak, Maier is advocating a:

> woman-interrogated' approach to translation, which she explains as 'an endeavour to work less from confidently held definitions than from a will to participate in re-definitions, to counter the restrictions of a gender-based identity by questioning gender as the most effective or the most appropriate point of departure for a translator's practice. (Maier, 1998: 102)

This may seem paramount to striking the first paradigm from translation and translation studies – yet, as Maier explains, though gender may no longer be a clearly identifiable or even an important issue, this contingency need not lead to a feeling of impotence. Translation is always a representation, always a performance of another author's work, and hence, is invested with power. The point is that translators may choose to privilege women authors, say, or emphasise their own understanding of gender issues in a text, yet these are selective, performative aspects of the translation and do not represent intrinsic qualities of the text. An example of such 'selected' performativity has been noted and criticised by Harveen Sachdeva Mann (1994) in her article on the massive two-volume collection entitled *Women Writing in India* (see Tharu & Lalita, 1991, 1993). Mann points out that the editors of the collection focused on first paradigm gender in compiling the materials, with the major criteria being that the work be written by women. Mann sees this as eliding issues of class differences and ethnicity, which she considers of far greater importance in the Indian context. Similarly, Maier's 'woman-interrogated' translation practice leads her to produce a translation of *Delirio y destino. Los veinte años en la vida de una española* (Zambrano, 1999), a book on the philosophical writings of Maria Zambrano, that first-paradigm translation practitioners would doubtless find hard to understand. Maier translates the second part of the title as 'Twenty Years in the Life of a Spaniard', deliberately eliding the fact that *'una española'* refers to a Spanish *woman*.[3] Maier's explanation is that, since the book has appeared in a series on women writers, there is a danger of misrepresenting Zambrano, who did not see herself as a *woman* philosopher (Godayol Nogué, 2000).

Similar ideas about gender as a contingent and only subjectively meaningful aspect of texts and translations are evident in recent studies focusing on gay men's writing and translation (with the exception of brief passages in De Lotbinière-Harwood (1991) there is very little material on lesbian textuality in translation.) Echoing the realisation that there is no one definition of woman that would hold within one culture or across diverse cultures, Keith Harvey's recent work notes the 'whole range of homosexual identities in French and English fiction' (Harvey, 1998: 295), which must be taken into account in the evaluation and translation of 'camp' talk. There is no one homosexual identity either. Instead, diverse contexts produce diverse identities, and performances of these. Harvey argues that the camp style privileged by certain of these (Anglo-American) homosexual groups signifies 'performance rather than existence' which leads to 'a deliberately exaggerated reliance on questions of (self)-representation' (Harvey, 1998: 304). He also describes 1990s queer theory notions of identity as a 'pure effect of performance' (Harvey, 1998: 305). Under this performance paradigm, then, certain types of writing and speech, in this case 'camp', are 'extrasexual performative gestures' (Harvey, citing Butler, 1998: 305) that both denote and generate gay self-identificatory activity. In other words, 'camp' talk is a code used by some gay individuals to signal their 'gayness', identifying themselves to others in the public sphere, and generating a special exclusive language for a group of insiders.

Much like earlier feminist thinkers, Harvey is concerned with the translation of a coded, encrypted, neologistic language across cultural boundaries where different linguistic markers, and different socio-political contexts, influence linguistic performativity. The same question arises: how can linguistic phenomena that both derive from and generate a particular socio-cultural phenomenon be translated across cultural/language borders? Harvey notes the tendency on the part of the French translator of Gore Vidal's *The City and the Pillar*, for instance, to tone down the 'camp' language, and surmises that this may be due to French homosexuals' reluctance to 'self-identify according to the variable of sexuality' (Harvey, 1998: 311). It may indeed be an expression of a certain scepticism about the construction of a subcultural community that challenges and parodies heterosexual hegemony, while the 'gayed' English translation of Tony Duvert's *Paysage de fantaisie* reflects the self-confident existence of such a community in the Anglo-American sphere.

In more recent work (2000), Harvey pays even closer attention to the presence of gay communities and their influence in allowing and encouraging certain types of textual, translational, transformances. This is also a topic explored by Eric Keenaghan (1998) in his work on the 'gayed' American rewriting of García Lorca's encrypted homosexual images. Though Lorca can hardly be seen as having produced discursively performative gay texts of the type Harvey describes, his American translator/adaptor, Jack Spicer, with the gay community as a backdrop, could turn Lorca's subtleties into a 'vulgar (some might say obscene) and sexual register [...] importing a concrete sense of male sexuality and rendering the male body and sexual activity highly visible poetic objects' (Keenaghan, 1998: 274). Here, too, are echoes of the assertive 'feminist translator' who takes charge of the text and rewrites it for her identity-reinforcing purposes. As Matthew Kayahara (2002) has argued, Alberto Mira (1999: 112) makes this question of gay identity and consciousness-raising through translation central to his argument that 'bringing homosexuality in translation out of the closet has to be regarded, first and foremost, as a political gesture'. Again, much like translators working under the first paradigm, Mira takes the position that translators must locate and recognise gay meaning in texts, and then activate it through translation for the sake of community building. Questions about where that meaning is located – in explicit sexual references, in 'camp' dialogue or slang, in subtle evocations of homoeroticism, in intertextual appropriations from pop culture or in some other discursively performative gesture – are complicated, essentially located in the culture of the moment, and therefore contingent.

It is interesting to note the close parallels between the translation challenges that the two gender paradigms have triggered and the strong similarities between the strategies and solutions they call for. In terms of the activist positions taken by translators and by many researchers on gender in the past decades, both paradigms are based on identity-formation and group affiliations, and it is up to the translator to accept or refuse this identification. Moreover, both are constructivist (Nussbaum, 1999), viewing sexual identity as either being unwittingly constructed from childhood or deliberately constructed and acted out as an adult. Both paradigms are reflected in language and can be evoked, displayed, activated, enacted, suppressed or erased both in source texts, and in translated texts when this language is carried over into other cultures and contexts. In this transfer, political or ideological reasons play an important role. Under both paradigms, the producers – translators, publishers, editors – can choose to take assertive activist positions, rendering gender aspects and their own interventions deliberately visible, choosing to translate only those authors/ texts that suit their politics, [4] or deliberately intervening to make a text fit their particular mindset. Similarly, translation research in historical areas, such as Limbeck's (1999) work on the translations of Plautus that erase all intimations of homosexuality and DeJean's (1989) work on the many French versions of Sappho, can exploit the theoretical and epistemological categories devised in these gender paradigms to do revisionist analyses, and propose new readings of classical and more recent writers, and other key texts. Though deemed to be different, or theorised as differently constructed, the two gender paradigms have so far provoked stimulating versions of similar types of work. Even the warnings about erasing differences, engaging in imperialist processes, or stabilising an identification that is inherently unstable or diffident apply to both, and can be heeded.

Notes

1. Interestingly, three books on 'gender and translation were written in Canada (De Lotbiniere-Harwood, 1991; Simon, 1996; von Flotow, 1997). Located within the Anglo-American 'gender realm', Canada has also been strongly affected by translation owing to its politics of bilingualism.
2. The Vatican document was published in several languages, yet only the English has a subheading clearly entitled Gender; the German and French consist of numbered paragraphs and include a conciliatory justification of this ban on inclusive language. Reproduced here is the first part of the German text plus explanation (my italics mark the text missing from the English), which even recognises and employs the word 'inclusive':

In vielen Sprachen gibt es Substantive and Pronomina, die für das männliche und weibliche Genus dieselbe Form aufweisen. Darauf zu bestehen, dass dieser Sprach-gebrauch geändert wird, darf nicht notwendigerweise als Wirkung oder Zeichen echten Fortschritts der jeweiligen Sprache gelten. Obwohl mit Hilfe der Katechese dafür zu sorgen ist, dass solche Wörter weiterhin in diesem 'inclusiven' Sinn verstanden werden, kann es in den Überseztungen selbst dennoch nicht oft vorkommen, dass verschiedene Wörter verwendet werden, ohne dass die im Text geforderte Genauigkeit, der Zusammenhang seiner Wörter und Ausdrücke und seiner Stimmigkeit Schaden nehmen.

The special title and the lack of explanation in the English version make it much more pre-emptory.

3. The published version of this subheading reads 'A Spaniard in her Twenties' (Zambrano, 1999), thus maintaining, or returning to pre-feminist notions of the feminine being included in or connoted by masculine/neutral forms. Maier had surmised that the final version might remain untranslated as 'una española', which could have avoided the problem (Maier, 1998: 22ff).

4. The 'lesbian and gay translation project' located in Budapest at is a wonderful example of a publisher's initiative.

Chapter 7

Theatre and Opera Translation

MARY SNELL-HORNBY

Introduction: Page or Stage?

Up until the 1980s the theatre was a neglected field in translation studies. In the world of academe the stage play was traditionally viewed as a work of literature, and in translating the dramatic text the same scholarly criteria (such as equivalence or faithfulness) were applied as to other types of literary translation. There were of course notable exceptions: in 1848 Ludwig Tieck, in his famous 'Letter to the Translator of *Elektra*', wrote as follows:

> *Denn das scheint mir ein Hauptvorzug Ihrer Übersetzung, dass die Sprache so ganz dramatisch, so ungeschwächt und ungezwungen ist, dass sie jedes Mal Leidenschaft richtig ausdrückt, ohne die oft etwas linkischen und erzwungenen Wendungen zu gebrauchen, in welche der Gelehrte, der Philologe oft verfällt, der sich nicht die wirkliche Rede, den natürlichen wahren Dialog des Theaters deutlich machen kann.* (Tieck, 1848: 420f.)

(For to me it seems to be one of the chief merits of your translation that the language is so entirely dramatic, so natural and undiluted that it is always a genuine vehicle of passion, without resorting to the often rather awkward and strained expressions frequently adopted by the scholar, the man of letters, who is unable to produce real spoken language, the true and natural dialogue of the theatre. *My translation.*)

Among literary scholars and the theatre world, the question of the faithful scholarly translation of dramatic dialogue on the one hand and the 'actable', 'performable' stage text on the other has been a common bone of contention. In the late 1950s there was a furore created among German academics – and fought out in the national weekly *Die Zeit* – by the Shakespeare translator Hans Rothe. His explicit aim was to produce, not a faithful reproduction of the printed English version with its wealth of imagery and meanwhile barely comprehensible allusions, but a text to be performed and understood on the mid-20th century German stage (Schröder *et al.*, 1959).

The Stage Play in Translation Studies

The 1970s: New approaches and new concepts

At this time translation studies had not yet established itself as a modern academic discipline, and the topic of translating for the stage was broached by only a few individual literary scholars (e.g. Levý, 1969; Mounin, 1967; Bednarz, 1969) and translators (e.g. Corrigan, 1961; Brenner-Rademacher, 1965; Hamberg, 1966; Hartung, 1965; Sahl, 1965). Once again, the debate centred round the question of the 'actable', 'performable' stage text on the one hand and the faithful scholarly translation on the other. Theatre practitioners also objected that translated theatre texts often had to be changed during rehearsals to make them suitable for a stage performance (cf. Snell-Hornby, 1984). Early impulses from the emerging interdisciplinary perspectives of translation studies, though still within the framework of literary studies, came in the 1970s, in particular from the international colloquium 'Literature and translation' held in Leuven in April 1976. In her contribution, 'Translating spatial poetry: An examination of theatre texts in performance', Susan Bassnett described a play as 'much more than a literary text, it is a combination of language and gesture brought together in a harmonious frame of timing' (Bassnett-McGuire, 1978: 161), and she presents 'patterns of tempo-rhythm' and 'basic undertextual rhythms' as new key concepts. In the French-speaking scientific community a semiotic approach was adopted: Anne Übersfeld (1978:153) describes the theatre text as one that merges into a dense pattern of synchronic signs, and Patrice Pavis (1976) equates the staging of a written text, the *mis en scène*, with a *mis en signe*.

The 1980s and 1990s: Developing independent theoretical approaches

The early contributions on stage translation unanimously point out that at the time this was an area previously ignored by translation theory, and it was during the course of the 1980s that the deficit was corrected. The first major step was to describe the specific characteristics of the dramatic text and what makes it so different from other kinds of literary text. One striking feature is that the stage text as such consists of two clearly separate components: the stage directions on the one hand and the spoken dialogue on the other. It is above all this latter component that is meant when the term 'stage translation' is used. In her text typology of 1971 the German translation scholar Katharina Reiß had already identified 'audiomedial' (later 'multimedial') texts as those written, not to be read silently, but to be spoken or sung, and that are hence dependent on a non-verbal medium or on other non-verbal forms of expression, both acoustic and visual, to reach their intended audience. Unlike the case of the novel, short story or lyric poem, in multimedial texts the verbal text is only one part of a larger and complex whole – and this poses particular problems for translation. Examples of multimedial texts in this definition are film scripts, radio plays, opera libretti and drama texts. The latter two share the characteristic that they are written specifically for live performance on the stage, and they have been compared with a musical score which only realises its full potential in the theatrical performance (Snell-Hornby, 1984; Totzeva, 1995).

The semiotic approach

The theatrical sign as icon, index and symbol

In the early 1980s semiotics, as the study of signs, was systematically applied as a basis for the theoretical discussion of drama (Fischer-Lichte, 1983). The concept of the sign is indeed helpful in explaining the basic workings of theatre, particularly in the famous trichotomy established by Charles S. Peirce, according to which a sign can be an *icon*, an *index* or a *symbol*:

> A sign can refer to an Object by virtue of an inherent similarity ('likeness') between them (*icon*), by virtue of an existential contextual connection of spatiotemporal (physical) contiguity between sign and object (*index*), or by virtue of a general law or cultural convention that permits sign and object to be interpreted as connected (*symbol*). (cf. Gorlée, 1994: 51)

The system of signs belonging to the world of the theatre presents a kaleidoscope of these three types, and the differentiation between them is essential for the spectator's interpretation of what he/she is seeing and hearing on stage. An iconic sign (such as a Tudor costume in a naturalistic production or a table set for dinner) can be taken as it stands, and it is fully interpretable as long as the spectator can situate it in context. An indexical sign is interpretable as long as the spectator can understand the point of connection (e.g. that smoke can stand for fire). A symbolic sign is only understandable if the spectator is familiar with its meaning in the culture concerned (e.g. that in Western cultures black is the colour of mourning). The theatrical experience varies with the spectator's previous experience and knowledge, and hence with his/her ability to arrange and interpret the abundance of sensory perceptions conveyed to him/her by the performance. The problem for stage translation is that the interpretation of the signs can also vary radically from one culture to another (particularly so with symbolic signs: the colour of mourning in Asiatic cultures for example is white), and much even depends on the acting styles and stage conventions of the country or cultural community concerned.

The above observations referred only to non-verbal signs. What is important for verbal language, and is therefore of special significance for translation, is the insight that the linguistic sign is essentially arbitrary and symbolic. In other words it is interpretable only if the recipient (or spectator) is familiar with its position or meaning within the language system and culture concerned. And this is where the stage text assumes its significance as dramatic potential.

Paralanguage, kinesics, proxemics and the stage text

As well as their potential for interpretation as signs, the naked words of the printed stage text provide a basis for action and co-ordination with the immediate environment of the dramatic world in which they are to be embedded. The means for such co-ordination are *paralinguistic, kinesic* and *proxemic*. The basic paralinguistic features concern vocal elements such as intonation, pitch, rhythm, tempo, resonance, loudness and voice timbre leading to expressions of emotion such as shouting, sighing or laughter. Kinesic features are related to body movements, postures and gestures and include smiling, winking, shrugging or waving (Poyatos, 1993). Proxemic features involve the relationship of a figure to the stage environment, and describe its movement within that environment and its varying distance or physical closeness to the other characters on stage.

The performability of a stage text as a dramatic 'score' is closely connected with the possibilities it offers for generating such vocal elements, gestures and movements within the framework of its interpretability as a system of theatrical signs. An outstanding example of the performable stage text – not unsurprisingly taken from Shakespeare – with paralinguistic, kinesic and proxemic potential is Macbeth's famous monologue before the murder of Duncan, 'Is this a dagger which I see before me?' What is generated by the text is a kind of optical illusion, described by Nicholas Brooke in his edition of *The Tragedy of Macbeth* as follows:

> Words play a great part here, but not words alone: The invisible dagger is necessarily created also by his body, gesture, and above all by his eyes, which focus on a point in space whose emptiness becomes, in a sense, visible to the audience. (Brooke, 1990: 4)

The focusing of the eyes on a point in space is the natural consequence of various verbal elements in the text – including the reiterated phrase 'I see (thee)'. It is also a consequence of the personification of the object throughout the passage, whereby its presence is established in a quasi-dialogue as a kind of partner with whom the speaker naturally maintains eye contact. In this case the dramatic effect arises from the interaction of word, gesture and motion needed to create the ominous vision of the poised dagger. Usually, however, in dramatic discourse such interaction takes place within the framework of real dialogue involving two or more partners. Here, too, the same principle applies: the performability of the verbal text depends on its capacity for generating non-verbal action and effects within its scope of interpretation as a system of theatrical signs (cf. Snell-Hornby, 1997). Sometimes the methods used by the dramatist are amazingly simple: misunderstandings arising from puns, for example, differing social conventions, irony or multiple associations have for centuries been the essence of stage dialogue.

The holistic approach

For the concert-goer the musical score is usually an abstract entity rationally analyzed only by the musicologist or critic: what counts is the global sensory effect of the music itself. A similar relationship exists between the stage text and the dramatic performance. But it is quite possible to analyse the dramatic score and identify the basic factors that make up its theatrical potential. The key words, much discussed over the last 20 years but still only vaguely defined, are *performability/actability (jouabilité/Spielbarkeit)* as discussed above, *speakability (Sprechbarkeit),* and in the case of the opera or musical *singability (Sangbarkeit)*. What is considered performable, speakable or singable depends to a great extent on the theatrical tradition and on the acting styles of the language community involved. Back in 1985 Susan Bassnett aptly described the difference between British, German and Italian acting styles:

> British classical acting requires the actor to physicalise the text, to reinforce possible textual obscurities with kinesic signs, to push forward through the language of the text, even at times *against* the text. The German tradition, which is more intensely intellectual, tends to the opposite extreme – the text acquires a weightiness that the spatial context reinforces and it is the text that carries the actor forward rather than the reverse. The Italian tradition of virtuosity on the part of the individual actor creates yet another type of performance style: the text of the play becomes the actor's instrument and the performance of that play is an orchestration of many different instruments playing together. (Bassnet-Maguire, 1985: 92)

Given such divergences, it seems inevitable that precise and at the same time generally accepted definitions will remain utopian. The term *speak-*

ability (Sprechbarkeit) was discussed in detail in the 1960s by Jiri Levý (1969), for whom speakable language depends on the interplay of syntax and rhythm, vowels and consonants. More recently, in 1984, the term was complemented by the concept of *Atembarkeit* (*'breathability'*), which was introduced by the German stage director Ansgar Haag (1984) and means that stress patterns and sentence structures should fit in with the emotions expressed in the dialogue. All these features contribute towards making a text performable, a phenomenon that I investigated in the 1980s, partly on the basis of interviews with a stage producer and an actor from the Schauspielhaus in Zürich (Snell-Hornby, 1984). The conclusions I then reached, which contain various criteria of performability, can be summarised as follows (cf. Snell-Hornby, 1996):

(1) Theatre dialogue is essentially an *artificial language,* written to be spoken, but never identical with ordinary spoken language. If we compare a stage dialogue with a transcription of normal conversation, we find that the dialogue is characterised by special forms of textual cohesion, by semantic density, highly sophisticated forms of ellipsis, often rapid changes of theme, and special dynamics of deictic interaction offering large scope for interpretation. This is what since Stanislavsky has been known as the sub-text, which, as Harold Pinter put it, is 'the language where, under what is said, another thing is being said' (Brown, 1972:18).

(2) It is characterised by an *interplay of multiple perspectives,* resulting from the simultaneous interaction of different factors and their effect on the audience. Eminently effective on the stage are elements of paradox, irony, allusion, wordplay, anachronism, climax, sudden anticlimax and so on (as demonstrated in innumerable examples by Shakespeare or Stoppard).

(3) Theatre language can be seen as *potential action in rhythmical progression;* in this sense rhythm does not only refer to stress patterns within sentences, but also involves the inner rhythm of intensity as the plot or action progresses, the alternation of tension and rest, suspense and calm. This also applies to the structure of the dialogue, whereby rhythm is closely bound up with the tempo, which is faster in an exchange of short, sharp utterances and slows down in long sentences with complicated syntax.

(4) For the actor his/her lines combine to form a kind of individual idiolect, a *'mask of language'.* For him or her, language is primarily a means of expressing emotion, through the voice, facial expression, gestures and movements. The dramatic discourse and the actor's performance

should form a coherent and convincing whole, hence the demand for translations which are speakable, breathable and performable.

(5) For the *spectator* in the audience, language and the action on stage are perceived sensuously, as a more or less personal experience; he/she is not just a bystander, looking on curiously but uninvolved. As long as the stage events are convincing, the spectator should feel drawn into them and respond to them – either through empathy or alienation.

Theatre and audience: The sociocultural perspective

A 'good' theatre text is invariably described by theatre practitioners as one that 'works', and hence it must be interpretable by both actors and audience. To explain these mechanisms in terms of stage translation, Sirkku Aaltonen extended the semiotic approach to include a sociocultural perspective:

> In order to understand what is going on stage, the audience needs to be able to decode, if not all, at least a sufficient minimum of the signs and sign systems within the text. In consequence, adjustments may be made in the translation process in relation to the general cultural conventions covering the language, manners, moral standards, rituals, tastes, ideologies, sense of humour, superstitions, religious beliefs, etc. (Aaltonen, 1997: 93)

In other words, a translated text is closely bound up with the sociocultural circumstances of its conception:

> Although the text will always mean different things to different individuals and a multitude of meanings will always arise from the interaction between the content of the signs it emits and the spectator's competence to decode them, it all still happens in particular social and historical circumstances. When John Millington Synge wrote *The Playboy of the Western World*, it gave rise to riots in Dublin. It could never have the same impact again in another time or culture. The further the text recedes in time, the less relevant become the original meanings, and the more different the 'message'. The great advantage of stage drama lies in the fact that each translation and performance can take the particular cultural, social, historical and geographical situation of its audience into account and adapt the play to these changing circumstances. (Aaltonen, 1997: 94)

These apt observations focus on yet another special characteristic of stage translation as compared with the 'faithfulness' required for 'sacred originals' as in Bible translation or narrative prose. The need to adapt the play to changing circumstances applies particularly where, as with *The Playboy of the Western World*, specific historic circumstances or outdated ethical principles are involved. Similar scandals accompanied the first productions of Molière's *Tartuffe*, Oscar Wilde's *Salome* and Arthur Schnitzler's *Reigen*, for example – for reasons that would be completely foreign to a modern audience.

The relationship between stage text and audience has been further investigated by Fabienne Hörmanseder (2001) who, in her list of basic criteria for a successful stage text, has added to those discussed above the features *Hörbarkeit* ('audibility'), *Fasslichkeit* ('comprehensibility') and *Klarheit* ('clarity').

It is, however, important to stress that no concrete, universally applicable rules can be drawn up for applying the terms discussed here. Actors are given intensive training in articulation and breathing techniques, and hence can master language that the layperson might consider 'unspeakable', but which the dramatist used deliberately to create tension or special effects, and terms like 'speakability' or 'comprehensibility' must remain relative to the production and situation concerned.

Opera Translation

With texts written to be sung on stage – as in the case of opera or musicals – the problems only increase. The issue of opera translation has been investigated by Klaus Kaindl (1995), who advocates an approach that is interdisciplinary (combining insights from theatre studies, literary studies and musicology) and holistic – whereby the opera text becomes a synthesis of the libretto, music and performance (both vocal and scenic). The criteria of 'performability' and 'breathability' are here complemented by that of 'singability' (*Sangbarkeit*). The call for singable opera texts is nothing new in the field – back in 1935 Edward Dent (1935: 83) stated clearly: 'It is essential to have words which can be easily sung and pronounced on the particular notes or musical phrases where they occur'. One of the basic rules here is that open vowels like /a/ are especially suitable for high notes and /o/ and /u/ for low notes, whereas consonant clusters are problematic. This applies especially with fast tempos that require rapid articulation from the singer.

This means that the translator of musical texts is faced with a challenging task. In her study of the translation of modern musicals, Claudia Lisa (1993) interviewed Herbert Kretzmer, the translator of the English text of *Les Misérables*; who correlated singability with characterisation. In describing his work, Kretzmer made the following remarks:

I never finish a translation for Aznavour until I hear him sing a song.

When I hear him sing the song there is (*sic*) always half a dozen ideas that come to me or certain words can be mistaken or misconstrued, or I can see that on that particular note of music the word I have given it does not sound right. It is to nasal or whatever and it needs a more open sound. (Lisa, 1993: 66)

Examples of the interplay of music, vocal performance and language are given by Kaindl (1995) in his discussion of *Carmen* and of various renderings through the centuries of the aria '*Fin ch'han dal vino*' in *Don Giovanni*, where it becomes clear that in opera, to an even more drastic extent than in spoken drama, the verbal text is only one of a whole complex of elements simultaneously at work. For the translator Edward Dent's words may still be valid:

An opera libretto is not meant to be read as a poem, but to be heard on the stage as set to music; if the translator feels that his words may appear bald and commonplace he must remember that it is the musician's business to clothe them with beauty. (Dent: 1935: 82)

Surtitling

In recent years opera houses have been adopting the practice of staging a work in its original language version and providing surtitles with the translated content of the verbal text similar to the subtitles of works on screen. Such translations are purely informative texts, of course, and criteria such as performability and singability do not apply. Surtitles are, however, growing increasingly sophisticated: apart from technical innovations such as installing small monitors in the seating so that the individual spectator can decide whether or in which language a text can be used, there have been attempts to integrate the translated text into the production on stage. Christina Hurt (1996) has compared French and English surtitles of Wagner's *Siegfried* based on the two different translation policies at the Royal Opera House Covent Garden and the Théâtre du Châtelet in Paris. While at Covent Garden the surtitles are seen as part of the general service provided by the house, and standard versions are offered that are valid for all productions, at the Théâtre du Châtelet surtitles are considered to be an integral part of the individual production and are created as part of an artistic whole. Hurt (1996) reaches the conclusion that the quality of the surtitles is superior if they form part of the production as in Paris, and if the translator is integrated into the production team – as an artist who uses technological media, but who can by no means be replaced by a machine.

The Stage Translator and the Production Team

Not only for surtitles has the need arisen for the translator to join the production team. In recent years this has been recommended by many scholars who have written on stage translation. Aaltonen describes two categories of translators:

> The first category of translators are those whose only connection with the stage is the translation work. They are fairly powerless and their relationship to the dramatic text is comparable to that of an actor. The text sets the parameters of the work, and both the translator and the actor must bow to the text. Their role is seen as that of mediators rather than of creators. The second category are translators who work within the theatre, such as dramaturges or directors. They exercise more power and retain this power when they work as translators. As translators they are closer to being creators than mediators. They can, if they so wish, make adjustments or interpret the text according to need. (Aaltonen, 1997: 92)

It is clearly this second category of translator who has the means and the influence to create and then produce the performable text. This does not only mean that stage directors can take over the translator's job, as has frequently been the case, but also that professional translators, as experts in text design, can cooperate with the production team. Working with Justa Holz-Mänttäri's (1984) concept of '*translatorisches Handeln*' (translatorial action), Klaus Kaindl (1995: 164–168) has sketched modalities of interaction for opera translation, and Fabienne Hörmanseder (2001: 256–309) has made detailed and concrete suggestions for such cooperation in producing translated stage plays. Herbert Kretzmer, as indicated in the above quotation, has shown how such cooperation has already worked for the English production of *Les Misérables*. The German translator of the same musical, the rock-singer Heinz Rudolf Kunze – in an interview with Claudia Lisa (1993) – describes virtually ideal conditions for his work in the Vienna production. Kuntze approached his task holistically (as did Kretzmer for the English version): he first read Victor Hugo's novel, then saw the London and New York musical productions several times. He bought dictionaries of slang (including 19th century expressions) and listened to Claude Michel Schönberg's music, writing down his thoughts and ideas, which were later used in his text. As he was given 18 months to complete his task, he had time for contemplation and revision. During rehearsals and the preparation period, he was completely integrated into the production team, and like Kretzmer, he was able to change the text where necessary to make it more singable. He quotes one of the singers as saying: '*Ich kann das nicht singen. Ich muss dabei tanzen, und da stolpere ich über die Konsonanten. Mach' das ein bisschen einfacher*' (Lisa, 1993: 77: 'I can't sing that. I've got to dance at the same time and I stumble over the consonants. Make it a bit easier', my translation). Kuntze was only too willing to cooperate, and although he was not a dramaturge or director and so does not strictly speaking belong to Aaltonen's second category of translators, he was given the time and scope to work creatively and was given the necessary influence in the production. The result was a high-quality German text – and a resoundingly successful production.

Translation or adaptation?

A question frequently raised is whether the creative, performable foreign language version of a theatre text is actually a translation at all. It is probably the low prestige and the lack of influence associated with the work of the translator that makes anyone who does more than merely transcode want to see the result as being a creative adaptation. Herbert Kretzmer was quite vehement in his refusal to see his work as a translation:

> The work that I did for *Les Misérables* can be described in any terms other than direct translation. It is a term that I absolutely reject. About a third of the piece might be described as translation of a kind, a rough translation following the line of the story, which was of course important to the project. Another third might be described as rough adaptation and the other third might be described as original material because there are at least six or seven songs now in the show that did not exist in the original French production at all. (Lisa, 1993: 62)

These remarks may be partially explained by the fact that Kretzmer – following common practice in stage translation – was provided with an interlinear translation of the French text along with English material from James Fenton, the first translator engaged for the project, and he did indeed add new material of his own. However, on being asked the reasons why he so vehemently rejected the term 'translation' for his work, he replied:

> I resist and resent the word 'translator' because it is an academic function and I bring more to the work than an academic function. It is very unacademic in fact. (...) I like to think that I brought something original to the project, that I was not a secretary to the project or a functionary, that I was as much a writer of *Les Misérables* than (*sic*!) Boublil and Schönberg and anyone else. So that is why I reject the term 'translator'. It is a soulless function. You do not have to bring intelligence, you do not

have to bring passion to the job of translation, you only have to bring a meticulous understanding of at least another language. You have to understand the language and you have to translate it into another language. You do not bring yourself, you just bring knowledge and skill. (Lisa, 1993: 62)

It is interesting that Heinz Rudolf Kuntze – as well as being a rock singer he is a graduate in German Literature – did not pretend to do anything other than translate. However, he sees this absolutely as a creative and poetic activity (*'Nach- und Neudichten'*) that aims at evoking a 'similar effect' in the target language, and not at merely reproducing individual linguistic items (Lisa, 1993: 76). Kunze expresses complete disdain for those producers in London and the USA who, in the early stages of the venture, gave him no scope for creativity, but ' ... *sich nicht nur Zeile für Zeile, sondern Silbe für Silbe alles haben übersetzen lassen'* ('had everything translated, not only line for line, but even syllable for syllable') (Lisa 1993: 75).

As indicated above, interlinear versions such as these are common in theatre practice, reducing the translator's contribution even more to hack-work which is then refined and improved by the 'creative' expert who produces the final version. This is especially the case when the expert concerned is not familiar with the language of the source version. An outstanding example is Tom Stoppard, who has created English versions of a Polish play (*Tango* by Slawomir Mrozek), a Spanish play (*La casa de Bernarda Alba* by Garcia Lorca), German plays by Arthur Schnitzler (*Liebelei* and *Das weite Land*), Nestroy's *Einen Jux will er sich machen*, and Pirandello's *Henry IV*, without being proficient in any of the source languages involved (cf. Snell-Hornby, 1993). The ensuing translation process was described by Stoppard as follows (he is referring to his version of Schnitzler's *Das weite Land*):

[...] the National Theatre provided me with a literal transcript which aspired to be *accurate and readable rather than actable*. I was also given the services of a German linguist, John Harrison. Together – he with the German text, I with the English – we went through the play line by line, during which process small corrections were made and large amounts of light were shed on the play I had before me. After several weeks of splitting hairs with Harrison over alternatives for innumerable words and phrases, the shadings of language began to reveal themselves: carving one's way by this method into the living rock is hardly likely to take one around the third dimension, but as the relief becomes bolder so does the translator, until there is nothing to do but begin. (Stoppard, 1986: ix, *emphasis added*)

Stoppard goes on to describe how during rehearsals further changes between source and target texts:

> [...] were often provoked by the sense that in its original time and place the text gave a sharper account of itself than it seemed to do on the page in faithful English in 1979. The temptation to add a flick here and there became irresistible. (Stoppard, 1986: ix)

It is interesting that Stoppard has no inhibitions about describing himself as 'the translator' – though definitely of Aaltonen's second category – but he does have reservations about calling the resulting version – *Undiscovered Country* – a translation:

> So the text here published, though largely faithful to Schnitzler's play in word and, I trust, more so in spirit, departs from it sufficiently to make one cautious about offering it as a 'translation': it is a record of what was performed at the National Theatre. (Stoppard, 1986: x)

One might well ask if the same remarks could not be made about any foreign language theatre text, and one can only take up Susan Bassnett's words in discussing the issue back in 1985:

> Because of the multiplicity of factors involved in theatre translation, it has become a commonplace to suggest that it is an impossible task. Translators have frequently tried to fudge issues further, by declaring that they have produced a 'version' or 'adaptation' of a text, or even, as Charles Marovitz described his *Hedda Gabler*, a 'collage'. None of these terms goes any way towards dealing with the issues, since all imply some kind of ideal SL [source language] text towards which translators have the responsibility of being 'faithful'. The distinction between a 'version' of an SL text and an 'adaptation' of that text seems to me to be a complete red herring. It is time the misleading use of these terms were set aside. (Bassnett-McGuire, 1985: 93)

Conclusion: Future Prospects

After long years of heated debate, it is now accepted in translation studies that translation as it is understood today goes far beyond the mechanical and 'soulless' activity described by Herbert Kretzmer, performed by a secretary or functionary and needing only knowledge or skill, but no creativity or passion – although unfortunately outside translation studies such prejudices are still widespread. The conception of translation as mere interlingual transcoding unfortunately still exists in the minds of many who work with language, and it is also still kept alive in theatre practice when a translator is asked to provide raw material that is then 'recreated' by someone familiar with the needs of the stage. We have seen that the theatre text, and the task of translating for the theatre, is immensely complicated, and the result might seem most promising if the translator is given the scope of a creative artist working within the production team. From the 19th century 'man of letters' and the 20th century 'functionary' the theatre translator of the future might develop into an expert working with texts in the theatre, and translation studies should get the message across to a larger audience that the issues involved lie between disciplines and across boundaries.

Chapter 8

Screen Translation

EITHNE O'CONNELL

Introduction

Translation studies is a field of research that has developed exponentially over the last two decades. During that time, screen translation has slowly emerged as a relatively new area, clearly deserving of attention, not least because of its increasingly important role in the dissemination of popular culture through the audiovisual media. The focus of research work conducted in screen translation has gradually shifted from the vague articles of the early days on such topics as the 'impossibility' of achieving successful dubbing to some more discerning contemporary output that highlights the relevance of screen translation not just to translation and literary studies but also to cross-cultural, film/television/multimedia and communication studies as well.

For many years, the considerable emphasis in screen translation literature on studio work environments and technical equipment and constraints has drawn attention to the many external influences brought to bear on the translator. It has also served to alert others in the broader field of translation studies to the sometimes obscure but nonetheless powerful roles played by commissioners, editors and publicists in the translation industry.

In recent times, central debates in translation studies, such as those concerning the merits of abusive translation strategies (Lewis, 1985) or domesticating or foreignising approaches to translation (Venuti, 1995), have not left screen translation untouched. Indeed, it can be argued that subtitling, by virtue of its preservation of the source language soundtrack, is a quintessentially foreignising type of translation (Danan, 1991). Nornes (1999) has shown how fans of Japanese animation series have taken up writing and exchanging abusive subtitles amongst themselves, via the Internet, thus presenting a challenge to the anodyne output of mainstream commercial audiovisual interests. Moreover, some screen translation writing, which addresses agendas at work within the audiovisual industry (such as political, commercial or language planning), has contributed to intercultural and media studies by highlighting the inappropriateness of (non-native speaker) audiences' traditional acceptance of dubbed and subtitled dialogue as verbatim renderings of the source language script (Ganz-Blättler, 1994; O'Connell, 2002).

With the expansion in recent years of the travel, tourism, information technology and audiovisual sectors, ordinary citizens are coming into contact, often on a daily basis, with television programmes, films, videos, CD-ROMs and DVDs, many of which originated in other cultures and languages. This is only possible because of screen translation. But how long has screen translation been practised? How is it achieved? What equipment and training is required? What changes and challenges arise from new technology? What makes a good screen translator? Who evaluates screen translation? What commercial and political agendas underpin the selection and translation of material for the screen? What are the financial, cultural and linguistic implications of the expanding use of translated audiovisual material in individual countries and in general? To what extent can we expect the mediated material we view to reflect the source texts upon which it is based? In what ways can screen translation methods be used to deliberately alter or censor audiovisual material? These are just some of the questions that arise in relation to the theory and practice of screen transla-tion; each of them is worthy of investigation.

In this chapter it is only possible to address some of these questions rather briefly. However, it is to be hoped that this overview will encourage further reading on specific aspects of the subject of screen translation. The priority here is simply to clarify key concepts and terminology relating to screen translation, to outline the main forms of screen translation com-monly practised and to identify the factors that influence the choice of any particular method in a given situation. In this context, it is important to be mindful of the tensions that exist between screen translation as both an enabling and a constraining form of language transfer.

History of Screen Translation

When Al Johnson made his sound debut on screen with *The Jazz Singer* in 1927, a new era in film history began. Although *silent movies* continued to be made until the early 1930s, the *talkies* quickly became the norm. Once an actor's voice could be heard, many a career was lost if audiences did not like the sound of the voice. But even though the early cinema actors' voices could not be heard, silent film was, in reality, far from silent. Early cinema audiences could clearly see that actors were engaged in verbal communication on screen (King, 1996: 32). This visible, though not audible, linguistic element of early films was often supplemented by the intermittent use of intertitles, which helped to clarify dialogue and plot development. Intertitles, which may be viewed as the direct forerunners of subtitles, posed relatively little problem when a film was exported, as they could be 'removed, translated, drawn or printed on paper, filmed and inserted again in the film' (Ivarsson, 1992: 15). But, by their very nature, they were little more than a very cryptic, silent substitute for audible narration and dialogue. So until synchronised sound became technically and commercially feasible, it was quite common for cinemas to provide a commentator on or near the stage who guided the audience through the emotional highs and lows of the film (Dreyer-Sfard, 1965: 1034). Small venues showing standard commercial fare may have employed a single piano player to hammer away on the keyboard as much in order to drown out the sound of the projector as to add to audience enjoyment (Pisek, 1994: 31), but some of those engaged in filmmaking, who saw cinema as the emerging art form of the 20th century, went so far as to commission orchestral music specially for their work. [1]

Early days of dubbing and subtitling

From 1906 to 1913, the French film industry alone accounted for over one third of global box office receipts (Flynn, 1995: 15) and, in 1912, Italy was the most advanced national cinema in the world, with 717 films in production (Russo, 1997). But by the time the talkies came along, the effects of World War 1 had left the US in a leading position in the audiovisual world, which Europe has never again been able to challenge. While the European film industry waned, European cinemas showing American films thrived. According to Pruys (1997: 147), Germany had 223 cinemas ready to show sound films by the end of 1929, and a year later the number has risen to an amazing 1864. With the arrival of the talkie, continental cinema-goers represented a huge, but linguistically disparate, potential audience for Hollywood films, but language barriers would first have to be overcome. Thus dubbing and, subsequently, subtitling rapidly grew in importance in Europe, although Hollywood responded initially to the language problem by reshooting its films in several languages using foreign actors. Indeed, American film companies built large studios at Joinville in France for this purpose, though the procedure was soon considered uneconomical, inefficient and often deemed artistically poor. As standards were so low, the French public actually boycotted some productions, and the approach was abandoned as early as 1932/33. Thereafter, the studios were used instead for dubbing purposes (Danan 1991: 606–7).

Emergence of national screen translation preferences

The introduction of sound increased costs and militated against the growth of indigenous film industries in smaller countries with limited budgets, especially when the national language was not shared by some wealthier, larger neighbour. The result was that home production in small countries declined particularly sharply and these countries came to rely more and more on imports. From the early 1930s, with the development of subtitling technology, small European countries tended to subtitle rather than dub in order to keep costs down. Herein lies a partial explanation for the identification of larger European countries such as France, Spain and Germany as predominantly dubbing countries, while their smaller neighbours such as Belgium, Portugal and Denmark have traditionally relied much more on subtitling. Primarily Anglophone countries like Britain and Ireland, spoilt by easy access to huge volumes of original British and American films, have until recently maintained a certain reserve in respect of the use of screen translation methods of any kind. Even now, the main kind of screen translation practised in these countries is intralingual subtitling, i.e. teletext subtitling for the deaf.

What is Screen Translation?

Screen translation is currently the preferred term used for translation of a wide variety of audiovisual texts displayed on one kind of screen or another. While it is normally associated with the subtitling and lip-synch dubbing of audiovisual material for television and cinema, its range is actually much greater, covering as it does the translation of television programmes, films, videos, CD-ROMs, DVDs, operas and plays.[2] Other terms sometimes used include *media translation, language versioning* and *audiovisual translation*, although the first of these could also cover print media or radio, while the latter also covers, for example, simultaneous interpreting of films at film festivals. *Revoicing* is the superordinate term used to describe the various means of rendering a translated voice track, namely lip-synch dubbing, voice-over, narration and free commentary (Luyken et al., 1991: 71), while subtitling and surtitling describe the main means used to render the voice track in written form.

Revoicing

In screen translation circles, dubbing is generally taken to refer specifically to the preparation and recording of the *target language* voice track. But the strict meaning of the term *dubbing* is simply the laying down of a voice track, not necessarily a translated version. On the question of lip-synch dubbing, Whitman-Linsen (1992: 57) distinguishes between:

- *pre-synchronisation,* e.g. using the prerecorded music/lyrics of Broadway musicals on the soundtrack of filmed versions;
- direct synchronisation, e.g. when voice and picture are recorded simultaneously;
- post-synchronisation, which is the most common dubbing procedure and involves the recording/addition of sound after the visual images have been shot.

Voice-over is often used to translate monologues or interviews. It is relatively inexpensive and so may be an option for low-budget commercial videos (Mailhac, 1998: 207–223). The technique was widely used in former Communist countries as a cheap alternative to dubbing feature films. The translation is not subject to the same strict constraints that apply to lip-sync dubbing. It is usual for voice-over to retain the original voice, allowing the viewer a few seconds at the beginning to register it before the sound level is reduced so that the original merely provides a backdrop to the translated version. Often the voice-over actor is a native speaker of the source language with a pronounced accent in the target language, which adds authenticity to the translation.

Narration is 'basically an extended voice-over' (Luyken *et al.*, 1991: 80). The source language narrator to be revoiced may be either on-screen or off-screen. If the narrator is on screen, it is important to synchronise the translation with the original. If not, matching the sequence in which information is delivered with the visual information presented is the priority. Luyken observes that the only difference between a voice-over and narration is likely to be linguistic: the original narrative will probably have been prepared in advance and be more formal in tone and grammatical structure than the typical conversational language of the voice-over. De Linde and Kay (1999: 2) have pointed out that the narrated message may be summarised, whereas the voiced-over message tends to be of similar duration to the original.

Free commentary, unlike the other three kinds of revoicing, does not attempt to reproduce the original spoken text faithfully (Luyken 1991: 82). The purpose of the commentary is to adapt the original programme to the new target language audience. While the drafting of the text may be time-consuming, the recording of a free commentary is usually quicker and cheaper than other types of revoicing. Commentary and narration are most commonly used for children's programmes, documentaries and promotional videos (de Linde & Kay, 1999: 2). Different forms of revoicing may also be used within a single audiovisual production.

Subtitling

The term *screen translation* may seem to suggest that the process involves translation between two languages but this is not always the case where subtitles are concerned. As indicated above, subtitles can be either *interlingual* or *intralingual* (O'Connell, 1999). Intralingual subtitling is normally associated with television subtitles for the deaf or hard-of-hearing. (Real time subtitles, created and broadcast just seconds after the words on which they are based have been spoken live on screen, are usually intralingual.) Intralingual subtitles may be accessed on an optional basis and, as well as assisting the deaf, can also be of benefit to other minorities, such as immigrants, refugees, foreign students and others with literacy problems, who may improve their language skills by opting for bi-modal (audio and visual) input[3] when watching certain television programmes (Vanderplank, 1988). Indeed, various researchers (e.g. Danan, 1992; d'Ydewalle & Pavakanum, 1997; Vanderplank, 1999) have conducted studies on the exploitation of subtitled material for the purposes of foreign language learning as well as the development of first language reading skills. In this regard, screen translation also has much to offer the field of language pedagogy.

Open and closed subtitles

The provision of *closed* (i.e. optional) subtitles on television became possible in the 1970s thanks to the advent of *Teletext* technology, whereby subtitles could be broadcast, encoded in the transmission signal, and then selected by those viewers with a teletext television set and a decoder. While deaf viewers are glad to have access to subtitles of any kind, teletext subtitles are usually drafted with the particular needs of the deaf in mind and consequently tend to have longer exposure and to include explanatory information such as 'Door bell rings'. As a result, this type of subtitle tends to rely on summary to a greater extent than would normally be the case with interlingual subtitles.

Nowadays, those with digital television can also access closed subtitles, sometimes in a wide range of languages. These broadcasting developments in closed subtitling have been particularly welcomed by the deaf community as this group is still not well catered for in cinema environments. In recent years, the efforts of the National Captioning Institute (NCI) in the United States, on behalf of the deaf viewers, have resulted in the development of technology, which now also makes it possible to encode

closed subtitles on video. Many new English language video releases have
these encoded or *closed* intralingual subtitles,[4] which can be read by a small,
inexpensive decoding device, either incorporated in or attached to a
normal television set and videotape recorder. The advent of DVDs, which
typically carry closed subtitles in several languages, are another very
welcome development for those with hearing problems.

The opposite of *closed* is *open* subtitles.[5] Subtitles are *open* if the viewer
cannot remove them from the screen. This type of subtitle is characteristi-
cally used to carry interlingual translation when foreign language films are
shown in cinemas or on television with the original soundtrack. Open
interlingual subtitles are used on many foreign language videos, as subtitling usually proves a much cheaper option than dubbing.

Relative advantages and disadvantages of dubbing and subtitling

Apart from the fact that subtitling is often up to ten times cheaper than
dubbing, it has other advantages that contribute to its increasing popularity. It usually takes much less time to subtitle than it does to dub. Moreover, subtitling also leaves the original soundtrack intact. It is for this
reason that Danan (1991: 613) claims that interlingual subtitling 'indirectly
promotes the use of a foreign language as an everyday function in addition
to creating an interest in a foreign culture'. Dubbing on the other hand,
while more expensive and slower, can reach audiences with low literacy
rates, does not interfere with the visual integrity of the images on screen
and allows for less concentrated, more relaxed viewing. Because texts with
interlingual subtitles are bilingual, those who know both languages to a
greater or lesser extent have the chance to check the translation for themselves. Dubbed texts, on the other hand, have to be taken at face value, as
there is no access to the source text on screen. Thus there is much greater
scope for censorship or other kinds of undetectable textual manipulation
when dubbing is used.

Practical examples of how changes can be made when dubbing, either
by cutting entire scenes or by changing the meaning of the dubbed
dialogue, are provided by German versions of American television series.
Brandt (1993) cites incidents of what might be deemed cultural or stylistic
censorship, involving the removal of certain original scenes during the
dubbing process in the Federal Republic of Germany. He discovered that
the German dubbed episodes of the American *Kojak* television series have
far fewer scenes dealing with the detective's personal life than are in the
original (Brandt, 1993: 255–6). Thus German audiences, in contrast to
American ones, learned primarily about the main character in terms of how

he behaved on the job, not from his full range of social interactions as a rounded human being.

Viewed from Danan's political perspective, choosing to dub rather than subtitle can be viewed as 'an attempt to hide the foreign nature of a film by creating the illusion the actors are speaking the viewer's language [...] an assertion of the supremacy of the national language and its unchallenged political, economic and cultural power within the nation boundaries ...' (Danan, 1991: 612). Writing in much the same vein, Ballester (1995: 159–181) provides insights into the political motivations underlying dubbing activity in Franco's Spain.

Ganz-Blättler (1994: 245) supplies a wide variety of examples of censorship of political references in dubbed material. She cites, for example, the case of Germany's ARD television station broadcast of the American *Magnum P.I.* series in 1991. A number of references at the end of one episode, which referred to the Nuremberg Trials and Nazi war criminals, were omitted and replaced instead with references to PLO agents.

Factors influencing the choice of screen translation method

While it is true that there is good reason to distinguish between dubbing countries (e.g. France, Germany, Spain) and subtitling countries (e.g. Belgium, Denmark, Sweden) in terms of their traditional preferred screen translation practice, the decision to either dub or subtitle specific audiovisual material is usually taken after consideration of a number of different factors, of which a country's dominant tradition is only one. Certainly, as we have seen, larger, wealthier countries have tended to dub, while smaller ones have opted more often for subtitles. But if we look more closely, it becomes clear that the situation is really rather complex and continually evolving. This point is well illustrated by Karamitroglou's (2000) groundbreaking study of the subtleties of the Greek audiovisual translation landscape.

Nowadays, local custom balanced by new trends, available budget and time, programme genre, the status of the source and target languages (e.g. world, major, minority languages) and the power relations existing between them, may all be factors that affect to differing degrees the decision to opt for dubbing or subtitling. In Ireland, for instance, a minority speaks the minority language, Irish, while most have the world language, English, as their mother tongue. Thus when English language programmes are translated they are generally dubbed, rather than subtitled, into Irish, so as to keep the minority language medium of Irish language broadcasting monolingual. But Irish language programmes translated into English are subtitled because the lower cost associated with subtitling is a more important factor for the English-speaking audience than the avoidance of a bilingual broadcast.

Target audience profile plays, or certainly should play, a significant role in the process of selecting the most appropriate translation method. Relevant here are such factors as the age, sex, educational background and social class of the audience (O'Connell, 1998). Since the formulation of Skopos theory (Reiß & Vermeer, 1984), which emphasises the function of the translation in the target culture, the purpose of the translation has been considered a very important factor in translation theory. In the case of screen translation for television, such issues as the broadcaster's primary purpose are highly relevant to the decision to dub or to subtitle. Programmes that are intended primarily for entertainment, education, propaganda or some other purpose will be better served by one or other method (Karamitroglou, 2000). In these days of commercial channels vying for viewers, if the priority is to reach the largest possible audience, dubbing will probably be the chosen method, budget allowing.

Subtitling is often preferred by more educated audiences, especially if they have some knowledge of the source culture and language. The decision to use this translation method can prove a double-edged sword, however, as some members of the audience may be in a position to spot poor translation decisions. This problem is becoming compounded through globalisation, as the recent case of the Japanese subtitled version of *The Lord of the Rings* shows.

One of the consequences of the global village is that a considerable number of Japanese people are well-informed fans of the novels of the British author Tolkien. A second is that it is commercially important to release foreign language versions of blockbuster films as quickly as possible. A third is that ordinary cinema-goers can reach huge numbers of others to exchange ideas and voice their criticisms via the very democratic medium of the Internet and thus, ultimately, exert considerable pressure on the film industry. So it came to pass that the *The Lord of the Rings* distributors in Japan allotted only one week to a leading subtitler to prepare a Japanese version. Expert fans were horrified by some of her translation decisions, which revealed a lack of familiarity with both the original and translated versions of the literary works on which the film was based. Using the Internet, fans exchanged criticisms and alternative suggestions and built up a strong lobby for better quality screen translation. A petition with 1300 signatures was sent to the film distributor and ultimately to Peter Jackson, the director. The result has been that the film industry has learnt the lesson that more time plus expert subject knowledge input is necessary for some cult films to pass muster, when subtitled, in these days of globalisation (O'Hagan, 2003).

Subtitling as constrained translation

As shown above, the ultimate constraint on subtitling arises from the fact that it is an overt form of translation (Gottlieb, 1992), i.e. it can be evaluated by those who know the source language of the voicetrack. Time and space are further constraints. As regards time, people speak more quickly than they can read so most language needs to be summarised in subtitles. Space constraints arise because there is room for only about 30 or 40 characters/spaces across a screen, and also because of the technical constraints posed by a maximum limit of two to three lines of text across the bottom of a screen.

Real time subtitles

There are additional constraints associated with the production and transmission of the so-called real time or 'live' subtitles, now increasingly provided with news programmes and chat shows. Existing technology and expertise available for subtitling live broadcasts does not yet allow the delivery of anything like the same quality of work one can expect when subtitles are prepared in advance. Real time subtitling is delivered using scrolling word-by-word intralingual transcription of language spoken on screen. The huge time constraint in operation here is in itself highly problematic, with subtitles ideally required to match speaking speeds of up to 200 words per minute. The problems are compounded in the case of an entirely unscripted live broadcast, because 'the subtitles must be composed, entered, formatted and transmitted in a single pass through the programme' (ITC, 1999: 22). Furthermore, the text usually scrolls from the bottom of the screen in a way that is at variance with 'the readers' natural reading strategy' (ITC, 1999: 22). Fortunately, many 'live' programmes have prepared slots for which it is possible to prepare text in advance, thus saving time and improving accuracy. These are then simply input manually during the broadcast as required. Given the constraints involved, the broadcasting of real time subtitles is largely only possible owing to the innovative use of phonetic or chord keyboards and software more traditionally associated with court stenography (Ivarsson, 1992: 142–144). Recent developments based on applications using voice recognition software are likely to contribute to a significant improvement in the standard and cost of real time subtitling in the short and medium term (Mellor, 2000: 39-49).

Dubbing as constrained translation

The search for *synchrony* creates the key constraints in dubbing. Fodor (1976: 10) first extended the concept from the conventional meaning of lip-sync to a triad of synchronies:

(1) *phonetic synchrony,* matching sounds and lip movements;
(2) *character synchrony,* matching the dubbing voice (timbre, tempo, etc.) and the original actor's physique and manner and gestures; and
(3) *content synchrony,* matching the semantic content of the original and dubbed script versions closely.

Since dubbing is covert rather than overt translation, there is no scope for the primary target audience to evaluate the actual standard of content synchrony achieved and this is one reason why analyses of dubbed texts often reveal a high degree of adaptation.

Whitman-Linsen (1992: 19) more recently developed a more elaborate, alternative model of dubbing synchrony. She suggests that the general concept of dubbing synchrony be subdivided into:

(1) *visual/optical synchrony;*
(2) *audio/acoustic synchrony;*
(3) *content synchrony.*

Visual/optical synchrony is then broken down into *lip synchrony* proper, *syllable synchrony and kinetic synchrony.* Audio/acoustic synchrony, in Whitman-Linsen's model, covers *idiosyncratic vocal type, paralinguistic/ prosodic elements* (such as tone, timbre, intonation and tempo) and *cultural specifics* such as regional accents and dialects. Content synchrony is understood to encompass all the linguistic challenges involved in the dubbing process. However, there is nothing absolute about the subdivisions that Whitman-Linsen proposes. Indeed, in practice these classifications overlap. Those dyschronies that register as most jarring or annoying for viewers are the ones that should impose the greatest constraints on dubbers (Whitman-Linsen, 1992: 53). In this respect, it is interesting to note that Herbst (1994) has argued convincingly that the significance of both the lip-sync and content synchrony constraints have been exaggerated in the literature on dubbing. Herbst advocates a shift in dubbing practice so that translation would occur scene by scene rather than take by take, thereby producing much more appropriate and natural translations and allowing translators to address *nucleus synchrony* which he promotes in his research (Herbst, 1994: 244–5). Herbst explains the significance of *nucleus-sync* as follows:

movements of the body, slight nods, raising of the eyebrows, or making gestures always coincide with the uttering of stressed syllables, which [...] are referred to as nuclei ...]. However, while lip-sync is given priority in dubbing, this is not always the case with nucleus-sync so that the situation could occur when a character raised his eyebrows between two nuclei with such movements appearing completely unmotivated. (Herbst in Luyken *et al.*, 1991: 160–1).

Herbst argues that paying attention to nuclei is of primary importance for successful dubbing although in practice every effort must be made to strike a balance between 'the demands of lip-sync, nucleus-sync and naturalness of text' (Luyken *et al.*, 1991: 161).

Minority language screen translation

State-funded television stations such as the Welsh language S4C or the Irish language TG4, which aim to maintain and develop the minority language linguistic competence of their main audiences, are likely to dub into the minority language where at all possible. In such cases, although finances often prove to be the ultimate constraint, the argument that subtitling is the cheaper option may become irrelevant in the face of language planning considerations. After all, if minority language television services need to be set up in the first instance, it is usually as an attempt to address the drastic underprovision of audiovisual media in those languages. To opt for what might see from a simplistic perspective to be the most egalitarian of solutions (namely, to broadcast English or foreign language material with Welsh or Irish subtitles), is to ignore the fact that this would change a potentially all-too-rare monolingual minority language viewing experience into a very definitely bilingual one (O'Connell, 1994: 367–373). Such a solution is perfectly satisfactory for Anglophone audiences but potentially detrimental to the linguistic viability of vunerable minority language-speaking communities. Indeed, it may be surprising to learn that even the slightly more attractive bilingual option of broadcasting Welsh or Irish language programmes with open subtitles in English is likely to prove damaging to the viability of minority communities, if practised on anything other than an occasional basis. This is because research conducted in Belgium (e.g. d'Ydewalle *et al.*, 1987) has shown that it is impossible to avoid reading subtitles on screen and, since reading is a more complex cognitive activity than listening, the involuntary reading of English language subtitles while listening to the minority language has the effect of reinforcing the major language rather, than vice versa.

Surtitles

Surtitles[6] are relative newcomers on the international stage. They are usually used in order to provide opera goers with a translation of the libretto during a live performance of an opera sung in a foreign language. In a sense, therefore, they are rather like the interlingual subtitles provided on some foreign films. Surtitles are also now increasingly used for foreign-language theatre productions. Originally, they were always open, as they were projected on to a narrow screen above the stage. Nowadays, however, it is not unusual for leading opera houses to present closed LCD titles on tiny screens located on the back of each seat in the auditorium. These can be switched on or off at will. and in some cases it is even possible to select from a choice of languages, including the original. Surtitles first appeared on the screen translation scene in Canada when, in 1983, they were used for the first time on an experimental basis by the Canadian Opera Company in Toronto. The surtitles were English translations of the original German libretto of *Elektra*, by Richard Strauss. Later in the same year the innovative technology, which then involved the use of a slide projector,[7] was officially launched at the opening of an Italian production of Monteverdi's *L'Incoronazione di Poppea*.

Conclusion

It cannot be denied that recent developments in digital technology have greatly improved the speed and capabilities of the dedicated subtitling workstations and audio dubbing studios used by screen translators. Similarly, from the audience's point of view, the advent of the digital era has brought improved access and a greater choice of screen translation modes, e.g. multilingual DVD and digital television closed subtitles. Exciting and potentially beneficial though these recent changes in the audiovisual translation landscape may be, there is a danger that future research could be tempted to focus primarily on new technological advances and the possibilities they offer, to the detriment of the linguistic, pedagogical, cultural, commercial and political issues that continue to lie at the heart of screen translation in its various forms. The best way to guard against this may be to pursue research projects that are interdisciplinary in nature, bringing together those from the audiovisual industry who commission and carry out screen translation and those who can situate and evaluate the work of the former in the broader context of intercultural, translation, language, communication and (multi)media studies.

Notes

1. Saint-Saëns (1835–1921) agreed to compose for the cinema thereby conferring respectability on it in much the same way as the stage actress, Sarah Bernhardt, did when she agreed to act in front of the camera (King, 1996: 33).
2. Software localisation is not generally considered screen translation, but certainly could make a case to be included under my definition.
3. An example of bi-modal L2 input: English speakers viewing a German language film with German subtitles.
4. Closed subtitles are known as *captions* in the US.
5. Open subtitles are also known as *burnt-on* subtitles because in the past, open cinema subtitles were etched on to the film celluloid using acid. Now laser technology is commonly used for this purpose.
6. Although the term 'surtitle(s)' is now used in a general way to describe in situ theatre and opera translation titles, SURTITLES™ is actually a registered trademark of the Canadian Opera Company.
7. Computer projectors are now more commonly used.

Chapter 9
Politics and Translation

CHRISTINA SCHÄFFNER

Introduction

In an article on the enlargement of the European Union in 2005, the weekly *European Voice* comments:

> Not everyone is feeling so optimistic after Monday's signing by Romania and Bulgaria of treaties setting the terms for EU membership. 'Everyone knows that Bulgaria, and especially Romania, are not ready for EU accession,' says Austria's *Die Presse*. (*European Voice,* 28 April, 2005, p. 18)

An article in *The Economist* (7 May, 2005, p. 50) reports on the shortage of Arabic translators working for the FBI. An article in the German weekly *Der Spiegel* (14 May, 2005) informs that a German publishing company decided to publish on the very same day both a German and a Turkish translation of a Dutch book, written by Ayaan Hirsi Ali and criticising radical Islamist practises. In February 2004, a number of newspapers reported that the British government had dropped charges against Katharine Gun, an intelligence linguist who had been arrested for leaking secrets about preparations for the conflict with Iraq. What all these examples have in common is that they are related to the topic of translation and politics.

Whether politics is viewed as struggle for power, or as the political institutions and practices of a state, the associated social interactions are kinds of linguistic action, types of discourse (for example, parliamentary debates, broadcast interviews, written constitutions or manifestos of political parties). All these types of discourse have specific characteristic features and fulfil specific communicative functions, such as persuasion, rational argument, threats and promises. Politics and language are, thus, closely related. As Neubert (2005: 149) argues, they 'form a complex bond bracketing the political reality and its symbolic representation'.

The relationship between language and politics has seen increasing interest within the last two decades, especially in the linguistic (sub)disci-

plines of critical linguistics, critical discourse analysis and political
discourse analysis (see Fairclough & Wodak 1997; Chilton, 2004, Chilton &
Schäffner, 1997), and also in the neighbouring disciplines of rhetorics,
philosophy and sociology (e.g. Habermas, 1981; Foucault, 1971; Bourdieu,
1982). Critical discourse analysis and political discourse analysis mediate
between linguistic structures as evident in a text and the social, political
and historical contexts of text production and reception. Scholars study the
textual or discursive manifestations of power structures and ideologies
and their specific linguistic realisations at lexical and grammatical levels,
with the aim of making visible the 'ideological loading of particular ways of
using language and the relations of power which underlie them' (Fairclough
& Wodak, 1997: 258).

In an increasingly globalised world, processes of text production and
reception are no longer confined to one language and one culture. This
applies to practically all spheres of human interaction, particularly to
politics. The universality of political discourse has consequences for
intercultural communication, and thus for translation. Political communication relies on translation, it is through translation (and also through interpreting) that information is made available to addressees beyond national
borders.

I have argued elsewhere (Schäffner, 2004) that political discourse analysis has not yet paid sufficient attention to aspects of translation. Within the
discipline of translation studies, aspects of politics have been considered
more frequently. This statement, however, needs to be put in perspective,
because the phenomenon of politics can be seen both in a wider and a
narrower sense. Concerning the narrower sense, i.e. translation of political
discourse, we do not have major monographs, and the keywords 'politics'
and 'political texts' do not show up in reference works (e.g. Baker, 1998;
Shuttleworth & Cowie, 1997; Snell-Hornby et al., 1998). Political texts in
translation have, however, been the object of study of a number of scholars.
In the wider sense, the activity of translation itself has been characterised as
being related to politics. For example, Alvarez and Vidal (1996: 2) define
translation in general as a political act, since translation is culture bound
and 'has to do with the production and ostentation of power and with the
strategies used by this power in order to represent the other culture'. They
argue that all the translator's choices, from what to translate to how to
translate, are determined by political agendas. In this wider sense, then,
politics is closely related to ideology.

In this chapter, the issue of translation and politics will be looked at from
three perspectives: the politics of translation, the translation of political
texts, and the politicisation of translation (studies). The focus will be on

how these three aspects have been covered in the discipline of translation studies, although the presentation here can only be selective.

The Politics of Translation

Translation studies is still a relatively young discipline, with roots in (applied) linguistics, comparative literature, and cultural studies. Linguistics-based theories, dominant in the 1950s and 1960s, which saw translation as meaning transfer between languages and cultures, did not explicitly study aspects of politics, ideology, and power. Since the mid-1980s, with the development of descriptive translation studies (e.g. Even-Zohar, 1978; Toury, 1995; Hermans, 1985b; Lefevere, 1992a) and, more importantly, with approaches inspired by cultural studies (e.g. Bassnett & Lefevere, 1990; Venuti, 1995), the complexity of the phenomenon of translation has been recognised. The focus is now on social, cultural and communicative practices, on the cultural and ideological significance of translating and of translations, on the external politics of translation, on the relationship between translation behaviour and socio-cultural factors, on social causation and human agency. This also means that questions such as the following are being asked: Who decides which texts get translated, and from and into which languages? Where are the translations produced? Which factors determine the translator's behaviour? How are translations received? What is the status of translations, of translating, and of translators in the respective cultures and systems? Who chooses and trains translators? How many? For which language combinations?

All these questions are related to politics: any decision to encourage, allow, promote, hinder or prevent to translate is a political decision. Translators perform their work in socio-political contexts and environments (cf. Toury's concept of translation event as the social, historical, cultural, ideological, etc. context of situation in which the act of translation, i.e. the cognitive aspects of translation as a decision-making process, is embedded; Toury, 1995: 249ff.). Studying these contexts in addition to the actual products (i.e. source texts and target texts) allows for deeper insights into translation than focusing solely on the (linguistics features of the) products.

In this respect, Lefevere's concept of patronage (Lefevere, 1992a), which he developed in his investigation into the role of power and ideology behind the production of translations (or rewritings, in a wider sense), is of relevance, Patronage has:

(1) *an ideological component*, which refers to the fact that literature should not be allowed to get too far out of step with the other systems in a

given society. This has consequences for the choice of topics and the form of presentation.

(2) *an economic component*, which refers to the fact that a patron assures the writer's livelihood by providing payment and similar support;

(3) *a status component*, which relates to the writer's position in society.

All three, interrelated, components are political in nature, in that they are linked to power relations in society. Lefevere himself analysed German translations of the Anne Frank diaries that were produced after the end of World War II, and he argued that specific decisions for the German target text were made on the basis of ideological and commercial deliberations (economic constraints of patronage). For example, the original sentence's reference to 'no greater enmity in the world than between Germans and Jews' had been modified to 'there is no greater enmity in the world than between these Germans and the Jews' (Lefevere, 1992a: 66). Lefevere sees the reasons for this modification in the publishers' aim to avoid any possible offence to the German readership, i.e. a readership that had to come to terms with its involvement in the Nazi atrocities.

Ben-Ari's (1992) study into the translation of children's literature from German into Hebrew revealed similar features. She illustrates that, owing to changed attitudes towards Germany after the Holocaust and World War II, references to Germany and German culture in the source texts were either omitted or changed in a systematic way in the Hebrew target texts, thus revealing both the ideologically motivated concerns of the translators and the publishers as well as the political power of publishers and governments. Methodologically, Ben-Ari's analysis is linked to polysystem theory (Even-Zohar, 1978) and norms (Toury, 1995), with the aim of discovering regularities in translators' behaviour and, ultimately, translational norms.

Although Lefevere developed the concept of patronage first of all for literary translation, it can equally be applied to all kinds of translation. Studies into the history of translation have brought to light a number of issues about power relations that are linked to patronage. For instance, the history of Bible translations is full of examples of material support for translators. Martin Luther finding refuge at the Wartburg castle and gaining the support of a German duke who allowed him to translate the Bible into German, is just one example that shows how a person in power acted as a patron. King James's role for the translation of the Bible into English is another example (Nicolson, 2003). Without any form of patronage, other translators were burnt at the stake for falsifying the word of God (see also Delisle & Woodsworth, 1995).

Institutions, associations and government bodies that provide funding for publications can act as patrons. For example, the German institution Inter Nationes provides half the cost of some translations, and the French Ministry of Culture supports, assists and encourages the translation of French texts. There is a long tradition of governments and authorities being interested in promoting knowledge of their culture abroad, or in enhancing it by ensuring the import of ideas.. Faiq (2000) illustrates this with reference to medieval Arab translators. He shows that translation was made 'part of government policy with its own budget and institutions', and that the Arab rulers had 'recognised the importance of translation for spreading their new faith and strengthening their new state' (Faiq, 2000: 90).

The opposite of promoting translation is hindering it, and this links to the issue of censorship. Censorship, too, can be considered with reference to Lefevere's concept of patronage, since it is perceived as ideological control by powerful institutions or individuals. That is, institutions have the authority to exercise explicit censorship, preventing translations from being published at all, or only in a specific form. The translation studies literature, includes quite a number of case studies of explicit censorship. The history of Bible translations can be cited again here, as can the cases of literary adaptations (e.g. Kohlmayer, 1996, whose study of the German translations and reception of Oscar Wilde's comedies includes sections on the ideologically determined translations for the German stage during the Nazi period). The contributions in Burrell and Kelly (1995) also reflect ideological and political aspects of religious, literary and philosophical texts, whereas Gordon (2002) explains that the erasure from Hebrew translations of segments of philosophical texts in English was performed in the service of Zionist identity politics.

Studies of translation policies under totalitarian regimes are dominant in this respect. Sturge (2004), for example, is a detailed account of policies and publication patterns in Nazi Germany. Her study examines the discourse on translation in Nazi literary journals, reveals practices of selection of texts for translation, and shows how foreign literature was viewed through the prism of national identity formation. Rundle (2000) comments on the activity of major publishers during Fascism in Italy in respect of Italian nation-building processes, focusing on translation from English (i.e.original texts produced by the political antagonist). On the basis of an analysis of the publication record of the Clube de Livro book club, Milton (2000) links the production of cheap and accessible literary translations for mass readership to censorship and the official ideology during the military regime of 1964–1989 in Brazil. Current projects in Spain and Portugal aim at 'tracing' patterns of censorship for literature, theatre and films at the time of the dictatorships in the 20th century (e.g. Rabadan, 2000). One such example is González Ruiz's (2000) empirical study into the translation of film titles into Spanish under the Franco regime, which reveals ideological manipulation to promote Catholic values through censorship. Censorship is also the topic of a special issue of the journal *TTR* edited by Denise Merkle (2002), in which most of the papers were devoted to literary translation.

Censorship, ideological and political aspects also play an important role for audiovisual translation. Even the decision to dub, rather than to provide subtitles, is a political decision, since dubbing prevents the audience from having access to the original text. But not all cases of dubbing necessarily reflect censorship, since differences in political systems and political traditions pose problems for translators both as dubbers and as subtitlers, as illustrated by Chang (1998) in his analysis of the Chinese version of the British TV series *Yes Prime Minister.*

The politics of translation also concerns translation directions, i.e. the choice of source and target languages. The fact that English has become the dominant language in translation is primarily a political fact. That is, both the power of the United States of America and the legacy of the colonial power of the United Kingdom have made English a lingua franca in various communicative contexts (including the lingua franca in former colonies, for commercial purposes, for academic exchanges, see Stoll, 2004). The inequality in translation directions has led to the concept of less(er) translated languages, illustrated in Branchadell and West (2005).

Translation and interpreting occur practically on a daily basis in bilingual or multilingual countries, although this phenomenon has not yet seen substantive research. Feinauer (2004) for example, commented on government initiatives to translate health care texts into a variety of ethnic languages in South Africa. In contrast to such encouraging developments, Kofoworola and Okoh (2005) explain that the many different worldviews and cultural traditions in Nigeria pose huge problems for translation. Political conflicts and mistrust between ethnic groups are barriers to translation activities. Direct translations between Yoruba and Haussa, two of the three main languages that function as lingua franca in Nigeria, do not (yet) exist. English therefore often functions as an intermediary language for translation. A more extreme case is reported by Kuhiwczak (1999) who illustrates how, in the former Yugoslavia, nationalists turned translation into a tool that helped to separate, using interpeters at meetings to 'prove that communities which once happily used a common language are now so deeply divided and distinct that they need to be interpreted to each other and the outside world' (Kuhiwczak, 1999: 221).

Revealing the (often hidden) power structures and the asymmetrical cultural exchanges involved in translation is a main concern of approaches to translation that have been inspired by postmodern and postcolonial theories. In the context of translating into or out of the language(s) of the former coloniser, concepts such as hybridity, intercultural space, space-in-between and hybrid identity have been frequently used (e.g. Tymoczko, 1999; Niranjana, 1992; Spivak, 1993; Robinson, 1997a). Power has become a keyword in postmodern translation theories, and scholars have also studied translators' engagement to resist and subvert power, as illustrated in Álvarez and Vidal (1996), Tymoczko and Gentzler (2002) and Venuti (1998b, 1998c). One specific topic in this respect of power is translation and gender, addressed, for example, in Simon (1996), von Flotow (1997) and Godard (1990). All these publications operate with the key concepts power, resistance, identity and ideology (Leung, 2002 speaks of an 'ideological turn' in translation studies), but the examples they use rarely belong to the domain of political discourse. The intention of post-modern theories is rather to show that power hierarchies are inherent in any translation event, independent of topics, genres, cultures and time.

With regard to political discourse, the politics of translation has been discussed in the context of institutions. For example, with reference to the role of translation in bilingual Canada, Mossop (1990) argues that translation from the Canadian federal government masks cultural differences. This is confirmed for legislative texts by Lavoie (2003) and for political texts by Gagnon (2003). Translation policies in international, multinational or supra-national organisations (such as the United Nations, NATO, UNESCO and the European Union) need to cater for communication needs of a multitude of addressees. The translation policy of the institutions of the European Union (EU), for example, is determined by the EU's language policy, which stipulates, in Council Regulation No. 1, the principle of multilingualism, which is that everybody has the right to use his/her own national language in communicating with the EU institutions. This equality of languages has consequences for translation, although only the official languages of each member state are catered for (Spain has recently campaigned to have EU documents translated into regional languages, such as Catalan and Basque). The enlargement of the EU has made the enormity of the translation tasks obvious and has resulted in changes in the actual translation activities. Owing to the sheer impossibility of providing translators (let alone interpreters) for all possible language combinations, new procedures (such as pivot translation and relay interpreting) have been introduced, limits have been set on the length of texts, and not all types of texts get translated into all languages. All legal acts such as treaties, directives and regulations are translated into all official languages, but during the drafting process documents are translated only into a smaller number of specified languages. Not all texts translated for and in the EU-institutions belong to the category of political texts, but their production is determined by institutional and political constraints (for more on translation policy and practice in the EU-institutions see, for example, Arthern, 1994; Volz, 1993; Tosi, 2002; Wagner *et al.*, 2002; and Schäffner, 2001b).

The principle of equal authenticity of all languages and texts in the EU-institutions has led to the phenomenon that translation, although a huge enterprise, is not explicitly mentioned in the Council Regulation No. 1 (nor in the draft EU constitution). Instead, the reference is to 'language versions'; in other words, translations are invisible. This political aim of equal authenticity results in specific linguistic features of the various language versions, as illustrated by Seymour (2002) and Koskinen (2000b), who speaks of an 'illusion of identity'.

Multilingual but equally authentic political texts play an important role in diplomatic negotiations. The authentic versions often exist in only a small number of languages; for example, the authentic texts of the UN Charter are Chinese, English, French, Russian, Spanish, and those of the Helsinki Final Act of 1975 are English, French, German, Italian, Russian and Spanish. Since such texts are usually linguistically and politically negotiated texts (i.e. the different language versions are the result of a mixture of parallel multilingual text production and translation), they reflect specific syntactic and lexical features. As with the texts produced in the EU-institutions, once published, it is impossible to identify any text as original source text. This has been illustrated, for example, with reference to the Helsinki Final Act (Schäffner, 1995), manifestos for the elections to the European Parliament (Schäffner, 1997b), legislative 'Eurotexts' (Schütte, 1993), and 'hybrid' texts in the context of the EU (Trosborg, 1997).

Such multilingual texts in the fields of politics and diplomacy can be interpreted differently for specific political or ideological purposes. For example, the authentic texts of the Quadripartite Agreement on Berlin signed in 1971 were in English, French and Russian. Political motivations were the reason for the production of two different German translations, one East German and one West German. The paragraph dealing with the relations between West Berlin and the Federal Republic of Germany says that the *ties* will be developed. *Ties* (French *liens*) had been translated as *Verbindungen* in the East German and as *Bindungen* in the West German version –*Verbindungen* denotes relations that are not so tight as those denoted by *Bindungen* (see Kade, 1980: 57ff.). Although neither of the two German versions was a politically valid document, political decisions and practical steps were nevertheless justified with reference to the wording (i.e. *Bindungen* or *Verbindungen*). That is, translations were used to achieve specific political and ideological purposes.

As noted above, studies into the politics of translations have primarily dealt with literary texts, revealing power hierarchies and (more or less) hidden ideological agendas. It has become obvious that the relationship between ideology and translation is multifarious. In a sense, it can be said that any translation is ideological since the choice of a source text and the use to which the subsequent target text is put are determined by the interests, aims and objectives of social agents. As Hatim and Mason say (1997: 146): 'The translator acts in a social context and is part of that context. It is in this sense that translating is, in itself, an ideological activity'. The social conditioning of translation events is reflected in the linguistic structure of the texts, and ideological aspects are thus particularly prominent in political texts. In other words, the politics of translation is more specific when it comes to the translation of political texts.

The Translation of Political Texts

Translation scholars interested in political topics have looked at specific features of political language, at individual political texts and/or genres, and at the socio-political causes and effects of particular translation solutions.

Newmark (1991), for example, devotes an entire chapter to 'the translation of political language', with a focus on lexical aspects. For example, he characterises political concepts as 'partly culture-bound, mainly value-laden, historically conditioned and [...] abstractions in spite of continuous efforts to concretise them' (Newmark, 1991: 149). He also mentions, albeit briefly, pronouns, political jargon, euphemisms, metaphors, neologisms, acronyms and euphony, and collocations as characteristic features of political language, and gives advice to translators on how to deal with such problems, noting that for political texts, 'the translator's neutrality is a myth' (Newmark, 1991: 161). Political concepts have often been the focus of analysis, since concepts not only evolve historically but they cannot be understood without linking them to the total historical process. With reference to political texts of the former Soviet Union, Markstein (1994: 105) speaks of a 'propagandistic linguistic nomenclature', i.e. words whose meanings have been ideologically determined and which are a 'code for insiders'. Knowledge of culture-specific and sensitive aspects of political concepts, of associated values and attitudes, as well as knowledge of political phenomena in source and target culture are thus listed as decisive elements of translation competence for political communication by Ivanova (2004).

Moving from a less specific label of 'political language' to the label 'political text' raises the problem of definition. 'Political text' can best be understood as an umbrella term covering a variety of text types, or genres, that fulfil different functions according to different political activities. Their topics are primarily related to politics, i.e. political activities, political ideas, political relations. Although one can make a distinction between institutional politics and everyday politics, it is predominantly institutional politics and its associated genres (e.g. parliamentary debates, speeches by politicians, political documents) that have been looked at from the point of view of translation. Such analyses of political texts have tackled specific phenomena, either in one individual text or in a series of interrelated texts. Translated political speeches are one genre that has been the basis of analyses. Using a conference address by Tony Blair, Aldridge (2001), for example, identifies humour, biblical references and narratives as potential translation problems. Stage (2002) compared three Danish versions of a speech by the former American president Bill Clinton – the speech had been interpreted simultaneously, subtitled for television, and subsequently translated for newspapers. Her study reveals potentials and constraints in these three different types of interlingual transfer. Al-Harrasi (2001) studied the treatment of ideological metaphors in translated political speeches from Arabic into English. Using a corpus of speeches by the Sultan of Oman, he shows that the translation choices for particular metaphors helped create an image of the speaker of the source text. Shunnaq (2000) looked at repetitive and emotive expressions in Nasser's political speeches, arguing that 'repetition' and 'emotiveness' are of 'paramount significance in translating Arabic political discourse' into English (Shunnaq, 2000: 207). Hatim and Mason (1997) analysed a translated political speech by the late Ayatollah Khomeini, which is characterised as a 'hybrid genre', appearing to be part-political, part-religious sermon, and part-legal deontology. Their study reveals variation of tenor, cohesion, transitivity and style-shifting.

Calzada Pérez (2001) applies a three-level model to the analysis of translated speeches in the European Parliament (Spanish/English). Her analysis, carried out through surface description, illocutionary explanation and (sociopolitical) perlocutionary explanation, reveals a broad variety of translational shifts that were intended to help target texts to be more readable, thus contradicting Koskinen's (2000b) findings that target texts mirror source texts in their linguistic structure. Calzada Pérez's analysis combines descriptive translation studies, critical discourse analysis and cultural studies. Critical discourse analysis combined with descriptive translation studies is also the methodological basis for the analysis of various English (and French) translations of Hitler's *Mein Kampf*. Baumgarten (2001) and Baumgarten and Gagnon (2005) explain how ideological factors shaped the textual make-up of translations. Among the translation strategies revealed are 'omission of sensitive political material, an overall flattening of the rhetorical style, shifts in register and the non-translation or adulteration of some linguistic features' (Baumgarten & Gagnon, 2005: 29). These strategies were found in translations that had been produced by translation agents who sympathised with National Socialist ideology, thus highlighting that the 'interplay of open censorship and political attitudes leads to subtle divergences from the original on the textual surface of the translations' (Baumgarten & Gagnon, 2005: 16f).

Political texts have also been studied from the point of view of interpreting. For example, Wadensjö (2000) explores the interpreter's performance in an interpreter-mediated political interview with the former Russian president Boris Yeltsin, which was broadcast live on Swedish radio. Wadensjö examines a variety of divergences between the original Russian and the interpreter's Swedish version. Based on an interactionistic approach to interpreter-mediated encounters, her study suggests that the 'interpreter's performance is affected first and foremost by the nature of the assignment and the communicative genre', i.e. by the 'conventions of 'news interview talk'' (Wadensjö, 2000: 233). Baker (1997) explores the effects of psychological and cultural constraints on interpreter strategies in political interviews. She uses as a case study a televised interview with Saddam Hussein, broadcast by the British channel ITN in 1990, i.e. at the tense period after the Iraqi invasion of Kuwait and before the start of the first Gulf War. Baker illustrates possible 'implications of the use of certain strategies in terms of reinforcing cultural stereotypes, constructing a convenient image of the enemy, and enabling or obstructing an understanding of the other's points of view and priorities' (Baker, 1997: 112).

The link between political and legal aspects has already been hinted at above with reference to politically-relevant texts produced and translated in and for the EU institutions. In a wider context, Garre (1999) looks at legal concepts with regard to human rights in translation. She argues that inconsistencies in Danish translations of international human rights texts can create confusion and uncertainty as to how such texts are to be understood.

In my own research on political discourse and translation, I have commented on the importance of political background knowledge for text comprehension (or lack of such knowledge on the part of translators), for example in the context of German unification and also in the wider context of the revolutions in Eastern Europe in 1989/1990 (illustrated in translated speeches and/or essays of politicians, writers and intellectuals, see

Schäffner, 1992, 1993, 1997a; Schäffner & Herting, 1994). Other issues of concern have been political influences on the choice of specific translation solutions, especially with reference to British/German relations in the context of European integration. For example, see Schäffner (1997c) on a political dispute in 1994 caused by the choice of 'hard core' for 'fester Kern' in the English translation of a German document; Schäffner (2003) on the more-or-less subtle differences in the English and German versions of the Blair/Schröder paper, which reflected ideological phenomena and an awareness of political sensitivities in the two countries; and Schäffner (2001a) on the role of translation in distorted media presentation of political information. Mass media play an important role in disseminating politics and in mediating between politicians and the public, and translation is highly relevant in this context as well. In the media, however, political discourse in translation appears mostly in 'fragmented' form, with the translations often done by journalists themselves (see, for example, http://www2.warwick.ac.uk/fac/arts/ctccs/research/tgn/ on an ongoing research project on Translation in Global News).

Politicisation of Translation

As noted above, politically relevant documents (relevant for decision-taking or for implementing practical political steps, for example) that are produced in international or multinational organisations (such as United Nations, EU) usually exist in several languages. Such texts are the result of translation activities, even if the label 'translation' is not used but is replaced by 'language versions'. When such texts are put to use for political purposes (i.e. 'the politicisation of translation'), the different language versions may give rise to different political interpretations or activities. Resolution 242 of the UN Security Council, adopted in 1967, is a case in point. The English version of the text speaks of 'withdrawal of Israeli armed forces from territories occupied in the recent conflict', whereas the other language versions have more specific references to territories, e.g. the French text says 'retrait des forces armées israéliennes des territoires occupés lors du récent conflit'. The (non-)use of a definite article allows for two different readings, i.e. withdrawal from some of the territories or withdrawal from all the territories. In other words, a language-specific phenomenon produced considerable controversy, and moreover, resulted in different, politically-motivated interpretations of this multilingual resolution.

Many countries have more or less official translation services that usually operate under the auspices of the foreign ministries. They produce translations (for example of speeches or press releases) predominantly for information purposes; in other words, they serve embassies, diplomats, governments, and the media. Such texts are increasingly made available on the Internet. It may, however, also be the case that translations are intended for propaganda purposes and/or for the transfer of political ideologies to other cultures. For example, the works of Marx and Engels (especially *The Communist Manifesto*), Lenin, and Mao Zedong have been translated with the intention of making their ideas more widely known, spreading their ideology, and thus inspiring the working classes in their struggle. It was quite common in Eastern European Communist countries at the time of the Cold War for speeches delivered at the congresses of the communist parties and related important documents (such as five-year plans and party manifestos) to be translated into the languages of the other Eastern European countries for immediate publication in daily newspapers. Translations into 'Western' languages, especially English, French and Spanish, were published in brochures and distributed via the embassies.

Translations, as products, are thus used as tools for political action, i.e. they are politicised. Such a use of translations for more or less hidden political action is not confined to political texts in a narrower sense. For example, Kadric and Kaindl (1997) illustrate how, as a result of textual shifts, the *Asterix* translations into Croatian reinforced negative feelings towards the former war-time enemy, Serbia. Issues like this have recently been discussed in the context of translation and ethics (see, for example, the special issue of the journal *The Translator* edited in 2001 by Anthony Pym).

It is in the context of translation theories inspired by cultural studies that aspects of power, asymmetry in cultural exchanges, ethics and the engagement of translators have been discussed in a forceful and committed way. An example is the work by Venuti (1995, 1998b), who defines translation as a socio-political practice and who recommends a translation method of 'foreignisation' in order to respect and represent the 'otherness' of the foreign text, language and culture. Translation, via a method of foreignisation, thus becomes a form of political action and engagement (on the scope and limitations of engagement in respect of translation (cf. Tymoczko, 2000). Engagement on the part of translators themselves can also take forms that go beyond linguistic choices for the target text. Baker (2004), for example, comments on commitments and political activities of recently established networks of translators. For example, the constitution of the network Translators for Peace states:

> The Association was established by the undersigned promoters in order to publish, as far as possible in every language and by whatever channel, every message against: war in general; and in particular,

against the use of war as a means of resolving international disputes. (http://www.traduttoriperlapace.org/index.htm)

Such networks of translators are voluntary organisations, and their activities, too, are examples of what can be called politicisation of translation. At the time of the Cold War, the political role of translators working in Communist countries was stressed as well, albeit the political context and the underlying ideology were very different from the new networks. For example, translator training in the former German Democratic Republic stressed that an awareness of the social mission and commission and acting in conformity with ideology of the Communist party were essential elements of the professional profile of socialist translators and interpreters; see, for example, the contributions in Lenschen (1998) on the political context in which literary translators in East Germany worked. Such a focus on Communist ideology was extended to the discipline itself, with translation studies being defined as belonging to the social sciences, and thus governed by principles of Marxist-Leninist epistemology. In other words, the discipline itself was put into a political context and thus politicised.

To sum up: the relationship between translation and politics is manifold, as can be revealed by studies of translations as products as well as by exploring the socio-political conditions in which translations are produced and received (see Chesterman, 1998, on causal models of translation). Translation, as product and as process, can highlight sociocultural and political practices, norms, and constraints, which can be of particular relevance in the field of political discourse. Analysing political discourse in translation can yield many detailed and useful insights into the intricate political scenery of our increasingly globalised world. Exploring the interrelationship of the politics of translation, the translation of political texts, and the politicisation of translation (studies) could thus make a significant contribution to an emerging critical translation studies.

Bibliography

Aaltonen, S. (1996) *Acculturation of the Other: Irish Milieux in Finnish Drama Translation*. Joensuu: Joensuu University Press.

Aaltonen, S. (1997) Translating plays or baking apple pies: A functional approach to the study of drama translation. In M. Snell-Hornby, Z. Jettmarová and K. Kaindl (eds) *Translation as Intercultural Communication* (pp. 135–46). Selected papers from the EST Congress, Prague 1995. Amsterdam: John Benjamins.

Aaltonen, S. (2000) *Time-Sharing on Stage: Drama Translation in Theatre and Society*. Clevedon: Multilingual Matters.

Aijmer, K. (forthcoming) Investigating discourse particles in a translation corpus. In G. Anderman and M. Rogers (eds) *Translation and Corpus Linguistics*. Clevedon: Multilingual Matters.

Aijmer, K. and Altenberg, B. (eds) (1991) *English Corpus Linguistics*. London: Longman.

Aijmer, K., Altenberg, B. and Johansson, M. (eds) (1996) *Languages in Contrast: Papers from a symposium on Text-based Cross-linguistic Studies, Lund 4–5 March 1994*. Lund: Lund University Press.

Aijmer, K. and Hasselgård, H. (eds) (2003) Selected papers from the Goteborg-Oslo Symposium, 18–19 Oct, Gothenburg Studies in English, Gothenburg.

Aitchison, J. (1996) *The Seeds of Speech: Language Origin and Evolution*. Cambridge: Cambridge University Press.

Aldridge, E-M. (2001) Connotations in public and political discourse. In L. Desblanche (ed.) *Aspects of Specialised Translation* (pp. 79–87). Paris: Maison du dictionnaire.

Al-Harrasi, A.N.K. (2001) Metaphor in (Arabic-into-English) translation with specific reference to metaphorical concepts and expressions in political discourse. PhD thesis, Aston University Birmingham.

Allen, B. (1999) Paralysis, crutches, wings: Italian feminisms and transculturation. On WWW at http://pum.12.pum.umontreal.ca/revues/ surfaces/vol13/allen. html. 1–19. Accessed 1999.

Álvarez, R. and Vidal, C-Á.M. (eds) (1996) *Translation, Power, Subversion*. Clevedon: Multilingual Matters.

Ammann, M. (1994) Von Schleiermacher bis Sartre: Translatologische Interpretationen. In M. Snell-Hornby, F. Pöchhacker and K. Kaindl (eds) *Translation Studies: An Interdiscipline* (pp. 37–44). Amsterdam: John Benjamins.

Amos, F.R.R. (1973) *Early Theories of Translation*. New York: Octagon (original work published 1920).

Anderman, G. (2005) *Europe on Stage: Translation and Theatre*. London: Oberon Books.

Anderman, G. and Rogers, M. (eds) (1996) *Words, Words, Words: The Translator and the Language Learner*. Clevedon: Multilingual Matters.

Anderman, G. and Rogers, M. (eds) (1999) *Word, Text, Translation: Liber Amicorum for Peter Newmark*. Clevedon: Multilingual Matters.

Anderman, G. and Rogers, M. (eds) (2007) *Incorporating Corpora: The Linguist and the Translator*. Clevedon: Multilingual Matters.

Anderson, A. and Dibble, C.E. (trans.) (1950) *Bernadino de Sahagun: General History of the Things of New Spain*. Salt Lake City: University of Utah Press.

Arberry, A.J. (1955) *The Koran Interpreted*. London: Allen & Unwin.

Armstrong, N. (2005) *Translation, Linguistics, Culture*. Clevedon: Multilingual Matters.

Arnold, M. (1865/1907) The function of criticism at the present time. In *Essays in Criticism*. First Series (pp. 1–41). London: Macmillan.

Arrojo, R. (1993) *Tradução, Desconstrução e Psicanálise*. Rio de Janeiro: Imago.

Arrojo, R. (1994) Fidelity and the gendered translation. *TTR. Traduction Terminologie, Rédaction* 7 (2), 147–63.

Arrojo, R. (1996) Postmodernism and the teaching of translation. In C. Dollerup and V. Appel (eds) *Teaching Translation and Interpreting* (pp. 97–105). Philadelphia: John Benjamins.

Arrojo, R. (1997) Asymmetrical relations of power and the ethics of translation. *TEXTconTEXT* 11, 5–25.

Arrojo, R. (1998) The revision of the traditional gap between theory and practice and the empowerment of translation in postmodern times. *The Translator* 4 (1), 25–48.

Arrowsmith, W. and Shattuck, R. (eds) (1961) *The Craft and Context of Translation*. Austin: University of Texas Press.

Arthern, P.J. (1994) European community translation in Belgium. *Meta* 39 (1), 150–158.

Ascheid, A. (1997) Dubbing as cultural ventriloquism. *The Velvet Light Trap* 40 (Fall), 32–41.

Avery, P. and Heath-Stubbs, J. (trans.) (1979) *The Ruba'iyat of Omar Kayyam*. Harmondsworth: Penguin Books.

Badawi, A. (1968) *La transmission de la philosophie grecque au monde arabe*. Paris: Vrin.

Bachmann, T.E. (ed.) (1960) On translation: An open letter. In *Word and Sacrament: Luther's Works* (Vol. 35; Part 1). Philadelphia: Muhlenburg Press.

Baker, M. (1992) *In Other Words: A Coursebook on Translation*. London: Routledge.

Baker, M. (1993) Corpus linguistics and translation studies. In M. Baker, G. Francis and E. Tognini-Bonelli (eds) *Text and Technology: In Honour of John Sinclair* (pp. 233–50). Amsterdam: John Benjamins.

Baker, M. (1995) Corpora in translation studies: An overview and suggestions for future research. *Target* 7, 223–44.

Baker, M. (1997) Non-cognitive constraints and interpreter strategies in political interviews. In K. Simms (ed.) *Translating Sensitive Texts: Linguistic Aspects* (pp. 111–129). Amsterdam: Rodopi.

Baker, M. (1998) (ed.) *Routledge Encyclopedia of Translation Studies*. London: Routledge.

Baker, M. (2000) Towards a methodology for investigating the style of a literary translator. *Target* 12 (2), 241–66.

Baker, M. (2004) Contesting dominant narratives. Paper delivered at a conference on Translation and Conflict, University of Salford.

Ballard, M. (1992) *De Cicéron à Benjamin: Traducteurs, traductions, réflexions*. Lille: Presses Universitaires de Lille.

Ballard, M. (ed.) (2000) *Oralité et traduction*. Arras: Artois Presses Université.

Ballester, A. (1995) The politics of dubbing. Spain: A case study. In P. Jansen (ed.) *Translation and the Manipulation of Discourse: Selected Papers of the CETRA research Seminars in Translation Studies 1992–1993* (pp. 159–181). Leuven: CETRA.

Barnstone, W. (1993) *The Poetics of Translation: History, Theory, Practice.* Yale: Yale University Press.

Barret-Ducrocq, F. (ed.) (1992) *Traduire l'Europe.* Paris: Payot.

Bassnett, S. (1980/2002) *Translation Studies* (3rd rev. edn). London: Routledge.

Bassnett, S. (1993) *Comparative Literature: A Critical Introduction.* Oxford: Blackwell.

Bassnett, S. (ed.) (1997) *Translating Literature.* Cambridge: D.S. Brewer.

Bassnett, S. (2001) 'Shakespear's in danger'. *The Independent Education Supplement,* 15 November, pp. 6–7.

Bassnett, S. (2005) Literature teaching in the twenty-first century: A hopeless endeavour or the start of something new? *Cambridge Quarterly* 34, 203–212.

Bassnett, S. (2006) Reflections on comparative literature in the twenty-first century. *Comparative Critical Studies* 3 (1–2), 3–11.

Bassnett, S. and Lefevere, A. (eds) (1990) *Translation, History and Culture.* London: Pinter.

Bassnett, S. and Lefevere, A. (1998) *Constructing Cultures: Essays on Literary Translation.* Clevedon: Multilingual Matters.

Bassnett, S. and Trivedi, H. (eds) (1999) *Post-colonial Translation: Theory and Practice.* London: Routledge.

Bassnett-McGuire, S. (1978) Translating spatial poetry: An examination of theatre texts in performance. In J. Holmes, J. Lambert, R. Van den Broeck *Literature and Translation: New Perspectives in Literary Studies* (pp. 161–76). Leuven: ACCO.

Bassnett-McGuire, S. (1985) Ways through the labyrinth: Strategies and methods for translating theatre texts. In T. Hermans (ed.) *The Manipulation of Literature: Studies in Literary Translation* (pp. 87–102). London: Croom Helm.

Baugh, A.C. and Cable, T. (1994) *A History of the English Language.* London: Routledge (original work published 1951).

Baumgarten, S. (2001) Uncovering ideology in translation: An analysis of English translations of Hitler's *Mein Kampf.* In M. Olohan (ed.) *CTIS Occasional Papers* (pp. 21–54). Manchester: UMIST, Centre for Translation and Intercultural Studies.

Baumgarten, S. and Gagnon, C. (2005) Written political discourse in translation: A critical discourse-perspective on *Mein Kampf.* In W. Thiele, J. Schwend and C. Todenhagen (eds) *Political Discourse: Different Media, Different Intentions, New Reflections* (pp. 11–32). Tübingen: Stauffenburg.

de Beaugrande, R. (1978) *Factors in a Theory of Poetic Translating.* Assen: Van Gorcum.

de Beauvoir, S. (1949) *The Second Sex* (H.M. Parshley, trans.). Harmondsworth: Penguin.

Bednarz, K. (1969) *Theatralische Aspekte der Dramenübersetzung: Dargestellt am Beispiel der deutschen Übersetzungen und Bühnenbearbeitungen der Dramen Anton Cechovs.* Vienna: Notring.

Beer, J. and Lloyd-Jones, K. (eds) (1995) *Translation and the Transmission of Culture Between 1300 and 1600.* Kalamazoo, MI: Medieval Institute Publications, Western Michigan University.

Belitt, B. (1978) *Adam's Dream: A Preface to Translation.* New York: Grove Press.

Ben-Ari, N. (1992) Didactic and pedagogic tendencies in the norms dictating the translation of children's literature: The case of postwar German–Hebrew translations. *Poetics Today* 13 (1), 198–221.

Benjamin, A. (1989) *Translation and the Nature of Philosophy: A New Theory of Words.* London: Routledge.

Benjamin, W. (1955) *Schrifte.* Band 2, Frankfurt am Main: Suhrkamp.

Benjamin, W. (1970) The task of the translator (H. Zohn, trans.). In W. Benjamin (H. Arendt, ed.) *Illuminations* (pp. 69–82). London: Fontana (original work published in 1923).

Benson, L.D. (ed) (1988) *The Riverside Chaucer.* Oxford: Oxford University Press (based on the F.N. Robinson edition).

Bergonzi, B. (1990) *Exploding English: Criticism, Theory and Culture.* Oxford: Clarendon Press.

Berman, A. (1984) *L'épreuve de l'étranger: Culture et traduction dans l'Allemagne romantique.* Paris: Gallimard.

Berman, A. (1985) La traduction et la lettre: Ou l'auberge du lointain. In A. Berman (ed.) *Les Tours de Babel* (pp. 35–100). Mauvezin: Trans-Europ-Repress.

Berman, A. (1992) *The Experience of the Foreign: Culture and Translation in Romantic Germany* (S. Heyvaert, trans.). Albany: State University of New York Press.

Berman, A. (1995) *Pour une critique des traductions: John Donne.* Paris: Gallimard.

Berman, A. (2000) Translation and the trials of the foreign. In L. Venuti (ed.) *The Translation Studies Reader* (pp. 276–289). London: Routledge.

Bernheimer, C. (ed.) (1995) *Comparative Literature in the Age of Multiculturalism.* Baltimore: Johns Hopkins University Press.

Beylard-Ozeroff, A., Králová, J. and Moser-Mercer, B. (eds) (1998) *Translators' Strategies and Creativity: In Honor of Jiří Levý and Anton Popovič.* Amsterdam: John Benjamins.

Biber, D., Conrad, S. and Reppen, R. (1998) *Corpus Linguistics: Investigating Language Structure and Use.* Cambridge: Cambridge University Press.

Bigelow, J. (1978) Semantics of thinking, speaking and translation. In. F. Guenthner and M. Guenthner-Reutter (eds) *Meaning and Translation: Philosophical and Linguistic Approaches* (pp. 109–135). London: Duckworth.

Biguenet, J. and Schulte, R. (eds) (1989) *The Craft of Translation.* Chicago: University of Chicago Press.

Blanchot, M. (1949) Traduit de... In M. Blanchot *La Part du feu* (pp. 173–187). Paris: Gallimard.

Blane, S. (1996) Interlingual subtitling in the languages degree. In P. Sewell and I. Higgins (eds) *Teaching Translation in Universities: Present and Future Perspectives* (pp. 183–208). London: CILT.

Bloom, P. (in preparation) Gender masks in translation: Delmira Agustini and Gabriela Mistral. PhD thesis, New York University.

Bloomfield, L. (1933) *Language.* New York: Henry Holt and Company.

Blumenfeld-Kosinski, R., von Flotow, L. and Russell, D. (eds) (2001) *The Politics of Translation in the Middle Ages and Renaissance.* Ottawa: Ottawa University.

Bly, R. (1983) *The Eight Stages of Translation.* Boston: Rowan Tree.

Boase-Beier, J. and Holman, M. (eds) (1999) *The Practices of Literary Translation. Constraints and Creativity.* Manchester: St Jerome.

Bolinger, D. (1965/66) Transformulation: Structural translation. *Acta Linguistica Hafniensia* 9, 130–44.

Botterill, S. (ed.) (1996) *Dante: de Vulgari Eloquentia*. Cambridge: Cambridge University Press.

Bourdieu, P. (1982) *Ce que parler veut dire*. Paris: Fayard.

Bourdieu, P. (1994) *In Other Worlds: Essays Towards a Reflexive Sociology*. Cambridge: Polity Press.

Bowker, L. and Kenny, D. (eds) (1998 onwards) *Bibliography of Translation Studies*. Manchester: St Jerome.

Bowker, L. and Pearson, J. (2002) *Working with Specialized Language: A Practical Guide to Using Corpora*. London: Routledge.

Bowman, M. (2000) Scottish horses and Montreal trains: The translation of vernacular to vernacular. In C-A. Upton (ed.) *Moving Target: Theatre Translation and Cultural Relocation* (pp. 25–33). Manchester: St. Jerome.

Branchadell, A. and West, L.M. (eds) (2005) *Less Translated Languages*. Amsterdam: John Benjamins.

Brandt, U. (1993) Krimistandards: Motive, narrative Strategien und Standardsituationen der amerkanischen Freitagabend-Krimiserien in der ARD von 1962–1978. PhD thesis, University of Siegen.

Brenan, G. (1951/1962) *The Literature of the Spanish People*. Cambridge: Cambridge University Press.

Brenner-Rademacher, S. (1965) Übersetzer sprachen mit Bühnenkünstlern. *Babel* 11, 8–9.

Brink, C.O. (1971) *Horace on Poetry: The Ars Poetica*. London: Cambridge University Press

Brisset, A. (2000) The search for a native language: Translation and cultural identity. In L. Venuti (ed.) *The Translation Studies Reader* (pp. 343–75). London: Routledge.

Brooke, N. (ed.) (1990) *The Tragedy of Macbeth* (The Oxford Shakespeare). Oxford: Oxford Universssity Press.

Brotherston, G. (2002) Tlaloc roars: Native America, the West and literary translation. In T. Hermans (ed.) *Crosscultural Transgressions: Research Models in Translation Studies II: Historical and Ideological Issues* (pp. 165–79). Manchester: St Jerome.

Brower, R.A. (ed.) (1959a) *On Translation*. Cambridge, MA: Harvard University Press.

Brower, R.A. (1959b) Seven Agamemnons. In R.A. Brower (ed.) *On Translation* (pp. 173–195). Cambridge, MA: Harvard University Press. (Reprinted in R.A. Brower (1974) *Mirror on Mirror: Translation, Imitation, Parody* (pp. 159–80). Cambridge, MA: Harvard University Press.)

Brown, J.R. (1972) *Theatre Language: A Study of Arden, Osborne, Pinter and Wesker*. London: Allen Lane.

Brown, P. and Levinson, S.C. (1987) *Politeness: Some Universals in Language Usage*. Cambridge: Cambridge University Press.

Bruce, F.F. (1961) *The English Bible: A History of Translations*. London: Lutterworth Press.

Bruner, G. and Temple, R.Z. (eds) (1968) *Literatures of the World in English Translation: A Bibliography*. New York: Ungar.

Bryan, G.B. (1984) *An Ibsen Companion*. London: Greenwood Press.

Bryson, B. (1990) *Mother Tongue: The English Language*. Harmondsworth: Penguin Books.

Budick, S. and Iser, W. (eds) (1996) *The Translatability of Cultures: Figurations of the Space Between*. Stanford: Stanford University Press.

Bühler, K. (1934) *Die Sprachtheorie*. Jena: Gustav Fischer.

Burge, T. (1978) Self-reference and translation. In F. Guenther and M. Guenther-Reutter (eds) *Meaning and Translation: Philosophical and Linguistic Approaches* (pp. 137–153). London: Duckworth.

Burnley, D. (1992) *The History of the English Language: A Sourcebook*. London: Longman.

Burrell, T. and Kelly, S.K. (eds) (1995) *Translation: Religion, Ideology, Politics*. Binghamton: Centre for Research in Translation.

Bush, P. and Malmkjær, K. (1998) *Rimbaud's Rainbow: Literary Translation in Higher Education*. Amsterdam: John Benjamins.

Butler, J. (1990) *Gender Trouble: Feminisms and the Subversion of Identity*. London and New York: Routledge.

Calzada Pérez, M. (2001) A three-level methodology for descriptive-explanatory translation studies. *Target* 13 (2), 203–39.

Calzada Pérez, M. (2003) (ed.) *Apropos of Ideology: Translation Studies on Ideology: Ideologies in Translation Studies*. Manchester: St Jerome.

Carson, D.A. (1988) *The Inclusive Language Debate: A Plea for Realism*. Grand Rapids Michigan: Baker Book House.

Catford, J.C. (1965) *A Linguistic Theory of Translation: An Essay in Applied Linguistics*. London: Oxford University Press.

Chadwick, L. (2000) *Translating Words, Translating Cultures*. London: Duckworth.

Chamberlain, L. (1992) Gender and the metaphorics of translation. In L. Venuti (ed.) *Rethinking Translation* (pp. 57–74). London: Routledge.

Chance, J. (1998) Gender subversion and linguistic castration in fifteenth century English translations of Christine de Pizan. In A. Roberts (ed.) *Violence Against Women in Medieval Texts* (pp. 161–93). Gainesville, FL: University Press of Florida.

Chang, N.F. (1998) Politics and poetics in translation: Accounting for a Chinese version of *Yes, Prime Minister*. *The Translator* 4 (2), 249–72.

Chau, S.S.C. (Chau Suicheong) (1984) Hermeneutics and the translator: The ontological dimension of translating. *Multilingua* 3 (2), 71–7.

Chaudhuri, S. (1999) *Translation and Understanding*. Delhi: Oxford University Press.

Chesterman, A. (1989) *Readings in Translation Theory*. Helsinki: Oy Finn Lecture Ab.

Chesterman, A. (1993) From 'is' to 'ought': Laws, norms and strategies in translation studies. *Target* 5 (1), 1–20.

Chesterman, A. (1997) *Memes of Translation: The Spread of Ideas in Translation Theory*. Amsterdam: John Benjamins.

Chesterman, A. (1998) Causes, translations, effects. *Target* 10 (2), 201–30.

Chesterman, A. (1999) The empirical status of prescriptivism. *Folia Translatologica* 6, 9–19.

Chesterman, A. and Wagner, E. (2002) *Can Theory Help Translators? A Dialogue Between the Ivory Tower and the Wordface*. Manchester: St Jerome.

Cheyfitz, E. (1991) *The Poetics of Imperialism: Translation and Colonization from The Tempest to Tarzan*. Oxford: Oxford University Press.

Chilton, P. (2004) *Analysing Political Discourse: Theory and Practice*, London: Routledge.

Chilton, P. and Schäffner, C. (1997) Discourse and politics. In T. van Dijk (ed.) *Discourse Studies: A Multidisciplinary Introduction* (Vol. 2): *Discourse as Social Interaction* (pp. 206–30). London: Sage.

Chomsky, N. (1957) *Syntactic Structures*. The Hague: Mouton.

Chomsky, N. (1965) *Aspects of the Theory of Syntax*. Cambridge, MA: MIT Press.
Chomsky, N. (1980) *Rules and Representations*. New York: Columbia University Press.
Chomsky, N. (2000) *New Horizons in the Study of Language and Mind*. Cambridge: Cambridge University Press.
Classe, O. (ed.) (2000) *Encyclopedia of Literary Translation into English*. London: Fitzroy Dearborn.
Cline, S.L. (1988) Revisionist conquest history: Sahagun's revised book XII. In J.J. Klor de Alba, H.B. Nicholson and E.Q. Keber (eds) *The Work of Bernadino de Sahagun*. New York: The Institute for Mesoamerican Studies, Albany State University.
Coelsch-Foisner, S. and Klein, H. (eds) (2005) *Drama Translation and Theatre Practice*. Frankfurt: Peter Lang.
Corbett, J. (1999) *Written in the Language of the Scottish Nation: A History of Literary Translation into Scots*. Clevedon: Multilingual Matters.
Corrigan, R. (1961) Translating for actors. In W. Arrowsmith and R. Shattuck (eds) *The Craft and Context of Translation* (pp. 95–106). Austin, TX: University of Texas Press.
Cronin, M. (1996) *Translating Ireland: Translation, Languages, Cultures*. Cork: Cork University Press
Cronin, M. (2000) *Across the Lines: Travel, Language,Translation*. Cork: Cork University Press.
Cronin, M. (2003) *Translation and Globalization*. London: Routledge.
Crotch, W.J. (ed.) (1956) *The Prologues and Epilogues of William Caxton*. E.E.T.S. London: Oxford University Press.
Crystal, D. (2004) *The Stories of English*. London: Allen Lane.
Culler, J. (1997) *Literary Theory: A Very Short Introduction*. Oxford: Oxford University Press.
Danan, M. (1991) Dubbing as an expression of nationalism. *Meta* 36 (4), 606–614.
Danan, M. (1992) Reversed subtitling and dual-coding theory: New directions for foreign language instruction. *Language Learning* 42 (4), 497–527.
Danan, M. (1994) *From Nationalism to Globalization: France's Challenges to Hollywood's Hegemony*. Michigan: Ann Arbor.
Davidson, D. (1984) *Enquiries into Truth and Interpretation*. Oxford: Clarendon Press.
Davis, K. (2001) *Deconstruction and Translation*. Manchester: St Jerome.
Day Lewis, C. (1970) *On Translating Poetry*. Abingdon-on-Thames: Abbey.
DeJean, J. (1989) *Fictions of Sappho*. Chicago: The University of Chicago Press.
Delabastita, D. (1993) *There's a Double Tongue: An Investigation into the Translation of Shakespeare's Wordplay*. Amsterdam: Rodopi.
Delabastita, D. (ed.) (1997) *Traductio: Essays on Punning and Translation*. Manchester: St Jerome.
Delabastita, D. and D'hulst, L. (eds) (1993) *European Shakespeares: Translating Shakespeare in the Romantic Age*. Amsterdam: John Benjamins.
Deleuze, G. (1977) Intellectuals and power: A conversation between Michel Foucault and Gilles Deleuze. In M. Foucault *Language, Counter-Memory, Practice: Selected Essays and Interviews by Michel Foucault* (D.F. Bouchard, ed.; S. Simon, trans.). Ithaca, NY: Cornell University Press.
Delisle, J. (ed.) (2002) *Portraits de traductrices*. Ottawa: University of Ottawa Press.
Delisle, J. and Woodsworth, J. (eds) (1995) *Translators through History*. Amsterdam: John Benjamins.

Delphy, C. (1995) The invention of French feminism: An essential move. *Yale French Studies* 87, 190–221.

Dent, E.J. (1935) The translation of opera. *Proceedings of the Musical Association for the Investigation and Discussion of Subjects Connected with the Art and Science of Music 1934/1935: 61st Session* (pp. 81–104). Leeds: Whithear and Miller.

Derrida, J. (1967/1976) *De la grammatologie*. Paris: Les Éditions de Minuit. (English version: G.C. Spivak (trans.) (1976) *Of Grammatology*. Baltimore: Johns Hopkins University Press.)

Derrida, J. (1968) La pharmacie de Platon. *Tel Quel* 32, 3–48, and 33, 18–59. (English version: B. Johnson (trans.) (1981) *Dissemination*. Chicago: University of Chicago Press.)

Derrida, J. (1985) Des tours de Babel (English and French versions, J. Graham, trans.). In J. Graham (ed.) *Difference in Translation* (pp. 165–207; 209–248). Ithaca, NY: Cornell University Press.

Derrida, J. (1988) *Limited Inc*. Evanston, IL: Northwestern University Press.

Derrida, J. (1992) This strange institution called literature: An interview with Jacques Derrida (G. Bennington and R. Bowlby, trans.). In D. Attridge (ed.) *Jacques Derrida: Acts of Literature* (pp. 33–75). London: Routledge.

Derrida, J. (1993) *Spectres de Marx*. Paris: Galilée.

D'hulst, L. (1987) *L'évolution de la poésie en France (1780–1830): Introduction à une analyse des interférences systémiques*. Leuven: Leuven University Press.

D'hulst, L. (1990) *Cent ans de théorie française de la traduction: De Batteux à Littré (1748–1847)*. Lille: Presses Universitaires de Lille.

D'hulst, L. and Milton, J. (eds) (2000) *Reconstructing Cultural Memory: Translation, Scripts, Literacy*. Amsterdam: Rodopi.

Diaz-Diocaretz, M. (1985) *Translating Poetic Discourse: Questions on Feminist Strategies in Adrienne Rich*. Amsterdam: John Benjamins.

Di, J. (2003) *Literary Translation: Quest for Artistic Integrity* (W. McNaughton ed. and intro.). Manchester: St Jerome.

Dingwaney, A. and Maier, C. (eds) (1995) *Between Languages and Cultures: Translation and Cross-Cultural Texts*. Pittsburgh: University of Pittsburgh.

Dreyer-Sfard, R. (1965) *Die Verflechtung von Sprache und Bild: Sprache im technischen Zeitalter* 13, 1034–39.

Eagleton, T. (1983) *Literary Theory: An Introduction*. Oxford: Basil Blackwell.

Eliot, T.S. (1960) 'Euripides and Professor Murray'. In T.S Eliot *The Sacred Wood: Essays on Poetry and Criticism*. London: Methuen.

Ellis, R. and Oakley-Brown, L. (eds) (2001) *Translation and Nation: Towards a Cultural Politics of Englishness*. Clevedon: Multilingual Matters.

Enkvist. N.E. (1978) Contrastive text linguistics and translation. In L. Gähs, G. Korlén and B. Malmberg (eds) *Theory and Practice of Translation* (pp. 169–88). Bern: Peter Lang.

Essmann, H. (1992) *Übersetzungsanthologien: Eine Typologie und eine Untersuchung am Beispiel der amerikanischen Versdichtung in deutschsprachigen Anthologien 1920–1960*. Frankfurt: Lang

Essmann, H. (1998) Weltliteratur between two covers: Forms and functions of German translation anthologies. In K. Müller-Vollmer and M. Irmscher (eds) *Translating Literatures, Translating Cultures: New Vistas and Approaches in Literary Studies* (pp. 149–63). Stanford: Stanford University Press.

Essmann, H. and Schöning, U. (eds) (1996) *Weltliteratur in deutschen Versanthologien des 19 Jahrhunderts*. Berlin: Erich Schmidt.

Even-Zohar, I. (1978) *Papers in Historical Poetics*. Tel Aviv: Porter Institute for Poetics and Semiotics.

Even-Zohar, I. (1990) Polysystem Studies. *Poetics Today*, xi (1). Updated versions on WWW at www.tau.ac.il/~itamarez. Accessed 10.06

Even-Zohar, I. (2000) The position of translated literature within the literary polysystem. In L. Venuti (ed.) *The Translation Studies Reader* (pp. 192–197). London: Routledge.

Faiq, S. (2000) Culture and the medieval Arab translator. *Perspectives* 8 (2), 89–95.

Fairclough, N. and Wodak, R. (1997) Critical discourse analysis. In T.A. van Dijk (ed.) *Discourse Studies: A Multidisciplinary Introduction* (Vol. 2): *Discourse as Social Interaction* (pp. 258–84). London: Sage.

Fawcett, P. (1997) *Translation and Language*. Manchester: St Jerome.

Fawcett, P. (1998) Linguistic approaches. In M. Baker (ed.) *Routledge Encyclopedia of Translation Studies* (pp. 120–26). London: Routledge.

Feinauer, I. (2004) Bridging the gap between source text recipient and target text recipient in South Africa: Functionalism is not always the remedy. Paper delivered at the 4th Congress of the European Society for Translation Studies, Lisbon, Portugal, September.

Feleppa, R. (1988) *Convention, Translation, and Understanding: Philosophical Problems in the Comparative Study of Culture*. Albany, NY: State University of New York Press.

Felstiner, J. (1981) *Translating Neruda: The Way to Machu Picchu*. Stanford: Stanford University Press.

Fick, J.C. (1793) *Praktische englische Sprachlehre für Deutsche beiderlei Geschlechts: Nach der in Meidingers französischen Grammatik befilgten Methode*. Erlangen.

Findlay, B. (1998) Silesian into Scots: Gerhart Hauptmann's *The Weavers*. *Modern Drama* 41, 90–104.

Findlay, B. (ed.) (2004) *Frae Ither Tongues*. Clevedon: Multilingual Matters.

Firbas, J. (1999) Translating the introductory paragraph of Boris Pasternak's *Doctor Zhivago*: A case study in functional sentence perspective. In G. Anderman and G. Rogers (eds) *Word, Text, Translation* (pp. 129–41). Clevedon: Multilingual Matters.

Firth, J.R. (1968) Linguistics analysis and translation. In F.R. Palmer (ed.) *Selected Papers by J.R. Firth 1952–1959* (pp. 74–83). London: Longman.

Fish, S. (1980) *Is There a Text in this Class?* Cambridge, MA: Harvard University Press.

Fischer-Lichte, E. (1983) *Das System der theatralischen Zeichen*. Tübingen: Gunter Narr.

Fitzgerald, E. (1859) *Rubáiyát of Omar Khayyám*. London: Bernard Quaritch.

von Flotow, L. (1997) *Translation and Gender: Translating in the 'Era of Feminism'*. Manchester: St Jerome.

von Flotow, L. (1999) Genders and the translated text: Developments in transformance. *Textus* XII, 275–88.

von Flotow, L. (2000) Women, bibles, ideologies. *TTR. Traduction Terminologie, Rédaction* 13 (1), 9–20.

von Flotow, Luise (2001) *Gender in Translation: The Issues go on*. On WWW at http://www.orees.concordia.ca/numero2/essai/VonFlotow.html. Accessed 10.06.

von Flotow, L. (2003) Sacrificing sense to sound: Mimetic translation and feminist writing. *Bucknell Review* 2 (January).

von Flotow, L. and Schwartz, A. (eds) (2006) *The Third Shore: Contemporary Short Fiction by Women Writers from East Central Europe.* Evanston, IL: Northwestern University Press.

Fodor, I. (1976) *Film Dubbing: Phonetic, Semiotic, Esthetic and Psychological Aspects.* Hamburg: Buske Verlag.

Folkart, B. (1991) *Le conflit des énonciations: Traduction et discours rapporté.* Candiac: Balzac.

Føllesdal, D. (2001) *Indeterminacy of Translation: of Philosophy of Quine* (Vol. 3). London: Garland.

Foucault, M. (1966) *Les mots et les choses.* Paris: Gallimard.

Foucault, M. (1971) *L'ordre du discours.* Paris: Gallimard.

Foucault, M. (1986) 'What is an author' (J.V. Harari, trans.). In P. Rabinow (ed.) *The Foucault Reader* (pp. 101–120). London: Penguin.

Fowler, R. (1971) *The Languages of Literature.* London: Routledge and Kegan Paul.

Fowler, R. (1981) *Literature as Social Discourse: The Practice of Linguistic Criticism.* London: Batsford.

Flynn, R. (1995) Europa, Europa: Ireland and media II. *Film Ireland* April/May, 15–17.

France, P. (ed.) (2000) *The Oxford Guide to Literature in English Translation.* Oxford: Oxford University Press.

Fraser, R. (2001) Translating sex from Berlin's Cabarets. Unpublished paper, University of Ottawa.

Frege, G. (1984) *Collected Papers on Mathematics, Logic, and Philosophy* (B. McGuinness, ed. and M. Black, trans.). Oxford: Blackwell.

Frye, R.N. (ed.) (1975) *The Cambridge History of Iran* (Vol. 4). Cambridge, Cambridge University Press.

Gadamer, H-G. (1977) *Philosophical Hermeneutics* (D.E. Linge, trans. and ed.). Berkeley, CA: California University Press.

Gaddis Rose, M. (1997) *Translation and Literary Criticism.* Manchester: St Jerome.

Gagnon, C. (2003) Institution in translated political speeches: A Canadian example. In D. Hall, T. Markopoulos, A. Salamoura and S. Skoufaki (eds) *Camling* (pp. 433–39). Proceedings of First Postgraduate Conference in Language Research. University of Cambridge, April.

Gallego Roca, M. (1994) *Traducción y literatura: Los estudios literarios ante las obras traducidas.* Madrid: Jucar.

Gambier, Y. (ed.) (1998) *Translating for the Media.* University of Turku: Centre for Translation and Interpreting.

Gambier, Y. and Gottlieb, H. (eds) (2001) *(Multi)media Translation.* Amsterdam: John Benjamins.

Ganz-Blättler, U. (1994) Angelsächsische Krimiserien und ihre deutsche Bearbeitung. *Spiel* 13 (2), 231–255.

Garayta, I. (1998) Womanhandling the text: Feminism, rewriting and translation. PhD thesis, University of Texas at Austin.

García Yebra, V. (1994) *Traducción: Historia y teoría.* Madrid: Gredos.

Garre, M. (1999) *Human Rights in Translation: Legal Concepts in Different Languages.* Copenhagen: Copenhagen Business School Press.

Gauntlett, D. (2002) Judith Butler. On WWW at http://www.theory.org/ctr-butl.htm. Accessed 10.06.

Gavigan, J. (ed.) (1966) *Augustine: On Christian Instruction. Fathers of the Church* (Vol. 2). Washington: Catholic University of America Press.

Gellerstam, M. (1986) Translationese in Swedish novels translated from English. In L. Wollin and H Lindquist (eds) *Translation Studies in Scandinavia* (pp. 88–95). Proceedings from the Scandinavian Symposium on Translation Theory. SSOTT II, Lund 14–15 June 1985. Lund: CWK Gleerup.

Gellerstam, M. (1996) Translations as a source for cross-linguistic studies. In K. Aijmer, B. Altenberg and M. Johansson (eds) *Languages in Contrast* (pp. 53–63). Papers from a symposium on Text-based Cross-linguistic Studies, Lund 4–5 March 1994. Lund: Lund University Press.

Gellerstam, M. (2005) Fingerprints in translation. In G. Anderman and M. Rogers (eds) *In and Out of English: Translating into L1 and L2*. Clevedon: Multilingual Matters.

Gentikow, B. (1994) Zwei deutsche Olsenbanden: Übersetzung zwischen Kultur-transfer und kultureller Hegemonie. *Text & Kontext* 19 (1), 148–171.

Gentzler, E. (1993/2001) *Contemporary Translation Theories*. London: Routledge. Clevedon: Multilingual Matters.

Gillespie, S. and Hopkins, D. (eds) (2005) *The Oxford History of Literary Translation in English* (Vol. 3): *1660–1790*. Oxford: Oxford University Press.

Godard, B. (1990) Theorizing feminist discourse/translation. In S. Bassnett and A. Lefevere (eds) *Translation, History, Culture* (pp. 87–96). London: Pinter.

Godayol, P. (1998) Interviewing Carol Maier: A woman in translation. *Quaderns Revista de traducció* 2, 155–62.

Godayol Nogué, P. (2000) Living on the border: Feminine subjectivity in translation. In A. Beeby, D. Ensinger and M. Presas (eds) *Investigating Translation* (pp. 37–42). Selected papers from the 4th International Congress on Translation, Barcelona 1998. Amsterdam: John Benjamins.

González Ruiz, V.M. (2000) La traducción del título cinematográfico como objeto de autocensura: El factor religioso. In A. Beeby, D. Ensinger and M. Presas (eds) *Investigating Translation* (pp. 161–9). Selected papers from the 4th International Congress on Translation, Barcelona 1998. Amsterdam: John Benjamins.

Gordon, N. (2002) Zionism, translation and the politics of erasure. *Political Studies* 50, 811–828

Goris, O. (1993) The question of French dubbing: Towards a frame for systematic investigation. *Target* 5 (2), 169–190.

Gorlée, D.L. (1994) *Semiotics and the Problem of Translation: With Special Reference to the Semiotics of Charles S. Peirce*. Amsterdam: Rodopi.

Gottlieb, H. (1992) Subtitling: A new university discipline. In C. Dollerup and A. Loodegaard (eds) *Teaching Translation and Interpreting* (pp. 161–170). Amsterdam: John Benjamins.

Graham, J. (ed.) (1985) *Difference in Translation*. Ithaca, NY: Cornell University Press.

Grant, C.B. (1999) Fuzzy interaction in dialogue interpreting: Factual replacements, autonomy and vagueness. *Linguistica Antwerpiensa* 33, 85–100.

Grbic, N. and Wolf, M. (eds) (2002) *Zur Geschlechterdifferenz in der Übersetzung*. Graz: Institut für Translationswissenschaft.

Greenberg, J.H. (1963) Some universals of grammar with particular reference to the order of meaningful elements. In J.H. Greenberg (ed.) *Universals of Language* (pp. 73–113). Cambridge, MA: MIT Press.

Grice, H.P. (1975) Logic and conversation. In P. Cole and J.L. Morgan (eds) *Syntax and Semantics 3: Speech Acts* (pp. 41–58). New York: Academic Press.

Guenther, F. and Guenther-Reutter, M. (eds) (1978) *Meaning and Translation: Philosophical and Linguistic Approaches*. London: Duckworth.

Gutt, E-A. (1991) *Translation and Relevance: Cognition and Context*. Oxford: Blackwell.

Haag, A. (1984) Übersetzen für das Theater: Am Beispiel William Shakespeare. *Babel* 30, 218–24.

Habermas, J. (1981) *Theorie des kommunikativen Handelns*. Frankfurt: Suhrkamp.

Halverson, S. (1999) Conceptual work and the 'translation' concept. *Target* 11, 1–32.

Hamberg, L. (1966) Some practical considerations concerning dramatic translation. *Babel* 12, 91–94.

Hardwick, L. (2000) *Translating Words, Translating Cultures*. London: Duckworth.

Hart, W. D. (1970) On self-reference. *Philosophical Review* 79, 523–528.

Hartung, E. A. (1965) Was erwarten Theaterleute von einer Übersetzung? *Babel* 11, 10–11.

Harvey, K. (1998) Translating camp talk: Gay identities and cultural transfer. *The Translator* 4 (2), 295–320.

Harvey, K. (2000) Gay community, gay identity and the translated text. *TTR. Traduction Terminologie, Rédaction* 13 (1), 137–65.

Harvey, K. (2002) Translating the Queens' English: Parodic femininity in fictional representations of gay talk. A study of French representations of late 1970s American gay fiction. PhD thesis, UMIST Centre for Translation and Intercultural Studies, Manchester.

Hatim, B. and Mason, I. (1990) *Discourse and the Translator*. London: Longman.

Hatim, B. and Mason, I. (1997) *The Translator as Communicator*. London: Routledge.

Hatim, B. and Munday, J. (2004) *Translation: An Advanced Resource Book*. London: Routledge.

Haugerud, J. (1977) *The Word for Us: Gospels of John and Mark, Epistles to the Romans and the Galatians*. Seattle: Coalition of Women in Religion.

Healy, M. (in prepn) The cachet of invisibility: Women translators of scientific texts in England, 1650–1850. PhD thesis, University of Ottawa.

Heidegger, M. (1963) Excerpts from *Der Satz vom Grund* [1957]. In H.J. Störig (ed.) *Das Problem des Übersetzens* (pp. 395–409). Darmstadt: Wissenschaftliche Buchgesellschaft.

Herbst, T. (1994) *Linguistische Aspekte der Synchronisation von Fernsehserien* Tübingen: Max Niemeyer Verlag.

Hermans, T. (ed.) (1985a) *Second Hand: Papers on the Theory and Historical Study of Literary Translation*. Antwerp: ALW.

Hermans, T. (ed.) (1985b) *The Manipulation of Literature: Studies in Literary Translation*. London: Croom Helm.

Hermans, T. (1996) The translator's voice in translated narrative. *Target* 8, 23–48.

Hermans, T. (1997) The task of the translator in the European Renaissance. In S. Bassnett (ed.) *Translating Literature* (pp. 14–40). Cambridge: D.S. Brewer.

Hermans, T. (1999a) Translation and normativity. In C. Schäffner (ed.) *Translation and Norms* (pp. 50–71). Clevedon: Multilingual Matters.

Hermans, T. (1999b) *Translation in Systems: Descriptive Translation and System-oriented Approaches Explained*. Manchester: St Jerome.

Hermans, T. (ed.) (2002) *Crosscultural Transgressions: Research Models in Translation Studies II: Historical and Ideological Issues*. Manchester: St Jerome.

Hermans, T. (2006) *Translating Others*. Manchester: St Jerome.

Heylen, R. (1993) *Translation, Poetics and the Stage: Six French Hamlets*. London: Routledge.

Hirsch, A. (1995) *Der Dialog der Sprachen: Studien zum Sprach und Übersetzungsdenken Walter Benjamins und Jacques Derridas*. Munich: Fink.

Hirsch, A. (ed.) (1997) *Übersetzung und Dekonstruktion*. Frankfurt: Suhrkamp.

Hofstadter, D. (1997) *Le Ton beau de Marot: In Praise of the Music of Language*. New York: Basic Books.

Holmes, J. (1972) The name and nature of translation studies. In J. Holmes (1988) *Translated! Papers on Literary Translation and Translation Studies* (pp. 67–80). Amsterdam: Rodopi. (Reprinted in L. Venuti (ed.) (2000) *The Translation Studies Reader* (pp.172–85). London: Routledge.)

Holmes, J. (1978) Describing literary translations: Models and methods. In J. Holmes, J. Lambert and R. Van den Broeck (eds) *Literature and Translation: New Perspectives in Literary Studies* (pp. 69–82). Leuven: Acco. (Reprinted in J. Holmes (1988) *Translated! Papers on Literary Translation and Translation Studies* (pp. 81–91). Amsterdam: Rodopi.)

Holmes, J. (1988) *Translated! Papers on Literary Translation and Translation Studies*. Amsterdam: Rodopi.

Holmes, J., Lambert, J. and Van den Broeck, R. (eds) (1978) *Literature and Translation: New Perspectives in Literary Studies*. Leuven: ACCO.

Holz-Mänttäri, J. (1984) *Translatorisches Handeln: Theorie und Methode*. Helsinki: Academia Scientiarum Fennica.

Honig, E. (ed.) (1985) *The Poet's Other Voice: Conversations on Literary Translation*. Amherst: University of Massachusetts Press.

Horguelin, P. (ed.) (1981) *Anthologie de la manière de traduire: Domaine français*. Montréal: Linguatech.

Hörmanseder, F. (2001). Text und publikum. Kriterien für eine bühnenwirksame Übersetzung im Hinblick auf eine Kooperation zwischen Translatologen und Bühnenexperten. PhD thesis, University of Vienna.

House, J. (1977) A model for assessing translation quality. *Meta* 22 (2), 103–9.

House, J. (1981) *A Model for Translation Quality Assessment*. Tübingen: Gunter Narr.

House, J. (2003) English as lingua franca and its influence on discourse norms in other languages. In G. Anderman and M. Rogers (eds) *Translation Today: Trends and Perspectives*. (pp. 168–180) Clevedon: Multilingual Matters.

House, J. and Kasper, G. (1981) Politeness markers in English and German. In F. Coulmas (ed.) *Conversational Routine* (pp. 157–85). The Hague: Mouton.

Howatt, A. (1984) *A History of English Language Teaching*. Oxford: Oxford University Press.

Hubbell, H.M. (ed.) (1949) *Marcus Tullius Cicero: de Inventione; de Optime Genere Oratorum; Topica*. Cambridge, MA: Harvard University Press.

Hudson, A. (1988) *The Premature Reformation*. Oxford: Clarendon Press.

von Humboldt, W. (1836) *Über die Verschiedenheit des menschlichen Sprachbaues und ihren Einfluss auf die geistige Entwicklung des Menschengeschlechts*. Zweiter Nachdruck (1968 facsimile: Bonn-Hannover-Munich: Dümmlers Verlag).

Hung, E. and Wakabayashi, J. (eds) (2005) *Asian Translation Traditions*. Manchester: St Jerome.

Hurt, C. (1996) Übertitel als Teil einer Operninszenierung: Am Beispiel der französischen und englischen Fassung von Wagners *Siegfried*. Master's thesis, University of Vienna.

Ihwe, J. (ed.) (1971–2) *Literaturwissenschaft und Linguistik. Ergebisse und Perspektiven* (3 vols). Frankfurt: Athenäum.

Inclusive Language Lectionary (1983) Philadelphia: Westminster Press.

ITC (1999) *Guidance on Standards for Subtitling*. London: ITC.

Ivanova, L. (2004) Translatorische Kompetenz und politische Kommunikation. In E. Fleischmann, P. Schmitt and G. Wotjak (eds) *Translationskompetenz* (pp. 377–90). Tübingen: Stauffenburg.

Ivarsson, J. (1992) *Subtitling for the Media*. Stockholm: Transedit.

Ivarsson, J. (1995) The history of subtitling. In Y. Gambier (ed.) *Communication Audiovisuelle et Transferts Linguistiques [Audiovisual Communication and Language Transfer]* (pp. 294–302). Sint-Amandsberg: FIT.

Jääskeläiner, R. (1998) Think-aloud protocols. In M. Baker (ed.) *Routledge Encyclopedia of Translation Studies* (pp. 265–69). London: Routledge.

Jakobsen, A.L. (1986) Lexical selection and creation in English. In I. Lindblad and M. Ljung (eds) *Proceedings from the Third Nordic Conference for English Studies* (pp. 101–12). Stockholm: Almquist and Wiksell.

Jakobson, R. (1959/2000) On linguistic aspects of translation. In R.A. Brower (ed.) *On Translation* (pp. 232–239). Cambridge MA: Harvard University Press. (Reprinted in Venuti, L. (ed.) (2000) *The Translation Studies Reader* (pp. 113–18). London: Routledge.)

Jean, G. (1992) *Writing: The Story of Alphabets and Scripts* (J. Oates, trans.). London: Thames and Hudson.

Johnson, B. (1985) Taking fidelity philosophically. In J. Graham (ed.) *Difference in Translation* (pp. 142–48). Ithaca, NY: Cornell University Press.

Johnston, D. (ed.) (1996) *Stages of Translation: Essays and Interviews on Translating for the Stage*. Bath: Absolute Classics.

Jones, W., Sir (1970) *The Letters of Sir William Jones* (G.H. Cannon, ed.). Oxford: Clarendon Press.

Kade, O. (1980) *Die Sprachmittlung als gesellschaftliche Erscheinung und Gegenstand wissenschaftlicher Untersuchung* (Übersetzungswissenschaftliche Beiträge 3). Leipzig: Enzyklopädie.

Kadish, D. and Massardier-Kenney, F. (eds) (1994) *Translating Slavery: Gender and Race in French Women's Writing, 1783–1823*. Kent: Kent State University Press.

Kadric, M. and Kaindl, K. (1997) Astérix: Vom Gallier zum Tschetnikjäger: Zur Problematik von Massenkommunikation und übersetzerischer Ethik. In M. Snell-Hornby, Z. Jettmarová and K. Kaindl (eds) *Translation as Intercultural Communication: Selected Papers from the EST Congress Prague 1995* (pp. 135–46). Amsterdam: John Benjamins.

Kaindl, K. (1991) Stimme und Gestalt in der Opernübersetzung: Am Beispiel 'Carmen' von G. Bizet. *TEXTconTEXT* 6, 227–250.

Kaindl, K. (1995) *Die Oper als Textgestalt: Perspektiven einer interdisziplinären Übersetzungswissenschaft*. Tübingen: Stauffenburg.

Karamitroglou, F. (2000) *Towards a Methodology for the Investigation of Norms in Audiovisual Translation: The Choice between Subtitling and Revoicing in Greece*. Amsterdam: Rodopi.

Katan, D. (1999/2004) *Translating Cultures* (2nd rev. edn). Manchester: St Jerome.

Katz, J. (1978) Effability and translation. In F. Guenther and M. Guenther-Reutter (eds) *Meaning and Translation: Philosophical and Linguistic Approaches* (pp. 191–234). London: Duckworth.

Kayahara, M. (2002) Translators go both ways: A survey of gay translation theory. Unpublished paper, University of Ottawa.

Kaylor, N.H. (1992) *The Medieval Consolation of Philosophy: A Bibliography.* New York: Garland Publishing.

Keenaghan, E. (1998) Jack Spicer's pricks and cocksuckers: Translating homosexuality into visibility. *The Translator* 4 (2), 273–94.

Kelly, L. (1979) *The True Interpreter: A History of Translation Theory and Practice in the West.* Oxford: Blackwell.

Kelly, L. (1984) Bibliography of the translation of literature. *Comparative Criticism* 6, 347–59.

Kenny, D. (1998) Equivalence. In M. Baker (ed.) *Routledge Encyclopedia of Translation Studies* (pp. 77–80). London: Routledge.

Kenny, D. (2001) *Lexis and Creativity in Translation: A Corpus-based Study.* Manchester: St Jerome.

King, N. (1996) The sounds of silence. In R. Abel (ed.) *The Silent Film* (pp. 31–44). London: The Athlone Press.

Kirk, R. (1986) *Translation Determined.* Oxford: Clarendon Press.

Kirkwood, H. (1969) Aspects of word order and its communicative function in English and German. *Journal of Linguistics* 5, 85–107.

Kittel H. (ed.) (1992) *Geschichte, System, Literarische Übersetzung* [*Histories, Systems, Literary Translations*]. Berlin: Erich Schmidt.

Kittel, H. (ed.) (1995) *International Anthologies of Literature in Translation.* Berlin: Erich Schmidt.

Kittel, H. (1998) The 'Göttingen approach' to translation studies. In K. Müller-Vollmer and M. Irmscher (eds) *Translating Literatures, Translating Cultures: New Vistas and Approaches in Literary Studies* (pp. 3–13). Stanford, CA: Stanford University Press.

Kittel, H. and Frank, A.P. (eds) (1991) *Interculturality and the Historical Study of Literary Translations.* Berlin: Erich Schmidt.

Klaudy, K. (1998) Explicitation. In M. Baker (ed.) *Routledge Encyclopedia of Translation Studies* (pp. 80–4). London: Routledge.

Kofoworola, K. and Okoh, B. (2005) Landmines and booby traps: A look at the translation of literary texts in Nigeria. Paper presented at the International Conference of Translating and Interpreting as a Social Practice, Graz, 5–7 May.

Kohlmayer, R. (1996) *Oscar Wilde in Deutschland und Österreich: Untersuchungen zur Rezeption der Komödien und zur Theorie der Bühnenübersetzung.* Tübingen: Max Niemeyer.

Koller, W. (1989) Equivalence in translation theory. In A. Chesterman (ed.) *Readings in Translation Theory* (pp. 99–104). Helsinki: Oy Finn Lectura Ab.

Koller, W. (1979/1992) *Einführung in die Übersetzungswissenschaft* (4th rev. edn). Heidelberg and Wiesbaden: Quelle and Meyer.

Korsak, M.P. (1992) *At the Start: Genesis Made New: A Translation of the Hebrew Text.* London: Doubleday.

Koskinen, K. (2000a) *Beyond Ambivalence: Postmodernity and the Ethics of Translation.* Tampere: University of Tampere.

Koskinen, K. (2000b) Institutional illusions: Translating in the EU Commission. *The Translator* 6, 49–65.

Koster, C. (2000) *From World to World: An 'Armamentarium' for the Study of Poetic Discourse in Translation.* Amsterdam: Rodopi.

Kothari, R. (2003) *Translating India.* Manchester: St Jerome.

Kreiswirth, M. and Cheetham, M.A. (eds) (1990) *Theory between the Disciplines: Authority/ Vision/ Politics.* Ann Arbor: The University of Michigan Press.

Krieger, M. (1994) *The Institution of Theory.* Baltimore: The Johns Hopkins University Press.

Kuhiwczak, P. (1999) Translation and language games in the Balkans. In G. Anderman and M. Rogers (eds) *Word, Text, Translation: Liber Amicorum for Peter Newmark* (pp. 217–224). Clevedon: Multilingual Matters.

Kuhiwczak, P. (2002) Buried in translation. *The Cambridge Quarterly* 31 (3), 199–213.

Kuhiwczak, P. (2003) The troubled identity of literary translation. In G. Anderman and M. Rogers (eds) *Translation Today: Trends and Perspectives* (pp. 112–125). Clevedon: Multilingual Matters.

Kuhiwczak, P. (2005) Left untranslated: On the function of the 'untranslatable' in literary texts. *Forum* 3 (2), 131–146.

Kuhiwczak, P. and Korzeniowska, A. (1994/2005) *Successful Polish–English Translation* (3rd rev. edn). Warsaw: Polish Scientific Publishers.

Kullmann, D. (ed.) (1995) *Erlebte Rede und impressionistischer Stil: Europäische Erzählprosa im Vergleich mit ihren deutschen Übersetzungen.* Göttingen: Wallstein.

Labov, W. (1972a) *Language in the Inner City.* Oxford: Blackwell.

Labov, W. (1972b) *Sociolinguistic Patterns.* Oxford: Blackwell.

Ladmiral, J-R. (1979) *Traduire: Théorèmes pour la traduction.* Paris: Payot.

Lafarga, F. (ed.) (1996) *El discurso sobre la traducción en la historia: Antología bilingüe.* Barcelona: EUB.

Lambert, J. (1998) Literary translation: Research issues. In M. Baker (ed.) *Routledge Encyclopedia of Translation Studies.* London: Routledge.

Lambert, J. and Hyun, T. (eds) (1995) *Translation and Modernization.* Tokyo: ICLA Congress.

Lambert, J. and Lefevere, A. (eds) (1993) *Translation in the Development of Literatures* [*La traduction dans le développement des littératures*]. Bern: Peter Lang.

Landers, C. (2001) *Literary Translation: A Practical Guide.* Clevedon: Multilingual Matters.

Lane-Mercer, G. (1997) Translating the untranslatable: The translator's aesthetic, ideological and political responsibility. *Target* 9 (1), 43–68.

Lathrop, H.B. (1967) *Translations from the Classics into English from Caxton to Chapman 1477–1620.* New York: Octagon Books.

Laviosa, S. (ed.) (1998) *The Corpus-based Approach.* Special issue of *Meta* 43 (4).

Laviosa-Braithwaite, S. (1998) Universals of translation. In M. Baker (ed.) *Routledge Encyclopedia of Translation Studies* (pp. 288–91). London: Routledge.

Lavoie, J. (2003) Le bilinguisme législatif et la place de la traduction. *TTR. Traduction Terminologie, Rédaction* 16 (1), 121–139.

Laygues, A. (2001) Review article of Buber, Marcel, and Levinas. In A. Pym (ed.) *The Return to Ethics.* Special issue of *The Translator* 7 (2), 315–19.

Lefebvre, H. (1968) *La vie quotidienne dans le monde moderne.* Paris: Gallimard.

Lefevere, A. (ed.) (1977) *Translating Literature: The German Tradition from Luther to Rosenzweig.* Assen: Van Gorcum.

Lefevere, A. (1991) Translation and comparative literature: The search for the center. *TTR. Traduction Terminologie, Rédaction* 4, 1, 129–44.

Lefevere, A. (1992a) *Translation, Rewriting and the Manipulation of Literary Fame.* London: Routledge.

Lefevere, A. (1992b) *Translating Literature: Practice and Theory in a Comparative Literature Context*. New York: Modern Language Association of America.

Lefevere, A. (ed.) (1992c) *Translation/History/Culture: A Sourcebook*. London: Routledge.

Lefevere, A. (1999) Composing the Other. In S. Bassnett and H. Trivedi (eds) *Postcolonial Translation: Theory and Practice* (pp. 75–94). London: Routledge.

Leighton, L.G. (1991) *Two Worlds, One Art: Literary Translation in Russia and America*. Dekalb: Northern Illinois University Press.

Lenschen, Walter (ed.) (1998) *Literatur übersetzen in der DDR: La traduction littéraire en RDA*. Bern: Peter Lang.

Leppihalme, R. (1997) *Culture Bumps: An Empirical Approach to the Translation of Allusions*. Clevedon: Multilingual Matters.

Leung, M.W. (2002) The ideological turn in translation studies. Paper given at Translation (Studies): A Crossroads of Disciplines, EST Congress, Faculdade de Letras, Universidade de Lisboa, 14–15 November.

van Leuven-Zwart, K. (1989–90) Translation and original. Similarities and dissimilarities. *Target* 1 (1989), 151–82; 2 (1990), 69–96.

Levine, S.J. (1991) *The Subversive Scribe: Translating Latin American Fiction*. St Paul, MN: Graywolf.

Levý, J. (1967) Translation as a decision process. In *To Honor Roman Jakobson* (Vol. 2; pp. 1171–82). The Hague and Paris: Mouton. (Reprinted in L. Venuti (ed.) (2000) *The Translation Studies Reader* (pp. 148–59). London: Routledge.)

Levý, J. (1969) *Die literarische Übersetzung: Theorie einer Kunstgattung* (W. Schamschula, trans.). Frankfurt: Athenäum.

Lewis, P. (1985) The measure of translation effects. In J. Graham (ed.) *Difference in Translation* (pp. 31–62). Ithaca: Cornell University Press.

Limbeck, S. (1999) Plautus in der Knabenschule. In D. Linck (ed.) *Erinnern und Wiederentdecken: Tabuisierung und Enttabuisierung der männlichen und weiblichen Homosexualität in Wissenschaft und Kritik* (pp. 15–68). Berlin: Verlag Rosa Winkel.

de Linde, Z. and Kay, N. (1999) *The Semiotics of Subtitling*. Manchester: St Jerome.

Lisa, C. (1993) Die Übersetzung des modernen Musicals: Am Beispiel von 'Les Misérables'. Master's thesis, University of Vienna.

Lispector, C. (1992a) *Discovering the World* (G. Pontiero, trans.). Manchester: Carcanet Press.

Lispector, C. (1992b) *The Hour of the Star* (G. Pontiero, trans.). Manchester: Carcanet Press.

Littau, K. (1993) Performing translation. *Theatre Research International* 18 (1), 53–61.

Littau, K. (1996) Incommunication: Derrida in translation. In J. Brannigan, R. Robbins and J. Wolfreys (eds) *Applying: to Derrida* (pp. 107–123). London: Macmillan.

Littau, K. (1997) Translation in the age of postmodern production: From text to intertext to hypertext. *Forum for Modern Language Studies* 33 (1), 81–96.

Littau, K. (2000) Pandora's tongues. *TTR. Traduction Terminologie, Rédaction* 13 (1), 21–35.

Littau, K. (2005) Serial translation: Angela Carter's new reading of Pabst's Wedekind's *Lulu*. *Comparative Critical Studies* 2 (1), 45–65.

Liturgiam Authenticam. On the use of vernacular languages in the publication of the books of the Roman Liturgy. On WWW at http://www.vatican.va/roman_curia/congregations/ccdds/documents/rc_con_ccdds_doc_20010507_liturgiam-authenticam_en.html. Accessed 05.02

Lockhart, J. (1991) *Nahuas and Spaniards*. Stanford, CA: Stanford University Press.

Long, L. (2001) *Translating The Bible: From the 7th to the 17th Century*. Aldershot: Ashgate.

Long, L. (ed.) (2005) *Holy Untranslatable? Translating Sacred Texts*. Clevedon: Multilingual Matters.

López García, D. (ed.) (1996) *Teorías de la traducción: Antología de textos*. Cuenca: Universidad de Castilla-la Mancha.

de Lotbinière-Harwood, S. (1991) *Re-belle et infidèle: La traduction comme pratique de ré-écriture au féminin*. [*The Body Bilingual: Translation as a Re-writing in the Feminine*]. Montréal: Editions du Remue-ménage.

Luyken, G-M., with Herbst, T., Langham-Brown, J., Reid, H. and Spinhof, H. (1991) *Overcoming Language Barriers in Television*. Manchester: European Institute for the Media.

Macurara, V. (1990) Culture as translation. In S. Bassnett and A. Lefevere (eds) *Translation, History and Culture* (pp. 64–70). London: Pinter.

Maier, C. (1998) Issues in the practice of translating women's fiction. *Bulletin of Hispanic Studies* LXXV, 95–108.

Maier, C. and Massardier-Kenney, F. (1996) Gender in/and literary translation. In M. Gaddis Rose (ed.) *Translation Horizons: Beyond the Boundaries of Translation Spectrum* (pp. 225–42). Binghamton: Centre for Research in Translation.

Mailhac, J.P. (1998) Optimising the linguistic transfer in the case of commercial videos. In Y. Gambier (ed.) *Translating for the Media*. University of Turku: Centre for Translation and Interpreting.

Mailhac, J.P. (2000) Levels of speech and grammar when translating between English and French. In C. Schäffner and B. Adab (eds) *Developing Translation Competence* (pp. 33–50). Amsterdam: John Benjamins.

Mailloux, S. (1982) *Interpretive Conventions*. Ithaca: Cornell University Press.

Malmkjaer, K. (1998a) Analytical philosophy and translation. In M. Baker (ed.) *Routledge Encylopedia of Translation Studies* (pp. 8–13). London: Routledge.

Malmkjær, K. (1998b) Introduction. In K. Malmkjær (ed.) *Translation and Language Teaching* (pp. 1–11). Manchester: St Jerome.

Mann, H.S. (1994) Bharat Mein Mahila Lekhana, or women's writing in India: Regional literatures, translation and global feminism. *Socialist Review* XXIV (4), 151–72.

Markstein, E. (1994) Sprache als Realie: Intertextualität und Übersetzung. Am Beispiel totalitärer Sprachen. In M. Snell-Hornby, F. Pöchhacker and K. Kaindl (eds) *Translation Studies: An Interdiscipline* (pp. 103–111). Amsterdam: John Benjamins.

Marlowe, M.D. (2001) Online document: http://www.bible-researcher.com/inclusive.html. Accessed 05.02.

Mason, H.A. (1959) *Humanism and Poetry in the Early Tudor Period*. London: Routledge and Kegan Paul.

May, R. (1994) *The Translator in the Text: On Reading Russian Literature in English*. Evanston, IL: Northwestern University Press.

McFarlane, J. (1953) Modes of Translation. *The Durham University Journal* 45 (3), 77–93.

Meidinger, J.V. (1783) *Praktische französische Grammatik*. Erlangen.

Melby, A., with Warner, T.C. (1995) *The Possibility of Language: A Discussion of the Nature of Language, with Implications for Human and Machine Translation*. Amsterdam: Benjamins.

Mellor, B. (2000) Real-time speech input for subtitling. In G. Jones (ed.) *Proceedings of Mercator Conference on Audiovisual Translation and Minority Languages* (pp. 39–49). Aberystwyth: Mercator.

Merkle, D. (ed.) (2002) *Censure et traduction dans le monde occidental*. Special issue of *TTR. Traduction Terminologie, Rédaction* 15 (2).

Meschonnic, H. (1973/1999) *Poétique du traduire*. Paris: Verdier.

Messner, S. and Wolf, M. (eds) (2001) *Übersetzung aus aller Frauen Länder. Beiträge zu Theorie und Praxis weiblicher Realität in der Translation*. Graz: Verlag Leykam.

Milton, J. (2000) The translation of mass fiction. In A. Beeby, D. Ensinger and M. Presas (eds) *Investigating Translation* (pp. 171–79). Selected papers from the 4th International Congress on Translation, Barcelona, 1998. Amsterdam: John Benjamins.

Milton, J. (2001) Translating classic fiction for mass markets: The Brazilian Clube do Livro. *The Translator* 7 (1), 43–70.

Mira, A. (1999) Pushing the limits of faithfulness: A case for gay translation. In M. Holman and J. Boase-Beier (eds.) *The Practices of Literary Translation* (pp. 109–124). Manchester: St Jerome.

Monacelli, C. and Punzo, R. (2001) Ethics in the fuzzy domain of interpreting: A 'military' perspective. In A. Pym (ed.) *The Return to Ethics*. Special Issue of *The Translator* 7 (2), 265–82.

Mossop, B. (1990) Translating institution and 'idiomatic' translations. *Meta* 35 (2), 342–54.

Mounin, G. (1967) *Die Übersetzung: Geschichte, Theorie, Anwendung* (H. Stammerjohann, trans.). Munich: Nymphenburg.

Müller-Vollmer, K. and Irmscher, M. (eds) (1998) *Translating Literatures, Translating Cultures: New Vistas and Approaches in Literary Studies*. Stanford, CA: Stanford University Press.

Munday, J. (2001) *Introducing Translation Studies: Theories and Applications*. London: Routledge.

Munday, J. (2002) Systems in translation: A systemic model for descriptive translation studies. In T. Hermans (ed.) (2002) *Crosscultural Transgressions: Research Models in Translation Studies II: Historical and Ideological Issues* (pp. 76–92). Manchester: St Jerome Press.

Nabokov, V. (1955/2000) Problems of translation: Onegin in English. In L. Venuti (ed.) *The Translation Studies Reader* (pp. 71–83). London: Routledge.

Neubert, Albert (1981) Translation, interpreting and text linguistics. In B. Sigurd and J. Svartvik (eds) *AILA 81 Proceedings: Lectures Studia. Linguistica* 35, 130–145.

Neubert, A. (2005) Politics and language: The case of translation. In W. Thiele, J. Schwend, C. Todenhagen (eds) *Political Discourse: Different Media, Different Intentions, New Reflections* (pp. 149–74). Tübingen: Stauffenburg.

Neubert, A. and Shreve, G.M. (1993) *Translation as Text*. Kent, OH: Kent State University Press.

Newmark, P. (1981) *Approaches to Translation*. Oxford: Pergamon Press.

Newmark, Peter (1987) *A Textbook of Translation*. Hemel Hempstead: Prentice Hall.

Newmark, P. (1991) *About Translation*. Clevedon: Multilingual Matters.

Nicolson, A. (2003) *Power and Glory: Jacobean England and the Making of the King James Bible*. London: Harper Collins Publishers.

Nida, E. (1947) *Bible Translating: An Analysis of Principles and Procedures*. New York: American Bible Society.

Nida, E. (1964) *Towards a Science of Translating*. Leiden: Brill.

Nida. E. (1969) Science of translation. *Language* 45 (3), 483–98.

Nida, E. and Taber, C. (1969) *The Theory and Practice of Translating*. Leiden: Brill.

Niranjana, T. (1992) *Siting Translation: History, Post-structuralism and the Colonial Text*. Berkeley, CA: University of California Press.

Nissen, U. (2002) Aspects of translating gender. *Linguistik Online* 11, 25–37. On WWW at http://www.linguistik-online.de/11_02/nissen.html. Accessed 10.06.

Nouss, A. (2001a) In praise of betrayal. In A. Pym (ed.) *The Return to Ethics*. Special issue of *The Translator* 7 (2), 283–295.

Nouss, A. (2001b) *Métissages*. Paris: Pauvert.

Nord, C. (1988) *Textanalyse und Übersetzen: Theoretische Grundlagen, Methode und didaktische Anwendung einer übersetzungsrelevanten Textanalyse*. Heidelberg: Groos.

Nord, C. (1991) *Text Analysis in Translation: Theory, Methodology and Didactic Application of a Model for Translation-Oriented Text Analysis*. Amsterdam: Rodopi.

Nord, C. (1997) *Translating as a Purposeful Activity: Functionalist Approaches Explained*. Manchester: St Jerome.

Nornes, A.M. (1999) For an abusive subtitling. *Film Quarterly* 52 (3), 17–34.

Nussbaum, M. (1999) The Professor of Parody (pp.37–45). *The New Republic*, 22 February.

O'Connell, E. (1994) Media translation and lesser-used languages: Implications of subtitles for Irish-language broadcasting. In F. Eguíluz *et al.* (eds) *Transvases Culturales: Literatura, Cine, Traducción* (pp. 367–373). Vitoria: Facultad de Filologia.

O'Connell, E. (1996) Media translation and translation studies. In T. Hickey and J. Williams (eds) *Language, Education and Society in a Changing* World. Clevedon: Multilingual Matters.

O'Connell, E. (1998) Choices and constraints in screen translation. In L. Bowker, M. Cronin, D. Kenny and J. Pearson (eds) *Unity in Diversity? Current Trends in Translation Studies* (pp. 65–71). Manchester: St Jerome.

O'Connell, E. (1999) Subtitles on screen: Something for everyone in the audience? *Teanga* 18, 85–91.

O'Connell, E. (2002) The big picture: Children and minority language dubbing. In *MULTIMEDIA 2000: Proceedings of International Congress of the Italian Translators' and Interpreters' Association*. Rome: AITI.

O'Connell, E. (2003) *Minority Language Dubbing for Children*. Bern: Peter Lang.

O'Hagan, M. (2003) Middle Earth poses challenges to Japanese subtitling. *LISA Newsletter* XII, 1.5 (18 March). On WWW at www.lisa.org/archive/newsletters/2003/. Accessed 10.06

Olohan, M. (ed.) (2000l) *Intercultural Faultlines: Research Models in Translation Studies I: Textual and Cognitive Aspects*. Manchester: St Jerome.

Olohan, M. (2004) *Introducing Corpora in Translation Studies*. London: Routledge.

Olshtain, E. (1983) Sociocultural competence and language transfer: The case of apology. In S. Gass and L. Selinker (eds) *Language Transfer in Language Learning* (pp. 232–49). Rowley, MA: Newbury House.

Ouyang, E. (1993) *The Transparent Eye: Reflections on Translation, Chinese Literature, and Comparative Poetics*. Honolulu: University of Hawaii Press.

Orero, P. (2004) *Topics in Audiovisual Translation*. Amsterdam: John Benjamins.

Orero, P. and Sager, J. (eds) (1997) *The Translator's Dialogue: Giovanni Pontiero*. Amsterdam: John Benjamins.

Ortega y Gasset, J. (1937) Miseria y esplendor de la traducción. _Obras completas 5_, 433–52. The misery and the splendor of translation (E.G. Miller, trans.). In L. Venuti (ed.) (2000) _The Translation Studies Reader_ (pp. 49–63). London: Routledge.

Oseki-Dépré, I. (1999) _Théories et pratiques de la traduction littéraire_. Paris: Armand Colin.

Paizis, G. (1998) Category romances: Translation, realism and myth. _The Translator_ 4 (1), 1–24.

Parks, T. (1998) _Translating Style: The English Modernists and their Italian Translations_. London and Washington: Cassell.

Pavis, P. (1976) _Problèmes de sémiologie théâtrale_. Montréal: Université de Québec.

Pêcheux, M. (1975) _Les Vérités de la palice_. Paris: Maspero.

Peirce, C.H. (1931–58) _Collected Papers of Charles Sanders Peirce_ (8 vols)(C. Hartshorne, P. Weiss, and A. Burks, eds). Cambridge, MA: Harvard University Press.

Pisek, G. (1994) _Die Grosse Illusion. Probleme und Möglichkeiten der Filmsynchronisation_. Trier: Wissenschaftlicher Verlag Trier.

Poe, E.A. (2004) _Eureka_ (S. Levine and S.F. Levine, eds). Champaigne, IL: Illinois University Press (original work published 1894).

Pollard, A. (ed.) (1911) _Records of the English Bible_. Oxford: Oxford University Press.

Pollard, D. (ed.) (1998) _Translation and Creation: Readings of Western Literature in Early Modern China, 1840–1918_. Amsterdam: John Benjamins.

Pollard, D. and Chan, S. (eds) (1995) _An Encylopaedia of Translation_. Hong Kong: Chinese University Press.

Popovič, A. (1976) _Dictionary for the Analysis of Literary Translation_. Edmonton: University of Alberta Department of Comparative Literature.

Poyatos, F. (1993) Aspects of nonverbal communication in literature. In J. Holz-Mänttäri and C. Nord (eds) _Traducere navem: Festschrift für Katharina Reiß zum 70. Geburtstag_ (pp. 137–51). Tampere: University Press.

Poyatos, F. (ed.) (1997) _Nonverbal Communication and Translation: New Perspectives and Challenges in Literature, Interpretation and the Media_. Amsterdam: John Benjamins.

Polythress, V.S. and Gruden, W. (2000) _The Gender Neutral Bible Controversy: Muting the Masculinity of God's Words_. Nashville, TN: Broadman and Holman.

Potter, S. (1990) _Our Language_. Harmondsworth: Pelican Books.

Price, L. (2000) _The Anthology and the Rise of the Novel_. Cambridge: Cambridge University Press.

Pruys, G.M. (1997) _Die Rhetorik der Filmsynchronisation: Wie ausländische Spielfilme in Deutschland zensiert, verändert und gesehen werden_. Tübingen: Gunter Narr.

Pym, A. (1992) Discursive persons and the limits of translation. In B. Lewandowska-Tomaszczyk and M. Thelen (eds) _Translation and Meaning, Part 2_ (pp. 159–68). Maastricht: Rijkshogeschool Maastricht.

Pym, A. (1995) European translation studies, _une science qui dérange_, and why equivalence needn't be a dirty word. _TTR. Traduction Terminologie, Rédaction_ 8 (1), 153–176.

Pym, A. (1997) _Pour une éthique du traducteur_. Arras: Artois Presses Université.

Pym, A. (1998a) Getting translated: Nietzsche's Panama Canal. In M. Ballard (ed.) _Europe et traduction_ (pp. 181–2). Arras: Artois Presses Université.

Pym, A. (1998b) _Method in Translation History_. Manchester: St Jerome.

Pym, A. (2000) _Negotiating the Frontier: Translators and Intercultures in Hispanic History_. Manchester: St Jerome.

Pym, A. (ed.) (2001) _The Return to Ethics_. Special issue of _The Translator_ 7 (2).

Bibliography 169

Pym, A. and Turk, H. (1998) Translatability. In M. Baker (ed.) *Routledge Encylopedia of Translation Studies* (pp. 273–277). London: Routledge.
Quine, W.V.O. (1959) Translation and meaning. In R.A. Brower (ed.) *On Translation*. Cambridge, MA: Harvard University Press. (Reprinted in L. Venuti (ed). (2000) *The Translation Studies Reader* (pp. 94–112). London: Routledge.)
Quine, W.V.O. (1969) Linguistics and philosophy. In S. Hook (ed.) *Language and Philosophy*. New York: University Press.
Rabadán, R. (ed.) (2000) *Traducción y censura Inglés–Espanol 1939–1985: Estudio preliminar*. León: Universidad de León.
Radice, W. and Reynolds, B. (eds) (1987) *The Translator's Art: Essays in Honour of Betty Radice*. Harmondsworth: Penguin.
Raffel, B. (1971) *The Forked Tongue: A Study of the Translation Process*. The Hague: Mouton.
Raffel, B. (1988) *The Art of Translating Poetry*. University Park: Pennsylvania State University Press.
Reed, P. (2000) Jean-Paul Sartre 1905–1980. In O. Classe (ed.) *Encyclopedia of Literary Translation into English* (Vol. 2: pp. 1234–7). London: Fitzroy Dearborn.
Reiß, K. (1971) *Möglichkeiten und Grenzen der Übersetzungskritik: Kategorien und Kriterien für eine sachgerechte Beurteilung von Übersetzungen*. Munich: Hueber.
Reiß, K. (1976) *Texttyp und Übersetzungsmethode Der operative Text*. Kronberg: Scriptor Verlag.
Reiß, K. (1977) Texttypen, Übersetzungstypen und die Beurteilung von Übersetzungen. *Lebende Sprachen* 22 (3), 97–100.
Reiß, K. (1989) Text types, translation types and translation assessment. In A. Chesterman (ed.) *Readings in Translation Theory* (pp. 105–15). Helsinki: Oy Finn Lectura Ab.
Reiß, K. (2000) *Translation Criticism* (E.F. Rhodes, trans.). Manchester: St Jerome (original work published in 1971).
Reiß, K. and Vermeer, H.J. (1984) *Grundlegung einer allgemeinen Translationstheorie*. Tübingen: Max Niemeyer.
Rener, F. (1989) *Interpretatio: Language and Translation from Cicero to Tytler*. Amsterdam: Rodopi.
Rhodes, E.F. and Lupas, L. (1997) *The Translators to the Reader*. New York: American Bible Society.
Richards, I.A. (1955) *Speculative Instruments*. London: Routledge and Kegan Paul.
Robinson, D. (1991) *The Translator's Turn*. Baltimore: Johns Hopkins University Press.
Robinson, D. (1992) Classical theories of translation from Cicero to Aulus Gellius. *TEXTconTEXT* 7, 15–55.
Robinson, D. (1996) *Translation and Taboo*. DeKalb: Northern Illinois University Press.
Robinson, D. (1997a) *Translation and Empire: Postcolonial Theories Explained*. Manchester: St Jerome.
Robinson, D. (ed.) (1997b/2001) *Western Translation Theory from Herodotus to Nietzsche*. Manchester: St Jerome.
Robinson, D. (2002) *Performative Linguistics: Speaking and Translating as Doing Things with Words*. London: Routledge.
Robyns, C. (1992) Towards a sociosemiotics of translation. *Romanische Zeitschrift für Literaturgeschichte* 16, 211–26.

Rundle, C. (2000) The censorship of translation in fascist Italy. *The Translator* 6 (1), 67–86.

Russo, V. (1997) History of motion pictures. In *Microsoft Encarta 97 Encyclopedia* CD-ROM.

Sabio Pinilla, J.A. and Fernández Sánchez, M.M. (eds) (1998) *O discurso sobre a tradução em Portugal: O proveito, o ensino et a crítica. Antología (c. 1429–1818)*. Lisboa: Colibri.

Sahl, H. (1965) Zur Übersetzung von Theaterstücken. In R. Italiaander (ed.) *Übersetzen: Vorträge und Beiträge vom Internationalen Kongress literarischer Übersetzer in Hamburg 1965* (pp. 104–05). Frankfurt: Athenäum.

Said, E. (1978) *Orientalism*. London: Pantheon Books.

Santaemilia, J. (ed.) (2005) *Gender, Sex and Translation: The Manipulation of Identites*. Manchester: St Jerome.

de Saussure, F. (1983) *Course in General Linguistics* (R. Harris, trans.). London: Duckworth (original work published in 1916).

Savory, T. (1957) *The Art of Translation*. London: Jonathan Cape.

Schacht, J. and Bosworth, C.E. (1974) *The Legacy of Islam*. Oxford: Clarendon Press.

Schaff, P. and Wace, H. (eds) (1979) Letter to Pammachius no. lviii. In *Nicene and Post-Nicene Fathers* (Vol. 6): *St Jerome*. Michigan: Eerdman.

Schäffner, C. (1992) Sprache des Umbruchs und ihre Übersetzung. In A. Burkhardt and K.P. Fritzsche (eds) *Sprache im Umbruch: Politischer Sprachwandel im Zeichen von 'Wende' und 'Vereinigung'* (pp. 135–53). Berlin: de Gruyter.

Schäffner, C. (1993) Meaning and knowledge in translation. In Y. Gambier and J. Tommola (eds) *Translation and Knowledge: Proceedings from the Scandinavian Symposium on Translation Theory IV, Turku 4–6 June 1992* (pp. 155–166). University of Turku: Centre for Translation and Interpreting.

Schäffner, C. (1995) CSCE documents from the point of view of translation. In A. Neubert, G.M. Shreve and K. Gommlich (eds) *Basic Issues in Translation Studies: Proceedings of the Fifth International Conference, Leipzig 1991* (Kent Forum on Translation Studies, Vol. II) (pp. 77–90). Kent: Kent State University Press.

Schäffner, C. (1997a) Strategies of translating political texts. In A. Trosborg (ed.) *Text Typology and Translation* (pp. 119–143). Amsterdam: John Benjamins.

Schäffner, C. (1997b) Where is the source text? In H. Schmidt and G. Wotjak (eds) *Modelle der Translation* [*Models of Translation.*]: *Festschrift für Albrecht Neubert* (pp. 193–211). Vervuert: Frankfurt.

Schäffner, C. (1997c) Metaphor and interdisciplinary analysis. *Journal of Area Studies*, 11, 57–72.

Schäffner, C. (ed.) (1999) *Translation and Norms*. Clevedon: Multilingual Matters.

Schäffner, C. (2001a) Attitudes towards Europe: Mediated by translation. In A. Musolff, C. Good, P. Points and R. Wittlinger (eds) *Attitudes towards Europe: Language in the Unification Process* (pp. 201–217). Aldershot: Ashgate.

Schäffner, C. (ed.) (2001b) *Language Work and the European Union*. Special issue of *Perspectives: Studies in Translatology* 9 (4).

Schäffner, C. (2003) Third ways and new centres: Ideological unity or difference? In M. Calzada Pérez (ed.) *Apropos of Ideology. Translation Studies on Ideology: Ideologies in Translation Studies* (pp. 23–41). Manchester: St Jerome.

Schäffner, C. (2004) Political discourse analysis from the point of view of translation studies. *Journal of Language and Politics* 3 (1), 117–150.

Schäffner, C. and Herting, B. (1994) The revolution of the magic lantern: A cross-cultural comparison of translation strategies. In M. Snell-Hornby, F. Pöchhacker and K. Kaindl (eds) *Translation Studies: An Interdiscipline* (pp. 27–37). Amsterdam: John Benjamins.

Schäffner, C. and Kelly-Holmes, H. (eds) (1995) *Cultural Functions of Translation*. Clevedon: Multilingual Matters.

Schiavi, G. (1996) There is always a teller in a tale. *Target* 8, 1–22.

Schleiermacher, F. (1838) Über die verschiedenen Methoden des Übersetzens. Lecture delivered in 1813. In *Sämtliche Werke, Dritte Abteilung: Zur Philosophie* (Vol. 2; pp. 207–245). Berlin: Reimer. (English version: On the different methods of translating. In D. Robinson (ed. and trans.) (1997) *Western Translation Theory from Herodotus to Nietzsche* (pp. 225–38). Manchester: St Jerome.

Schogt, H. (1988) *Linguistics, Literary Analysis and Literary Translation*. Toronto: University of Toronto Press.

Schröder, R.A. *et al.* (1959) Fünf Forscher protestieren gegen Rothes Shakespeare. *Die Zeit* 17 (4), 6.

Schulte, R. and Biguenet, J. (eds) (1992) *Theories of Translation: An Anthology of Essays from Dryden to Derrida*. Chicago: University of Chicago Press.

Schultze, B. (ed.) (1987) *Die literarische Übersetzung: Fallstudien zu ihrer Kulturgeschichte*. Berlin: Erich Schmidt.

Schütte, W. (1993) 'Eurotexte': Zur Entstehung von Rechtstexten unter den Mehrsprachigkeitsbedingungen der Brüsseler EG-Institutionen. In J. Born and G. Stickel (eds) *Deutsch als Verkehrssprache in Europa* (pp. 88–113). Berlin: de Gruyter.

Schwartz, A. and von Flotow, L. (2006) *The Third Shore: Women's Fiction from East Central Europe*. Evanston, IL: Northwestern University Press.

Scolnicov, H. and Holland, P. (eds) (1989) *The Play Out of Context: Transferring Plays from Culture to Culture*. Cambridge: Cambridge University Press.

Scott, C. (2000) *Translating Baudelaire*. Exeter: University of Exeter Press.

Searle, J.R. (1969), *Speech Acts: An Essay in the Philosophy of Language*. Cambridge: Cambridge University Press.

Searle, John (2002) End of the revolution. *The New York Review*, February 28, 33–6.

Seleskovitch, D. (1975) *Langage, langues et mémoire*. Paris: Minard.

Seleskovitch, D. and Lederer, M. (1989) *Pédagogie raisonnée de l'interprétation*. Paris: Didier.

Seymour, E. (2002) A common EU legal language? *Perspectives* 10 (1), 7–14.

Shapiro, M. (ed.) (1990) *De Vulgari Eloquentia: Dante's Book of Exile*. Lincoln: University of Nebraska Press.

Shunnaq, A. (2000) Arabic–English translation of political speeches. *Perspectives* 8 (3), 213–228.

Shuttleworth, M. and Cowie, M. (1997) *Dictionary of Translation Studies*. Manchester: St Jerome.

Siefert, M. (1995) Image/music/voice: Song dubbing in Hollywood musicals. *Journal of Communications* XLV (2), 44–64.

Simeoni, D. (1998) The pivotal status of the translator's habitus. *Target* 10 (1), 1–39.

Simon, S. (1996) *Gender in Translation: Cultural Identity and the Politics of Transmission*. London: Routledge.

Simon, S. and St Pierre, P. (eds) (2000) *Changing the Terms: Translating in the Postcolonial Era*. Ottawa: University of Ottawa Press.

Singerman, R. (2002) *Jewish Translation History*. Amsterdam: John Benjamins.

Siwak, E. (1998) Rewriting women's discourse across cultures: Reception and translation of Ingeborg Bachmann's prose in Poland and in the United States. PhD thesis, University of Texas at Austin.

Smith, J.E. (trans.) (1876) *The Holy Bible: Containing the Old and New Testaments*. Hartford, CT: American Publishing Company.

Snell-Hornby, M. (1984) Sprechbare Sprache: Spielbarer Text. Zur Problematik der Bühnenübersetzung. In R.J. Watts and U. Weidmann (eds) *Modes of Interpretation. Essays Presented to Ernst Leisi on the Occasion of his 65th Birthday* (pp. 101–16). Tübingen: Narr.

Snell-Hornby, M. (ed.) (1986) *Übersetzungswissenschaft: Eine Neuorientierung*. Tübingen: Francke.

Snell-Hornby, M. (1988)*Translation Studies: An Integrated Approach*. Amsterdam: John Benjamins.

Snell-Hornby, M. (1993) Der Text als Partitur: Möglichkeiten und Grenzen der multimedialen Übersetzung. In J. Holz-Mänttäri and C. Nord (eds) *Traducere navem: Festschrift für Katharina Reiß zum 70. Geburtstag* (pp. 335–50). Tampere: University Press.

Snell-Hornby, M. (1996) 'All the world's a stage': Multimedial translation, constraint or potential? In C. Heiss and R.M. Bollettieri Bosinelli (eds) *Traduzione multimediale per il cinema, la televisione e la scena* (pp. 29–45). Forlí: clueb.

Snell-Hornby, M. (1997): 'Is this a dagger which I see before me?': The non-verbal language of drama. In F. Poyatos (ed.) *Nonverbal Communication and Translation: New Perspectives and Challenges in Literature, Interpretation and the Media* (pp. 187–201). Amsterdam: John Benjamins.

Snell-Hornby, M. (2006) *The Turns of Translation Studies*. Amsterdam: John Benjamins.

Snell-Hornby, M.. Hönig, H.G., Kussmaul, P. and Schmitt, P.A. (1998) *Handbuch Translation*. Tübingen: Stauffenburg.

Snell-Hornby, M., Jettmarová, Z. and Kaindl, K. (eds) (1997) *Translation as Intercultural Communication: Selected Papers from the EST Congress Prague 1995*. Amsterdam: Benjamins.

Snell-Hornby, M. Pöchhacker, F. and Kaindl, K. (eds) (1994) *Translation Studies: An Interdiscipline*. Amsterdam: John Benjamins.

Spivak, G.C. (1993) The politics of translation. In G.C. Spivak *Outside in the Teaching Machine*. London: Routledge. (Reprinted in L. Venuti (ed.) (2000) *The Translation Studies Reader* (pp. 369–388). London: Routledge.)

Spivak, G.C. (1996) Diasporas old and new: Women in the transnational world. *Textual Practice* 10 (2), 245–69.

Sperber, D. and Wilson, D. (1986) *Relevance: Communication and Cognition*. Oxford: Blackwell.

Stage, D. (2002) Comparing types of interlingual transfer. *Perspectives* 10 (2), 119–134.

Stark, S. (1999) *'Behind Inverted Commas'. Translation and Anglo-German Cultural Relations in the Nineteenth Century*. Clevedon: Multilingual Matters.

Steiner, G. (1975/1998) *After Babel: Aspects of Language and Translation*. Oxford: Oxford University Press.

Steiner, G. (1995) *What is Comparative Literature?* Oxford: Clarendon.

Steiner, T.R. (1975) *English Translation Theory 1650–1800*. Assen: Van Gorcum.

Stoll, K-H. (2004) Englisch als Kommunikationsvernichter. In E. Fleischmann, P. Schmitt and G. Wotjak (eds) *Translationskompetenz* (pp. 443–61). Tübingen: Stauffenburg.
Stoppard, T. (1986) *Dalliance* and *Undiscovered Country*. Adapted from A. Schnitzler. London: Faber and Faber.
Stoppard, T. (1997) *Anton Chekhov: The Seagull*. London: Faber and Faber.
Strauss, M.L. (1998) *Distorting Scripture? The Challenge of Bible Translation and Gender Accuracy*. Downers Grove, IL: Intervarsity Press.
Sturge, K. (2004) *'The Alien Within': Translation into German during the Nazi Regime*. Munich: Iudicium.
Surtitles (2002). Online document: http://www.surtitles.com. Accessed 04.04.
Swann, B. (ed.) (1992) *On the Translation of Native American Literatures*. Washington: Smithsonian Institution Press.
Sweet, H. (1877) *A Handbook of Phonetics*. Oxford: Clarendon Press.
Sweet, H. (1890) *A Primer of Spoken English*. London: Arnold.
Talmy, L. (1985) Lexicalisation patterns: Semantic structure in lexical forms. In T. Shopen (ed.) *Language Typology and Syntactic Description* (Vol. 3): *Grammatical Categories and the Lexicon*. (pp. 57–149). Cambridge: Cambridge University Press.
Tarski, A. (1994) *Introduction to Logic and to the Methodology of the Deductive Sciences*. Oxford: Oxford University Press.
Tharu, S. and Ke, L. (eds) (1991) *Women Writing in India: 600 BC to the Present* (Vol. 1): *600 BC to the Early Twentieth Century*. New York: The Feminist Press at Cuny.
Tharu, S. and Ke, L. (eds) (1993) *Women Writing in India: 600 BC to the Present* (Vol. 2): *The Twentieth Century*. New York: The Feminist Press at Cuny.
Thirlwall, J. (1966) *In Another Language. A Record of the Thirty-Year Relationship between Thomas Mann and his English Translator, Helen Tracy Lowe-Porter*. New York: Alfred Knopf.
Tieck, L. (1848) *Kritische Schriften* (Vol. 2). Berlin: Georg Reimer.
Tosi, A. (2002) *Crossing Barriers and Bridging Cultures. The Challenges of Multilingual Translation for the European Union*. Clevedon: Multilingual Matters.
Tötösy de Zepetnek, S. (1998) *Comparative Literature: Theory, Method, Application*. Amsterdam: Rodopi.
Toury, G. (1978) The nature and role of norms in literary translation. In J. Holmes, J. Lambert, R. Van den Broeck (eds) *Literature and Translation: New Perspectives in Literary Studies*. Leuven: ACCO.
Toury, G. (1980) *In Search of a Theory of Translation*. Tel Aviv: Porter Institute.
Toury, G. (1995) *Descriptive Translation Studies and Beyond*. Amsterdam: John Benjamins.
Toury, G. (1999) A handful of paragraphs on 'translation' and 'norms'. In C. Schäffner (ed.) *Translation and Norms* (pp. 9–31). Clevedon: Multilingual Matters.
Totzeva, S. (1995) *Das theatrale Potential des dramatischen Textes: Ein Beitrag zur Theorie von Drama und Dramenübersetzung*. Tübingen: Narr.
Trivedi, H. (1993) *Colonial Translations: English Literature and India*. Calcutta, India: Papyrus.
Trosborg, A. (1997) Translating hybrid political texts. In A. Trosborg (ed.) *Text Typology and Translation* (pp. 119–143). Amsterdam: John Benjamins.
Trudgill, P. (1974) *The Social Differentiation of English in Norwich*. Cambridge: Cambridge University Press.

Tymoczko, M. (1998) The metonymics of translating marginalized texts. _Comparative Literature_ 47 (1), 11–24.

Tymoczko, M. (1999) _Translation in a Postcolonial Context: Early Irish Literature in English Translation_. Manchester: St Jerome.

Tymoczko, M. (2000) Translation and political engagement: Activisim, social change and the role of translation in geopolitical shifts. _The Translator_ 6 (1), 23–47.

Tymoczko, M. and Gentzler, E. (2002) (eds) _Translation and Power_. Boston. MA: University of Massachussetts Press.

Übersfeld, A. (1978) _Lire le théâtre_. Paris: Editions sociales.

Underwood, S. (1998) _English Translators of Homer_. Plymouth: Northcote House Publishers.

Upton, C-A. (ed.) (2000) _Moving Target: Theatre Translation and Cultural Relocation_. Manchester: St Jerome.

Vanderplank, R. (1988) The value of teletext sub-titles in language learning. _ELT Journal_ 42, 272–281.

Vanderplank, R. (1999) Global medium: Global resource? Perspectives and paradoxes in using authentic broadcast material for teaching and learning English. In C. Gnutzmann (ed.) _Teaching and Learning English as a Global Language: Native and Non-native Perspectives_ (pp. 253–266). Tübingen: Stauffenberg.

Vanderschelden, I. (2000) Quality assessment and literary translation in France. _The Translator_ 6 (2), 271–93.

Varela, F.J. (1992) _Un know-how per l'etica_. Roma-Bari: Editori Laterza,

Vega, M.Á. (ed.) (1994) _Textos clásicos de teoría de la traducción_. Madrid: Cátedra.

Venuti, L. (1986) The translator's invisibility. _Criticism_ 28 (2), 179–212.

Venuti, L. (1991) Genealogies of translation theory: Schleiermacher. _TTR. Traduction Terminologie, Rédaction_ 4 (2), 125–150.

Venuti, L. (ed.) (1992) _Rethinking Translation_. London: Routledge.

Venuti, L. (1995) _The Translator's Invisibility: A History of Translation_. London: Routledge.

Venuti, L. (1998a) Introduction. In L. Venuti (ed.) _Translation and Minority_. Special issue of _The Translator_ 4 (2), 135–144.

Venuti, L. (1998b) _The Scandals of Translation: Towards an Ethics of Difference_. London: Routledge.

Venuti, L. (ed.) (1998c) _Translation and Minority_. Special issue of _The Translator_ 4 (2).

Venuti, L. (ed.) (2000) _The Translation Studies Reader_. London: Routledge.

Vermeer, H.J. (1983) _Aufsätze zur Translationstheorie_. Heidelberg: Groos.

Vermeer, H.J. (1989) Skopos and commission in translational action. In A. Chesterman (ed.) _Readings in Translation Theory_ (pp. 173–87). Helsinki: Oy Finn Lectura. (Reprinted in L. Venuti (ed.) (2000) _The Translation Studies Reader_ (pp. 221–32). London: Routledge.)

Vermeer, H.J. (1996). _Das Übersetzen im Mittelalter (13. und 14. Jahrhundert)_ (2 vols). Heidelberg: TEXTconTEXT Verlag.

Vieira, E. (1999) Liberating Calibans: Readings of _Antropofagia_ and Haroldo decampos' _Poetics of Transcreation_ (pp. 95–113). In S. Bassnett and H. Trivedi (eds) _Post-colonial Translation: Theory and Practice_. London: Routledge.

Vinay, J-P. and Darbelnet, J. (1958/1977) _Stylistique comparée du français et de l'anglais_ (rev. edn). Paris: Les Editions Didier.

Vinay, J-P. and Darbelnet, J. (1995) _Comparative Stylistics of French and English_ (J.C. Sager and M.J. Hamel, trans.). Amsterdam: John Benjamins.

Volz, W. (1993) Deutsch im Übersetzeralltag der EG-Kommission. In J. Born and G. Stickel (eds) *Deutsch als Verkehrssprache in Europa* (pp. 64–76). Berlin: de Gruyter.

Wadensjö, C. (2000) Co-constructing Yeltsin: Explorations of an interpreter- mediated political interview. In M. Olohan (ed.) *Intercultural Faultlines: Research Methods in Translation Studies I: Textual and Cognitive Aspects* (pp. 233–252). Manchester: St Jerome.

Wagner, E. (2006) A tale of two industries. *The Linguist* 45 (2), 48–49.

Wagner, E., Bech, S. and Martínez, J.M. (2002) *Translating for the European Union Institutions*. Manchester: St Jerome.

Warren, R. (ed.) (1989) *The Art of Translation: Voices from the Field*. Boston: Northeastern University Press.

Watzlawick, P., Bavelas, J.B. and Jackson, D.D. (1967) *Pragmatics of Human Communication*. New York: Norton.

Wechsler, R. (1998) *Performing Without a Stage: The Art of Literary Translation*. New Haven: Catbird.

Weissbort, D. (ed.) (1989) *Translating Poetry: The Double Labyrinth*. London: MacMillan.

Weissbort, D. and Eysteinsson, A. (2006) *Translation: Theory and Practice*. Oxford: Oxford University Press.

Weißert, J. (2001) Einmal keine Sorgen haben. Zum Vergleich der englischen und der deutschen Gesangstexte des Musicals 'La cage aux folles' im Hinblick auf Gender- und Sexualitätsfragen. Unpublished paper, University of Vienna.

Wheeler Robinson, H. (ed.) (1940) *Ancient and English Versions of the Bible*. Oxford: Oxford University Press.

Whitman-Linsen, C. (1992) *Through the Dubbing Glass: The Synchronization of American Motion Pictures into German, French and Spanish*. Frankfurt: Peter Lang.

Whorf, B.L. (1956) *Language, Thought and Reality*. New York: Wiley.

Wilcock, R. (2000) *The Temple of Iconoclasts* (L. Venuti, trans. and intro.). San Francisco, CA: Mercury House.

Williams, D. (ed.) (1991) *Peter Brook and the Mahabharata: Critical Perspectives*. London: Routledge.

Williams, H. and Thorne, D. (2000) The value of teletext subtitling as a medium for language learning. *System* 28, 217–228.

Williams, J. and Chesterman, A. (2002) *The Map: A Beginner's Guide to Doing Research in Translation Studies*. Manchester: St Jerome.

Wolf, M. and Messner, S. (2000) *Mittlerin zwischen den Kulturen: Mittlerin zwischen den Geschlechtern. Studie zu Theorie und Praxis feministischer Übersetzung*. Graz: Institut für Translationswissenschaft.

Wolf, M. and Messner, S. (eds) (2001) *Übersetzung aus aller Frauen Länder: Beiträge zu Theorie und Praxis weiblicher Realität in der Translation*. Graz: Leykam.

Woods, M. (2006) *Translating Milan Kundera*. Clevedon: Multilingual Matters.

von Wright, G.H. (1968) *An Essay in Deontic Logic and the Theory of Action*. Amsterdam: North-Holland.

Yao, S. (2002) *Translation and the Languages of Modernism: Gender, Politics, Language*. Houndmills: Palgrave.

d'Ydewalle, G., Van Resnbergen, J. and Pollet, J. (1987) Reading a message when the same message is available auditorily in another language: The case of subtitling. In J. K. O'Regan and A. Lévy-Schoen (eds) *Eye Movements: From Physiology to Cognition* (pp. 233–248). Amsterdam: North-Holland.

d'Ydewalle, Gèry and Pavakanum, U. (1997) Could enjoying a movie lead to language acquisition? In P. Winterhoff-Spurk and T. Van der Voort (eds) *New Horizons in Media Pedagogy* (pp. 145–155). Opladen: Westdeutscher Verlag.

Zambrano, M. (1999) *Delirium and Destiny* (C. Maier, trans.). Albany, NY: SUNY Press.

Zanettin, F., Bernardini, S. and Stewart, D. (2003) *Corpora in Translation Studies*. Manchester: St Jerome.

Zatlin, P. (2005) *Theatrical Translation and Film Adaptation: A Practitioner's View*. Clevedon: Multilingual Matters.

Zima, P. (1992) *Komparatistik: Einführung in die vergleichende Literaturwissenschaft*. Tübingen: Francke

Zubert-Skerrit, O. (1984) *Page to Stage: Theatre Translation*. Amsterdam: Rodopi.

Index